Stan Weinstein's Secrets for Profiting in Bull and Bear Markets

Stan Weinstein's Secrets for Profiting in Bull and Bear Markets

Stan Weinstein

McGraw-Hill
New York   San Francisco   Washington, D.C.   Auckland   Bogotá
Caracas   Lisbon   London   Madrid   Mexico City   Milan
Montreal   New Delhi   San Juan   Singapore
Sydney   Tokyo   Toronto

McGraw-Hill

A Division of The McGraw·Hill Companies

Library of Congress Cataloging-in-Publication Data

Weinstein, Stan.
    Stan Weinstein's Secrets for profiting in bull
and bear markets.

        1. Stock-exchange—United States.   2. Securities—
United States.   3. Investment analysis.   I. Title.
II. Title: Secrets for profiting in bull and bear
markets.
HG4910.W363   1988   332.63'2   88-2817
ISBN 1-55623-079-6   1-55623-683-2

Printed in the United States of America

22 23 24 25 26 27 DOC/DOC 0 9 8 7 6 5 4 3

*To Rita, My Best Investment,
and Marcy, Marla, and Marni,
My Best Dividends*

ACKNOWLEDGMENTS

I'd like to thank those whose contributions made this book possible, beginning with those chart services whose graphs I drew on so extensively to clarify my points:

Commodity Research Bureau, 30 S. Wacker Drive, Suite 1820, Chicago, Ill. 60606 (Tel. #1–800–826–7685)

Daily Graphs, P.O. Box 24933, Los Angeles, Calif. 90024 (Tel. #213–820–7011)

Dow Theory Letters, P.O. Box 1759, La Jolla, Calif. 92038 (Tel. #619–454–0481)

M. C. Horsey & Co., 120 South Blvd., Salisbury, Md. 21801 (Tel. #301–742–3700)

Market Charts Inc., 20 Exchange Place 13 Floor, New York, N. Y. 10005 (Tel. #212–509–0944)

Mansfield Chart Service, 2973 Kennedy Blvd., Jersey City, N. J. 07306 (Tel. #201–795–0629). This is one chart service that I owe a special debt of appreciation to as they not only granted permission for the reproduction of many charts, but also supplied me with several old charts from their archives.

I'd also like to thank several colleagues for whom I have great respect:

Yale Hirsch and Arthur Merrill who were generous enough to let me draw on their studies of market cycles, and Richard Russell who allowed me to reproduce his historical charts on the Dow Jones Industrial Average.

Robert Diamond of Drexel Burnham who was extremely helpful in obtaining historical data.

Robert Fisher of Thompson McKinnon for keeping me and my staff in touch with the market's hourly moves while I worked on this book.

My *Professional Tape Reader* staff for helping in my research and for keeping their fingers in the dike while I gave my all to this book.

I appreciate the support and assistance of other special people including:

My many *Professional Tape Reader* subscribers who have so loyally supported my work over the years and made people want to read and hear my market opinions.

The very helpful and cooperative team at IRWIN Professional Publishing who made this book priority and helped bring it out so quickly. One special member of that team, my editor, Dick Luecke, was great to work with. His advice and guidance were very important in giving this book a cohesive direction and making it more readable. I am truly indebted to him.

My late father for first introducing me to the fascinating swings of the market and whetting my investment appetite at a very young age.

My mother for giving me my first market stake and always believing in me.

My daughter Marla for taking time out from her rigorous college schedule to both type and read the manuscript. Her suggestions were excellent and I appreciate her being available at all hours of the day and night.

My three wonderful daughters, Marcy, Marla, and Marni— who make my life just a bit more special every day—for giving me the time, space, and understanding to write this book while I secluded myself in my study.

My wife, Rita, for wrestling with the word processor and making many excellent suggestions about the content. I also want to thank her for always being there for me and for choosing to make the journey through life with me.

Writing this book was a really tough task and I thank you all.

Stan Weinstein

CONTENTS

Buying. Further Tips for Buying. Double-Barreled Action. Bigger Is Better. Stan's Don't Commandments. Quiz. Answers. Don't Put All Your Eggs in One Basket.

The Triple Confirmation Pattern. Quiz. Answers.

Don'ts for Selling. Selling Properly—The Investor's Way. Sell-Stop Orders. Sell-Stops in the Real World. The Trader's Way. Trending toward Profits. Measuring the Move. Learning How to Win by Learning How to Lose. The Philosophy of Selling, or Don't Give Back Profits Needlessly. Quiz. Answers.

Why Is Short Selling So Feared? Common Mistakes When Shorting. Other Short-Selling Errors. Summary of Short-Selling Don'ts. How to Do It Right. When to Sell Short. Taking Some Profitable Steps. Placing the Order. Never Too Late? Especially Profitable Formations. Projecting a Target. Protecting Your Short with a Buy-Stop. Using Buy-Stops the Trader's Way. Trendlines on the Downside. Another Way of Reducing Risk. Quiz. Answers.

Stage Analysis for the Market Averages. The Advance-Decline Line. Measuring the Market's Momentum. Simple but Effective. No Isolationism

Here. As GM Goes . . . Cheap or Dear. Going Against
the Crowd.

CHAPTER 1

IT ALL STARTS HERE!

Buy low, sell high! That's the shortcut to a fortune, right? Wrong! It is just one of many loss-causing clichés that the crowd chants as they lose money year after year.

There are many other do's on Wall Street that are really don'ts, such as the necessity of reading the financial pages and watching the evening TV business report so you are in touch with important developments in the economy and its leading industries. Or the need to get advice from a so-called Wall Street wunderkind who wears a three- piece suit and talks to other wunderkinds.

These aren't the answers and they won't put profits in your pockets. It's unfortunate that so many investors embrace these ideas as the key to financial well-being.

Buy low, sell high is a cliché, not a blueprint for action. It blinds investors to the professionals' approach of buying high and selling higher, which I'll teach you to do consistently.

Being in touch with all the financial and economic news won't put your investments in the plus column either. In a world of computers and instant communications, the financial markets respond to the latest news long before you read or hear about it in the press. In addition, the market sells on future rather than current earnings. In order to be successful you have to learn to use the many clues the market action provides. This book will show you how to uncover those clues and turn them into profits.

Finally, relying on the advice of Wall Street wunderkinds—the brokers and analysts—won't get you very far. The overwhelming evidence is that their advice is inferior to the advice you will get from a set of darts thrown at a stock page (and believe me, a set of darts is far less expensive). Too many of these people spend their time talking with other brokers and analysts. They go to luncheons where executives of the Fortune 500 companies treat them to chicken Kiev and information about current company performance. You don't have to go to more than a few of these functions to realize that both the chicken and the information being served have been on the warming tables for a long time.

The real market professionals, the specialists on the floors of the exchanges, don't adhere to any of these misguided approaches. They base their decisions on market actions, not the news. And while others follow the clichés into the loss column, the real market pros are making plenty of money. Mr. and Mrs. Average Investor declare that they are unlucky in the stock market, but this is nonsense. It isn't a matter of luck at all. They are playing the game by the wrong set of rules and until they learn what the winning rules are, they will continue to have poor results. What they need in order to get on the winning road is a consistent method of properly timing the market and controlling their two market enemies: greed and fear.

That's what this book is all about—winning! After having made plenty of mistakes, I've learned how to decipher the very obvious clues that the market gives us and then tactically respond to a given situation. I'm going to teach you a new set of stock market rules that will make the market much less stressful and far more profitable for you. These rules won't have you poring over balance sheets or listening to some company spokesman drone on about his firm's progress toward higher returns on shareholders' equity. These rules will require that you do two things: control your own greed and fear, and find and decipher the obvious clues that the market tosses your way.

That's what I'll teach you in this book, and what you'll learn will make you a winning investor. Best of all, once you get the hang of it, you only have to spend about an hour every week implementing this winning approach.

Over the past 25 years, I've learned what works and what doesn't, and I've refined this knowledge and experience into an approach for consistently staying on the winning side of the market. This method has enabled *The Professional Tape Reader* to forecast *every* bull and bear market during the past 15 years. You can use these techniques in any market, be it stocks, mutual funds, options, stock index futures, or commodities. While each of these markets will be covered in the following pages, the major emphasis will be on the stock market.

Before going further, I want to stress that this isn't a "get rich quick" book. Dozens of those books cross my desk each year, and most literally aren't worth the paper they are printed on. Many are so simplistic that they're practically worthless; others are so pedantic and theoretical that all you get out of them is a headache. Even worse, others promise you the sky and the moon. If you want a book that is going to turn $10,000 into $1 million by 4 P.M. next Tuesday, then stop reading right now. But if you are serious and want to learn how to *consistently* profit year in and year out—in both bull and bear markets—and want to amass a tidy sum over the next several years, then this book is for you!

Understand something else. We are a team. The more you put into learning my methods, the more chips you'll take from the table. It's no different than taking a tennis lesson from a pro. The one-hour lesson is just the start of the learning experience; the second and equally important step is to practice what you've learned. For my part, I will make the learning very easy. I've done it for years writing *The Professional Tape Reader* and conducting teaching seminars all over the country. So don't worry if you've never looked at a chart or plotted an indicator before. You will quickly understand and learn how to use my methods if you do your fair share.

Unlike some books on technical analysis which are so esoteric that only the author and a few academic types can understand them, this book will deal with only those factors that I rate a 10 in importance for making money, while leaving the 1s and 2s alone. In addition, this text will flow logically from chapter to chapter and will slowly develop your profit-making ability. To help you gauge even further just how quickly you are grasping the method, several of the chapters will end with a short quiz. If you find that a given chapter isn't 100 percent clear, quickly scan it again until you master the material before moving on.

MY PHILOSOPHY OF INVESTING

In the following pages you are going to learn exactly how I go about analyzing and beating the market. While it certainly isn't easy, it's not nearly as difficult as most investors and traders make it.

Lesson number one is *consistency*! For over 25 years, I have been consistent in my approach and discipline. This is so very important. Don't be a fundamentalist one week, and a technician the next.[1] And don't follow indicator A one month and switch to indicator B the next. Find a good method, be disciplined, and stick with it. If it doesn't regularly beat the market, then get a new method. But be absolutely disciplined and don't ever abandon a successful method because you think this time things are different.

Lesson number two is to learn what most investors never do: that you cannot consistently make money in the market by reading today's fundamentals in the newspaper and acting on that information. That is a prescription for disaster; it's a little draught of poison taken by most novice investors. You must learn that the market is a discounting mechanism, and that stocks sell on future and not current fundamentals. I therefore use a technical approach that deciphers the market's interpretation of all of the currently known news as well as future expectations. Don't be thrown off by the fancy name. All that technical analysis really consists of is the study of price and volume relationships to gain an insight into future trends.

In this book I'm going to teach you a new set of rules and a new market language that will make the market far more predictable, profitable, and enjoyable. Unfortunately, most traders and investors think that technical analysis is akin to black magic or astrology (and the way some technicians operate, that's not too far off the mark). Technical analysis is more an art than a science. And just as everyone who picks up a paintbrush is not a Picasso, everyone who opens a chart book is not a John Magee.[2] I'm going to teach you this approach. It will be a new set of rules for you. Properly used, however, this approach to the market will make winning much easier for you. Can you be perfect? Of course not!

---

[1] If these are unfamiliar terms, just understand this: fundamentalists base their buy and sell decisions on factors such as performance of the economy, an industry, and earnings trends of a specific company. Technicians look instead to market behavior itself as they concentrate on price/volume relationships which help to decipher the supply/demand equation.

[2] John Magee wrote *Technical Analysis of Stock Trends* in 1948 and is considered the father of technical analysis.

No quarterback in the National Football League can complete every pass, either.

You don't have to be right all of the time. By consistently following my methods, you will be right a very high percentage of the time. One secret that most professionals know is that you can rack up a fortune in the market by being right less than 50 percent of the time, as long as you let your profits run and cut your losses quickly. A future chapter will show you how to correctly deal with a losing situation, which is one of the most profit-enhancing secrets that you'll ever learn.

WHY THE TECHNICAL APPROACH

Now let's get to specifics. First of all, put aside all of your pre-conceived notions about the market and get ready to start anew. Just as when you embark on a weight loss program that requires you to first purge your system, here, too, the starting point is to put aside all of your prior beliefs and start over, slowly building step by step. If you are a confirmed fundamentals addict, don't worry. You will experience no withdrawal symptoms—not even hallucinations! After you've mastered this new approach, you'll be able to synthesize the two methods and better time your funda-mental buys and sells.[3]

On the other hand, if you really become polished in this tech-nical method, then the chances are very good that you'll do as I do and ignore the headlines while paying strict attention to the message of the tape. It's no coincidence that the motto at the top of each issue of *PTR* is "The Tape Tells All." That's more than a cute slogan, it's a market philosophy that works. What it simply means is that all of the relevant information about a company's earnings, new products, management, and so forth—the funda-mentals—that is currently known and cared about is already in-corporated in the price of its stock. It isn't that I don't care about

---

[3]Many fundamentally oriented institutional money managers subscribe to *The Professional Tape Reader* (*PTR*) and readily admit that the technical approach has improved their timing.

an important piece of fundamental news such as a pending takeover offer; rather I learned long ago that you and I aren't going to find out about that juicy news before it hits the broad tape—and by then it's too late. Sure, we'll hear rumors, but for every 100 that you'll hear, no more than one or two really pan out. That is not a way to rack up a winning percentage in the market. So accept the fact that unless you're willing to break the laws on insider trading, you aren't going to find out about that important piece of news ahead of time. And once you read the news in the paper, it's too late to act on it profitably. The remarkable thing is that when you learn how to properly interpret what's taking place on the tape— and on your chart—you'll often be buying or selling with the insiders without even knowing it.

You don't have to be Sherlock Holmes to know that something is up in stock XYZ if it has traded an average of 20,000 to 30,000 shares each week over the past several months while quietly moving back and forth in an 8 to 10 trading range; and then, suddenly, it breaks out above its ceiling, or what we technicians call *resistance*[4] on huge volume (say, 250,000 to 300,000 shares for the week).

Now look at the charts of Piedmont Aviation and Spectradyne (Charts 1–1 and 1–2). While you don't yet have the trained eye that you'll possess 100 pages from now, even the uninitiated can see some very unusual and exciting action starting to take place several months before the Piedmont announcement was made in early 1987, and before the mid–1987 Spectradyne announcement. While I wasn't privy to inside information, I listened to the message of the tape and recommended both of these issues in *PTR before* the takeover news and the huge gains took place. (see arrow for points in Charts 1–1 and 1–2.) Obviously, considerable insider buying was taking place. When you've finished reading this book, turn back to this page and you'll see even more clearly why you would never in a million years have considered selling these stocks— as many thousands of investors did day after day—while they moved higher. Even more importantly, you'll see why you should have called your broker with *buy* orders.

---

[4]In a moment I'll define all of the technical jargon you need to know for this book.

CHART 1–1

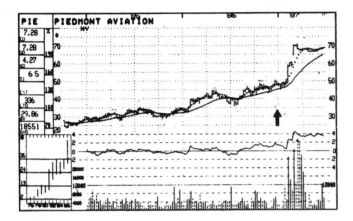

COURTESY OF MANSFIELD STOCK CHARTS
2973 KENNEDY BLVD.
JERSEY CITY, N.J. 07306
201-795-0629

CHART 1–2

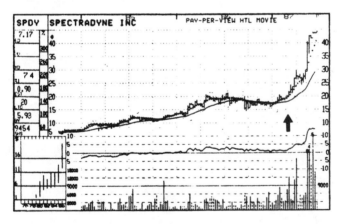

COURTESY OF MANSFIELD STOCK CHARTS

Furthermore, it doesn't have to be fundamental news as sensational as a takeover to see the merits of listening to the tape. Look at Charts 1–3 and 1–4 of Harrah's and TS Industries. In hindsight, Harrah's was a great buy in 1978 and TS Industries an even better purchase in 1986. But here are two interesting facts

CHART 1–3

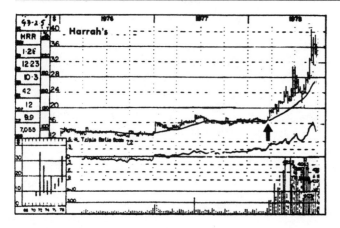

COURTESY OF MANSFIELD STOCK CHARTS

CHART 1–4

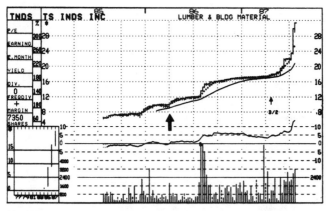

COURTESY OF MANSFIELD STOCK CHARTS

that should make you more open-minded to the technical approach. First, they were both recommended as buys in *The Professional Tape Reader* (see arrows). Second, they both had less-than-inspiring fundamentals when they were recommended and were rocketing higher. Harrah's trailing 12 months' earnings had just dropped down to $2.38 from $2.41. Then, over the next six months while the stock more than doubled, the earnings dropped even further to $2.16.

TS Industries' performance was even more spectacular in conjunction with even worse fundamentals. When the stock was recommended early in 1986, the latest 12 months trailing earnings were 37 cents—fair but not exciting. Then, 15 months later when the stock was 200 percent higher, earnings were an even worse 9 cents per share. Crazy? Not at all! Once you learn how the market really works, rather than how the ivory tower textbooks say it's supposed to function, you'll see that such action is commonplace. And rather than becoming confused, as you master my technique you will profit by such disparities.

When we examine the overall market, the same pattern shows up quite clearly on a grander scale. In late 1974, the Dow Jones Industrial Average had crashed from above 1050 down to 570. The gloom and doom was so thick you could just about touch it. The news headlines were absolutely ghastly (Chart 1–5). One leading financial newspaper ran a lead story titled "World Depression," and that was the good news! To top things off, one leading news

CHART 1–5

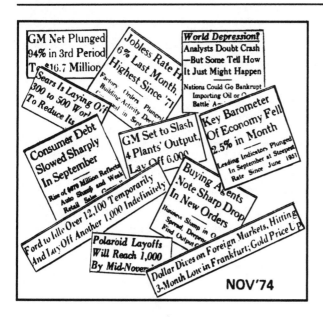

weekly featured a picture of a bear knocking down the pillars of Wall Street. Fear was widespread that the market was going to crash further—possibly to 250–300! Amidst all of this pessimism and fear, our technical indicators roared "buy," and a new bull market was born that soon took the Dow back above 1,000.

Now do you get the idea? There's a reason why savvy market professionals know that you buy on the bad news and sell on the good news. Stocks form bottoms when the current news is terrible and top out when the public is ecstatic about glowing earnings reports, stock splits, and so on. It's therefore not surprising that typical traders and investors buy near the top, when the news is great, and then dump their stock for big losses near the low, when the media are reporting ghastly news. It's not luck (good or bad) that causes consistent losses for the public and consistent profits for the real professionals, but the rules by which the two groups are playing. It's really no different from a professional poker player who understands the odds and refuses to pull to an inside straight, while the amateur lets his hunches and feelings lead him into losses.

Therefore, your philosophy should be simple:

1. Never buy or sell a stock without checking the chart.
2. Never buy a stock when good news comes out, especially if the chart shows a significant advance prior to the news release.
3. Never buy a stock because it appears cheap after getting smashed. When it sells off further, you'll find out that cheap can become far cheaper!
4. Never buy a stock in a downtrend on the chart (I'll soon show you specifically how to define a downtrend).
5. Never hold a stock that is in a downtrend no matter how low the price/earnings ratio. Many weeks later and several points lower, you'll find out why the stock was going down.
6. Always be consistent. If you find that you're sometimes buying, sometimes selling in practically identical situations, then there is something terribly wrong with your discipline.

So understand that chart reading and technical analysis is not some arcane science. It's not black magic or astrology. Very simply, it is learning to read the cardiograms of the market's health. Your physician runs X rays, blood tests, and EKGs on you before making a diagnosis. The competent technical analyst does the same to the market. Neither one is a witch doctor, though I have some reservations about certain MDs I've known. So let's move onward as I turn you into a stock market intern.

LET'S ALL SPEAK THE SAME LANGUAGE

Before charting your way to a profitable future, there are a few basic terms that you must become familiar with. Chart 1–6 will help you better understand what they mean. Even if you aren't technically oriented, you've probably heard and seen many of these terms, but you might be a little fuzzy about their exact meaning. No problem. A quick review will do the trick. Even if you're a seasoned technician, check how I define each term so we'll all be

CHART 1–6

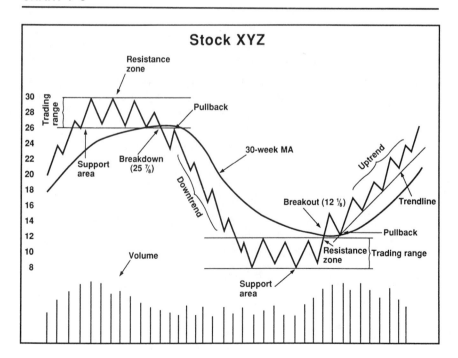

on the same wavelength. This is very important as these are the building blocks of my technical method, and they will be used repeatedly throughout this book. So take a minute or two to go over the definitions, and be sure you are clear about the meaning of each. If you pay your dues here in Chapter 1, the book will be easy to understand and very profitable for you. If you aren't 100 percent sure about a term, refer back to this section later on.

I'm not going to introduce these technical terms in strict alphabetical order since some become easier to grasp after you already understand a given definition. The first thing to do is to study Chart 1–6 of stock XYZ for a moment. Just look it over and try to initially grasp whatever makes sense to you. Then, on the next round, read one definition at a time, reflect on it, and study only that term on the chart in conjunction with the definition. Don't overwhelm yourself and try to remember all of the meanings at once. That's not really necessary. For many of you, it's a new language that you're learning, but if you go through this section slowly, it will start to make sense. After a few chapters, you'll feel like an old-time technician. Let's start with:

Support.   The area where a stock that has been declining is likely to stabilize and then bounce off and move higher (at least temporarily). It's like a floor. Be aware, however, that you can't become fanatical, as too many technicians often do, when talking about support as being at a certain point. It's really an area or *zone*. In Chart 1–6, support is first in the 26 to 26½ zone. The first low was at 26, the next at 26½. The third decline halted at 26¼, while the next selloff held at 26.

Be aware that a break below the absolute bottom of the support zone (in this case 26) has *very* negative implications for the price of the stock. The more times a given support level is tested, and the longer the time period during which the testing takes place, the more important the negative signal that is flashed *if* that zone is eventually violated. Also be aware that once a major decline or advance gets underway, new support levels will form along the way. In the case of XYZ, new support formed in the 8 to 8½ area (see Chart 1–6).

Resistance (also SUPPLY—the two terms are interchangeable).
The zone where a rallying stock is likely to run into trouble (at least temporarily) and then be turned back. The more times the given resistance area is tested, and again the longer the time period involved, the more important the bullish signal that is given if the resistance zone is eventually overcome. In our example on the chart, there is resistance first near the 30 level. After the major decline, the next valid resistance zone becomes 11½ to 12. The first rally failed at 12, the second at 11½, and the next at 11¾ before XYZ broke out above the top of the range. Always remember that a move above the top of the resistance range is a very bullish indication for the price of the stock. Once again, you must realize that when a major move gets going, new resistance (or supply) levels will form along the way. In the case of XYZ there was first resistance in the 29½ to 30 zone; later on in the 11½ to 12 area.

Trading Range.   The neutral zone in the ongoing battle between buyers and sellers. When a stock is in an uptrend, the buying army is obviously stronger than the selling side and rising prices result. A downtrend is the flip side of the coin, where the selling side is much more powerful than the buyers. But in a trading range, the two sides are equal in strength and the battle rages between the support zone (in this case 8 to 8½) and the resistance area (11½ to 12 on the accompanying chart). Note that there is also a second trading range on the chart (in the 26 to 30 area).

Moving Average (MA).   A very important technical tool that helps alert you to both shorter- and longer-term moves. All that a moving average really does is smooth out the major trend so the wild day-to-day gyrations—which the new buying and selling programs have made even wilder—do not throw off your market perspective. Over the years, I've found that a 30-week moving average (MA) is the best one for long-term investors, while the 10-week MA is best for traders to use. A 30-week MA is simply the closing price for this Friday night added to the prior 29 Friday weekly closings. Divide that figure by 30 and the answer is what's plotted on this week's chart.[5] Stocks trading beneath their 30-week MAs should *never* be considered for purchase, especially if the MA is declining. Stocks trading *above* their 30-week MAs should never be considered for short selling, especially if the MA is rising. For a long-term investor, the ideal time to buy a stock is when it breaks out above resistance and also moves above its 30-week MA, which must no longer be declining. For a trader, who wants action, the ideal time to buy a stock is when it's already above its 30-week MA, when the MA is rising. The trader's ideal entry point is after a stock consolidates in a new trading range and pulls back close to the moving average, then breaks out again above resistance.

Breakout.   When the price of a stock moves above the top of its resistance zone (12 on the XYZ chart). In this case, the breakout would occur at 12⅛ once the *top* of the resistance zone is cleared. Just as there are grades of eggs, there are different qualities of breakouts. Two hints to always remember are: (1) the longer the time spent below the resistance, the more significant is the eventual breakout; and (2) the greater the expansion of volume on the breakout, the more bullish the implications. (Don't worry: we'll go into much greater detail in the coming chapters. For now, remembering these two simple rules will add greatly to your profits.)

Breakdown.   The mirror image of breakout, as the price of a stock moves *below* the bottom of the support zone (26 in this example on the XYZ chart). In this case, the breakdown would occur at 25⅞ as the bottom of the support zone was pierced. Unlike a breakout, a breakdown doesn't need very heavy volume to be valid. Stocks can literally fall of their own weight, but there should be some increase in volume.

Pullback.   After a stock breaks out of its trading range and advances, there is usually at least one profit-taking correction that brings the price of the stock back close to the initial breakout point (in this case 12⅛). This is an ideal second chance to do further

---

[5] A 10-week MA is obviously this Friday's closing price for a given stock added to the prior nine Friday closings and then divided by 10.

buying (especially if the pullback occurs on sharply decreased volume). On the other hand, after a stock breaks down below support and declines, there is usually at least one pullback back up toward the breakdown level (in this case 25⅞). If this occurs on very light volume, it is an ideal entry point to sell the stock short.

Trendline. If you take a ruler and connect any two lows on a given chart, you've drawn a trendline. However, there is a big difference between a trendline and a *significant* trendline! A significant trendline will be touched at least three times. Chart 1–7 (Skyline) illustrates a significant trendline. It was hit four times before it broke on the fifth testing of the line. These are the lines that should set off sirens when they are violated, because the breaks signal major changes in the trend's direction. A break below an advancing trendline is negative, while a break above a declining trendline is bullish. (Note that once Skyline broke below its uptrend line, it literally crashed.) It's also important to realize that the greater the slope of a given trendline, the less meaningful its break is on the downside. If you have a very steep advancing trendline (Chart 1–8), a break below that trendline may merely mean that a stock (or a market average) is now going to move up at a slower rate of advance—because its prior rate was simply not sustainable. The closer a trendline is to being horizontal (Chart 1–9) the more negative the implications are when it is broken on the downside. Conversely, the steeper the angle of descent of a declining trendline

CHART 1–7

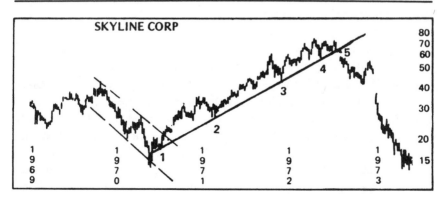

SOURCE: Data Graph

CHART 1–8

CHART 1–9

(Chart 1–10) the less bullish its implications are when it's over-come. All it may mean (especially if the stock is below its long-term MA) is that the stock is now going to decline at a slower rate of descent. However, the closer to horizontal the trendline is when it's broken on the upside (Chart 1–11), the more bullish the im-plications are. The most bullish signals are given when a very important trendline is broken on the upside, and within a matter of days the long-term MA is also overcome on the upside. Con-versely, the most negative implications are given when a significant

CHART 1–10

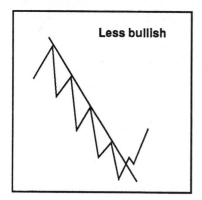

CHART 1–11

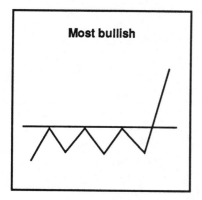

trendline is broken on the downside, and within a matter of days the long-term MA is also violated on the downside.

Uptrend.   Simply a series of higher peaks and higher lows on a given stock (or market average) that lasts for a minimum of several weeks to a maximum of years (see Chart 1–6).

Downtrend.   A series of lower peaks and lower bottoms on a given stock (or market average) that once again lasts from several weeks to years (see Chart 1–6).

Terms such as trader, investor, short term, and long term are relatively subjective. It's important for you to know what I mean when I use them, since one person's investing definition is another person's trading time frame.

Trader.   When I address traders in this book, I'm not talking about people who buy in the morning and sell in the afternoon. My definition of a trader is someone who wants to catch each *significant* two to four month move. This is what I consider intelligent trading. Buying on Monday and selling on Tuesday is smart only if you want to make your broker rich.

Investor.   My investing time frame is up to 12 months. That doesn't mean you can't end up holding a stock longer, but I don't feel it's relevant to talk about the market (or stocks) in terms of three, four, or five years. There are too many variables and too many cycles that can come into play over so long a time frame.

Short Term.   By my definition, short-term moves are those cycles that last from one to about six weeks.

Intermediate Term.   Those cycles which run from six weeks to approximately four months.

Long Term.   My definition of long term is 4 to 12 months. The major trends are long term and always the most important patterns to be aware of. If you are in harmony with a long-term trend, it will often bail you out of a short-term timing error.

Relative Strength.   How a given stock (or group) acts in relation to the overall market. For instance, if stock XYZ rallies 10 percent while the market moves ahead 20 percent, that's poor relative strength even though the stock has advanced. On the other hand, if stock XYZ declines 10 percent while the market averages decline 20 percent, that's favorable relative strength even though the stock has moved lower. The formula for measuring relative strength is simply the price of a stock (or group average) divided by the price of a market average.

Short Selling.   This is the most misunderstood and underutilized of techniques. The pros use it, but nine out of ten individual investors have never even tried it. Short selling is placing a sell order for shares you do not currently own in the expectation that the share price will drop in the future. If you sell short XYZ at 20, you simply borrow the shares from your broker for delivery to the buyer. If XYZ drops to 10, as you'd expected, you then buy XYZ shares in the market to replace those you owe your broker. In the process you make $10 per share. So who says you cannot make money in bear markets?

I'll devote an entire section to short selling at the right time!

Now that you've read each of the definitions and have at least a working knowledge go back to Chart 1–6 and study it again. It should now make much more sense to you. If, in the coming chapters, you forget what a term means or aren't 100 percent sure, just reread that term in this section.

The next exciting concept to move on to is the chart itself. But before you do that, here's a quick quiz so you can test yourself on how well you understand the basic building blocks. The answers follow the quiz.

QUIZ

1. Stock XYZ rallies from 50 to 60, which is a 20 percent   **T   F**
   advance. In the meantime, the Dow Jones Industrial
   Average advances by 25 percent. This is an example
   of good relative strength.
2. The more times a trendline is touched without being   **T   F**
   violated, the more significant that trendline is, and the
   more important an eventual break of that trendline.
3. The sharper the angle of ascent of a trendline, the less   **T   F**
   meaningful is a break below it.
4. It is a bullish signal when a stock moves into a trading   **T   F**
   range, as it shows that the buyers are more aggressive
   than the sellers.

5. A stock is in a trading range and drops down to 8   **T F**
   before bouncing higher. On the next dip it drops to
   8½ before rallying. On the third decline it falls to 8¼
   before bouncing back up. The entire 8 to 8½ area is
   considered the support zone.
6. The more times a resistance zone is hit without being   **T F**
   overcome, the more bullish the eventual breaking of
   that zone.
7. Never buy a stock that is trading below its declining   **T F**
   30-week MA no matter how exciting the fundamentals.
8. A stock that breaks out above its resistance zone on   **T F**
   decreased volume is a good buy because it shows that
   sellers are weak and getting weaker.

ANSWERS

1. False. Percentage-wise, the stock is advancing less than the
   market average, showing poor relative strength.
2. True.
3. True.
4. False. A trading range is a neutral situation where buyers and
   sellers show equal strength.
5. True.
6. True.
7. True.
8. False. Stocks that break out on increased volume are good buys.
   Low-volume breakouts have a higher probability of being false
   since they have less-powerful buying propelling them.

CHARTS—THEY COME IN ALL FORMS

While there are many different types of charts available (daily,
weekly, monthly), there are two basic kinds that we should be
familiar with. While I'm going to expose you to all of them, I'll

show you which are easiest and most effective to use for traders
and which for investors.

First, there is the line or bar chart, which depicts volume along
with the high, low, and closing price for a given time period. The
second chart style is the point-and-figure approach (see Chart 1–12
of Marion Labs), which records only price changes while ignoring
time and volume. Therefore, if a given stock swings wildly in one
day on a point-and-figure chart, there would be several entries for
that day. Then, if the stock trades basically unchanged (close to
the same price) for the next several days, there would be no further
entries made because there were no price changes to record. Point-
and-figure (P&F) charts are basically compact summaries of the
action (this P&F chart of Marion Labs shows 20 years of history).
They're very useful for spotting important formations, identifying
areas of support (where a stock will stop declining), and resistance
zones (where a given advance will run into trouble). While I use
them in conjunction with all of my other charts when analyzing a

CHART 1–12

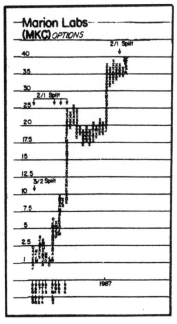

COURTESY: MARKET CHARTS
20 Exchange Pl.
New York NY 10005
212-509-0944

stock, they should *never* be used alone since there is no volume signal and no MA. In addition, they are much more difficult to master. So in this book, I am going to stick strictly with bar charts. When properly used, bar charts can help you reap some very substantial profits.

Now let's return to bar-chart analysis. It really doesn't matter what time period we are dealing with, but for this illustration (Chart 1–13) let's assume we are talking about one day's trading (a daily chart). If the high for this day is 18 and the low is 16½, all you do is place a dot at the high of the day (18) and at the low (16½) and draw a straight line. If XYZ closed that day at 17½, you put a horizontal tick line on the day's trading at 17½. As for the volume, there is a separate scale at the bottom of the chart on the same day's axis. If the volume for the day was 25,000 shares, you simply put a dot at the 25,000-share level and then bring that line down to the zero line on the volume scale. The next day, the high was 18, the low was 17, and the close was 17. One line over to the right on the time scale, you again plot the high of 18, the low (17), and

CHART 1–13

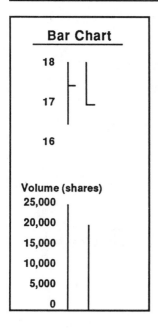

the close (17). The volume for this second day, we'll say, was 20,000 shares.

That's all there is to the plotting. It's not mystical and certainly not difficult once you do it a few times. The only difference on a weekly chart is that you plot the high, low, and close for the entire week (Monday trading through Friday). You also plot the volume for the entire week. On a very long-term chart, you can do the same thing for the entire month (high, low, close, and volume for the whole month). Charts 1–14, 1–15, and 1–16 show examples of each chart.

All three charts have a function. The daily chart (1–14) is definitely best for shorter-term trading where near term definition is important. The monthly chart (1–16) is on the other side of the spectrum and is a fine tool for very long-term investors who are looking for trends of several years. In between these two extremes are the Mansfield weekly charts (1–15), which are a good compromise of the other two. There is enough definition to trade (although very short-term traders should use daily charts), but they

CHART 1–14

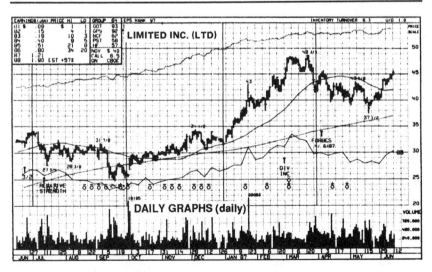

CHART COURTESY: DAILY GRAPHS AND LONG-TERM VALUES
P.O. BOX 24933
LOS ANGELES, CA 90024
(213)820-7011

CHART 1–15

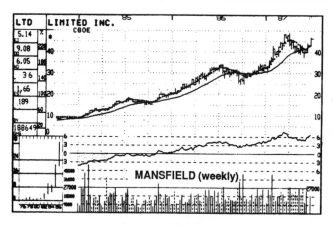

COURTESY OF MANSFIELD STOCK CHARTS

CHART 1–16

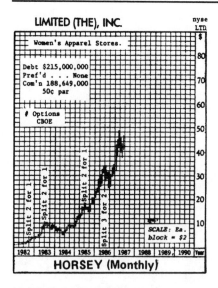

COURTESY OF HORSEY STOCK CHARTS
SALISBURY, MARYLAND 21801
301-742-3700

are especially valuable in showing the really important moves that matter to intermediate-term traders (several months) and investors.

While we will refer to all of these charts throughout this book, we will draw heaviest on the weekly Mansfield charts, as they are the best all-around charts for investors, especially since they show more than two years of history at a time. Nevertheless, be aware that all three are excellent chart services, and all serve their purpose.[6]

READING THE MANSFIELD CHART

Now let's get to the nitty-gritty and study a weekly Mansfield chart (Chart 1–17). If you've never looked at one before, don't be over-whelmed—I promise that in five minutes it will all make sense to you. If, however, you're an old hand at technical analysis, you can quickly skim the next page or two while everyone gets on an equal technical footing.

I won't bother you with all the features—many of which are fundamental—that are on the chart. Many are confusing and not necessary. Instead we'll stick to what's really important and profit-producing on the chart.

1. The first thing to look at is each high-low-close spike. The stock's price is the most important component of the chart because, over time, it forms the pattern that will give us clues and subtle insights into the next major move.

2. The second factor is the volume plot for the week. It's a favorable signal when volume expands as a stock rises and decreases as a stock declines. As we said earlier and will stress many more times throughout this book, it's *very important that volume is large and expanding on a breakout.* Heavy volume signals urgent and powerful buying that will propel the stock much higher.

3. The third important detail on this chart is the 30-week MA. Mansfield charts do not give a simple 30-week MA where all 30 weeks count equally. Instead, they use a weighted 30-week MA

---

[6]Before making a recommendation in *PTR*, I always check all three.

CHART 1–17

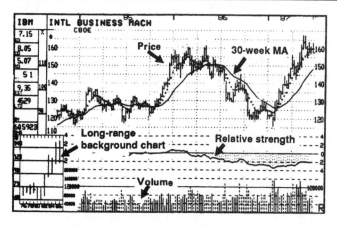

COURTESY OF MANSFIELD STOCK CHARTS

whereby the most recent action counts far more than the old input. This makes the MA more sensitive to current activity and helps it reverse direction faster. The drawback to their weighted average is that it leads to a few more whipsaws. Nevertheless, since it is such a long-term MA, the signals are still quite good. Remember, *never* buy a stock—no matter how cheap it appears based on fundamentals or a recent sharp decline—if it is trading below its declining 30-week MA. The price performance is giving you a clear signal that there's a worm in the apple! Don't even *think* of buying it! Conversely, never sell short any stock that is above its rising 30-week MA no matter how high the price/earnings ratio is.

4. The fourth item to be aware of is the long-range background. These are the yearly high-low figures located in the lower lefthand corner of the Mansfield chart. The value of the long-range background chart is that it helps you put current price activity into historical context. When an upside breakout moved Goodyear Tire to a new high for 1986 (see Chart 1–18), a quick glance at the background chart would tell you that it was also a new high for the past several years. That is an especially favorable situation, as it shows that there is no further resistance overhanging the stock. It is in virgin territory and there are no sellers who are looking to "get out even." In the absence of the sellers, the stock can move

CHART 1–18

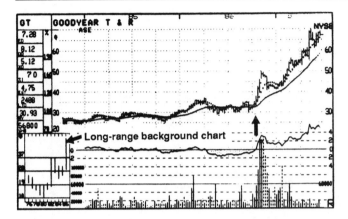

Long-range background chart

COURTESY OF MANSFIELD STOCK CHARTS

still higher. That's just what Goodyear Tire did in late 1986 through early 1987. It's no coincidence that it rallied more in the few months after it broke above the 37 high than in the several years prior to that break into virgin territory.

On the other hand, a breakdown on the chart that drops a stock to a new yearly low is a dangerous pattern. And when you look at the long-range background and see that a stock has also broken to a new low for the past several years, you should recognize this as an especially bearish and dangerous situation which should most definitely be avoided on the long side. Campbell Resources (Chart 1–19) provides us with a textbook example of what happens when a stock breaks down and there is no long term support beneath it. Campbell broke below 7½ and eventually hit bottom at 75 cents before reversing.

5. The final important part of the chart to be aware of is the relative-strength line. As long as this line is in a downtrend, *don't* consider buying the stock even if it breaks out on the high-low-close price chart. Poor relative strength shows that it is still an inferior performer compared to the overall stock market. On the other hand, if the relative strength line is in an uptrend, don't consider selling the stock short even if it breaks down on the price chart. Another important use for this relative-strength line is to

CHART 1–19

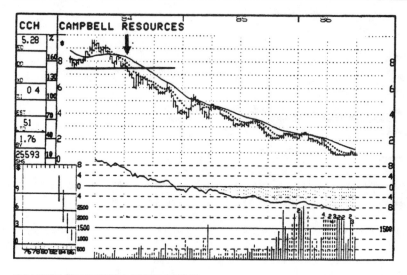

COURTESY OF MANSFIELD STOCK CHARTS

CHART 1–20

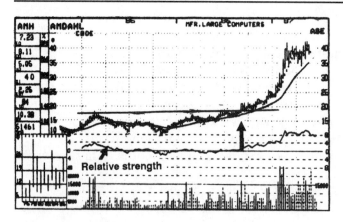

COURTESY OF MANSFIELD STOCK CHARTS

watch for those situations where it moves from negative territory (below the zero line) to positive territory. That is another favorable signal. In cases such as Amdahl (Chart 1–20) and Newmont Mining (Chart 1–21)—both *PTR* recommendations in the summer of 1986 (see arrows)—where an upside breakout also is accompanied by a move by the relative-strength line into positive territory, the probabilities of buying a big winner are increased substantially. Conversely, when a breakdown on the price chart goes hand in hand with a move into negative territory (below the zero line) by the relative strength line (see Charts 1–22 and 1–23) it's a case of "look out below"! Be sure to treat these as bearish situations no matter how cheap they may appear based on fundamentals. Both Ocean Drilling and Reading & Bates show you what can happen. Even though they had fallen substantially before their relative-strength line turned negative, once their relative-strength graphs dropped into negative territory, there was far more decline ahead of them.

That's it! That's all you need to know to be able to profitably read a chart. There is a lot more to be learned about chart analysis; many excellent volumes have been written on the subject. But you've just learned the lessons of chart reading that have the greatest payoff. With these simple but important tools you are now ready to start charting your way to a much more profitable future.

CHART 1–21

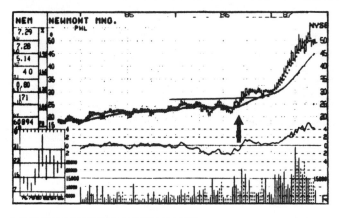

COURTESY OF MANSFIELD STOCK CHARTS

CHART 1–22

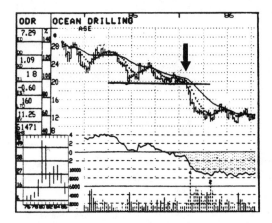

COURTESY OF MANSFIELD STOCK CHARTS

CHART 1–23

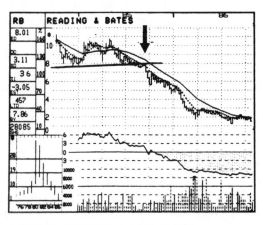

COURTESY OF MANSFIELD STOCK CHARTS

CHAPTER 2

ONE GLANCE IS WORTH
A THOUSAND EARNINGS
FORECASTS

The title of this chapter is something I really believe in. All you have to do is look at a stock like General Motors, which had improving earnings in 1981, as it dropped from 58 to 34; or a stock like Greenwich Pharmaceuticals, which moved from 3 to 19 in the 1986–1987 period while it registered deficits! So remember: it is really true that: "the tape tells all," and our job is to learn how to listen properly.

You are now ready to start working on your degree in technical analysis, and to start learning how to apply my methods so the market can become less mystical and more profitable for you. Look at this Stage Chart (Chart 2–1). If ever the cliché that a picture is worth a thousand words was true, this is a perfect example of it—in living color! Study Chart 2–1 for a minute. This is how you are going to start analyzing stocks and the market from now on. Once you grasp this profitable technique, the market game for stocks, options, mutual funds, commodities, or you-name-it will become much easier—and more profitable. You'll be able to flip through any chart book and immediately spot those few stocks worthy of further study and possible action, while eliminating the scores of issues that aren't worth another moment of consideration no matter how exciting the newspaper headlines. Just remember this basic fact: any stock has to be in one of four market stages, and the trick is to be able to identify each one. The four stages of a major cycle, as illustrated in Chart 2–1 are: (1) The basing area, (2) the advancing stage, (3) the top area, and (4) the declining stage.

CHART 2–1

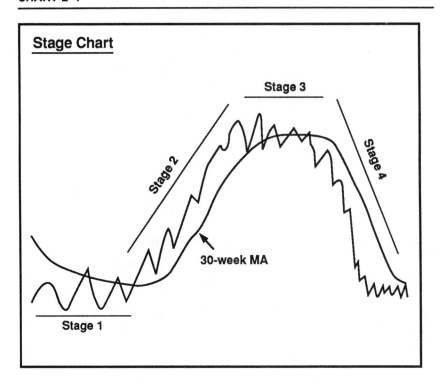

STAGE 1: THE BASING AREA

After stock XYZ has been declining for several months, it eventually will lose downside momentum and start to trend sideways. What's actually taking place is that buyers and sellers are starting to move into equilibrium, whereas previously the sellers were far stronger, which is why the stock had plummeted. Volume will usually lessen—dry up—as a base forms. But often volume will start to expand late in Stage 1, even though prices remain little changed. This is an indication that dumping of the stock by disgruntled owners is no longer driving down the price. The buyers who are moving in to take the stock off their hands are not demanding any significant price concession. This is a favorable indication.

Here's how it appears on the chart. Initially the 30-week MA loses its downside slope and starts to flatten out. In addition, intermittent rallies and declines will toss the stock above and below the MA. During this stage, there will usually be several swings between support at the bottom of the trading range and resistance at the top of the range. This basing action can go on for months or, in some cases, years.

This is the point where many market players get itchy to move in and catch the bottom price. But it doesn't do much good to buy yet. Even if you catch the exact low, your money could be tied up for a long time with little movement, and time is money. Even worse, premature investors often get impatient and end up selling after months of frustrating sideways action right *before* the big move starts.

Now study Chart 2–2—Bethlehem Steel, which is in Stage 1 (shaded area). Note that after dropping sharply from 22 to 4⅝, it finally managed to rally up to and then above the MA. The next decline took it slightly back below the MA, and then the next rally (on increasing volume) saw BS break above its horizontal trendline as the MA started edging higher. Once BS moved above 9⅜, it

CHART 2–2

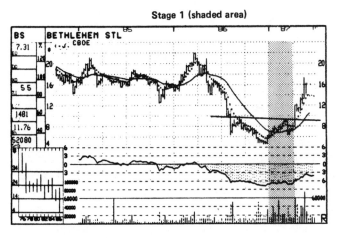

Stage 1 (shaded area)

COURTESY OF MANSFIELD STOCK CHARTS

was now ready for a Stage 2 advance, and it quickly soared to 17¼ over the next several weeks.

STAGE 2: ADVANCING PHASE

The ideal time to buy is when a stock is finally swinging out of its base into this more dynamic stage. Such a breakout above the top of the resistance zone and the 30-week MA should occur on impressive volume. This is the start of the advancing Stage 2 uptrend phase. However, before the really dynamic part of the advance gets rolling, be aware that there is usually an initial rally followed by at least one pullback. That dip brings the stock back close to the breakout point, which is a good second chance to do low-risk buying. Don't become a fanatic about saving a few cents per share! If the breakout occurs at 12⅛, for example, the pullback may turn out to be 12⅜ or 12⅝ but will come close. The less it pulls back, the more strength it actually is showing. Interestingly enough, at the breakout point—which is the perfect time to buy—the reported fundamentals will often be negative. And unless your stockbroker is technically oriented, he may try to talk you out of buying the stock.

In Stage 2, the 30-week MA usually starts turning up shortly after the breakout. The situation becomes a buyer's dream as each successive rally peak is higher than the last. In addition, the lows on corrections are also progressively higher. This is important! Don't expect the stock to be a one-way street no matter how bullish and powerful the pattern is. Chart 2–3 of International Paper illustrates what I am talking about. Once it moved into Stage 2 (shaded area) in early 1986, all downside corrections were contained above the rising 30-week MA, and each rally took IP to another new high. The market is always tricky and there is a reason why the overwhelming majority of investors lose money over the years in the market. The stock market (or any market for that matter) will do whatever is necessary to keep the majority from making money while amply rewarding the astute professional minority. So expect two steps forward and one sharp step back. As long as all of these wild swings and shakeouts take place *above* the stock's *rising* 30-week MA, don't worry—everything is proceeding according to Hoyle and is on schedule for a big profit!

CHART 2–3

Stage 2 (shaded area)

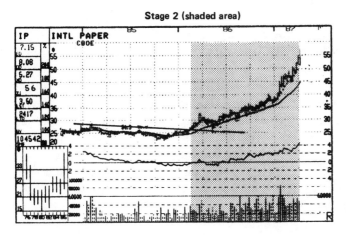

COURTESY OF MANSFIELD STOCK CHARTS

After several months of bullish bliss as the fundamentals start to improve and more and more investors belatedly jump on the bullish bandwagon, the stock will eventually start to sag closer and closer to its MA. The angle of ascent of the MA will slow down considerably. At this point, the stock is a "hold." Although it is still in Stage 2, this stock is now trading far above its support level and MA and is being discovered by the investment community; it is overextended and most definitely no longer a buy. This is the point where buying puts you at considerable risk.

From an investing point of view (we'll deal with trading in a later chapter), the right time to buy the stock was either on the initial breakout or on the later pullback toward the breakout level (12⅛ on our XYZ Chart 1–6 on page 11). At that time, when the stock was still close to its base, the downside risk was quite low and the upside potential considerable. The reward/risk ratio was totally in your favor. Now, however, that obviously is not the case. In addition, the later we get into Stage 2, the more erratic the price swings become as early buyers panic on selloffs because they don't want to lose their excellent profits. The Johnny-come-latelies buy in on each selloff as they want to get a bargain in their newly discovered hot stock. At this point the stock is the subject of rumors and glowing press reports. It's also the point where emotions are having a big impact on the decisions of both buyers and sellers. I can't stress how many times I've seen portfolios filled with big losses because the entry point for the given stock was poor. Be disciplined! If you are a long-term investor, buy only at the proper entry point early in Stage 2 (in the case of XYZ, near 12⅛). If you miss buying a stock, don't get panicky and chase it and just end up paying any old price. Be consistent. Either buy it right or don't buy it at all. Obviously a little common sense is needed. If you miss it at 12⅛, buying at 12⅞ is no big deal, but paying 25 or 26 sure is! If you've missed a good stock, don't fret about it. With thousands of listed and over-the-counter stocks to pick from, there will always be good stocks at great prices. It's similar to hailing a taxi; if you miss the first one, another one will soon come along.

STAGE 3: THE TOP AREA

Eventually, all good things come to an end. In the stock market, this takes the form of a Stage 3 top as the upward advance loses momentum and starts to trend sideways. What's going on beneath the surface is that buyers and sellers are once again about equal in strength. In Stage 2, the buyers were far stronger and overwhelmed the sellers. Now that the advance is ending, the stock is in equilibrium and the mirror image of a Stage 1 base starts to take shape.

Volume is usually heavy in Stage 3 and the moves are sharp and choppy. If you've ever heard the expression that a stock is "churning" (moving sideways on heavy volume), this stage is an outstanding example of it. The heavy volume on the part of buyers, who are excited by the improving fundamentals or "story," is met in equal measure by aggressive selling by the people who bought at considerably lower prices and are heading for the exits.

Here is how all of this takes shape on the chart. First the 30-week MA loses its upward slope and starts to flatten out. Whereas Stage 2 price declines always held at or above the MA, the stock will now tiptoe below and above the MA on declines and rallies. Once a Stage 3 top starts to form, traders should get the heck out with their profits! Investors, however, have more leeway. Once this stage is reached, I suggest that investors take profits on only half of their position. There is always the chance that the stock will break out on the upside again, beginning yet another Stage 2 upleg. If you still hold half of your original position, you'll then be able to benefit from the upward movement of this new Stage 2. But it's imperative that you protect your profits on the remaining half position with a protective sell stop set right beneath the bottom of the new support level (in this case, 25⅞, see Chart 1–6, pg. 11). For now, just accept this as good market tactics. In a later chapter, we will show you how to properly set your stops—which not one investor in a hundred knows how to do, and which is one of the real secrets of stock market success.

Chart 2–4 of ICH Corporation is a perfect illustration of Stage 3 (shaded area). Note how the moving average stopped rising, and how ICH broke below and then temporarily back above it. Even though the price/earnings ratio was only 10 at that time, and earnings were still on the upswing, this stock was clearly in trouble. Once it broke below 24, the Stage 3 top was complete and Stage 4 was ready to unfold. Now that ICH was in Stage 4, it dropped by more than 50 percent over the next six months, in the midst of one of the great bull markets in history!

Be very careful to keep your emotions in check in Stage 3, because the stories about the stock will usually be exciting and the

CHART 2–4

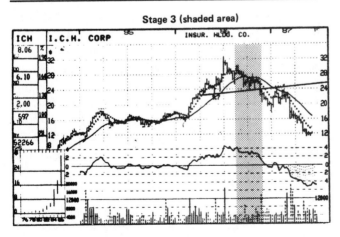

COURTESY OF MANSFIELD STOCK CHARTS

news glowing (good earnings, stock splits, and so on). As always, have faith in the chart, since—unlike you and I—it is not emotional. By learning the consistent discipline of following the market's message on the chart, we too can learn to be cool, calm, and calculating while others get consistently whipsawed by the greed-fear syndrome. So remember—no matter how powerful the fundamentals, no matter how convincing the story, you are *never* going to buy a stock in this stage because the reward/risk ratio is strongly stacked against you.

STAGE 4: THE DECLINING PHASE

This is a period when the factors that maintained a stock's price during the topping phase give way to the fatigue and pressures of fearful sellers. It shows up on the chart in the following manner: After moving back and forth in a neutral trading range, a stock eventually breaks below the bottom of its support zone. Our XYZ chart (1–6) shows a support zone of 26 to 26½, resistance near 30, and a basically flat MA. Unlike an upside breakout, which needs a *significant increase in volume* to be considered trustworthy, a downside break into Stage 4 doesn't necessarily need such a huge increase in volume to be considered valid. A volume increase on a breakdown followed by a volume decrease on a pullback to the breakdown point does signal a very dangerous situation; yet I've seen many cases where a stock moved into Stage 4 on relatively light volume and dropped substantially in the months ahead. Therefore, while a volume increase on the breakdown is even more bearish, don't ever let yourself get lulled into a false sense of security because the volume isn't heavy!¹ One way or another, you should get out of the stock. If your broker is a fundamentalist, he may try to dissuade you because the earnings and other fundamentals may be in pretty good shape. And the conventional thinking as Stage 4 starts to unfold is usually that the stock is just undergoing

---

¹However, when looking for short sales, those that break down on heavy volume are preferable since the big volume implies urgent selling, and these stocks usually decline far more rapidly.

a correction. This is nonsense. Once the stock breaks into Stage 4, the upside potential is very small (the old 26 to 26½ support zone of XYZ becomes the new ceiling, or resistance area, once the breakdown occurs), while the downside risk is considerable.

At this moment, stop and reflect for a second and then make a pledge to yourself. Take the oath that you are *never going to buy another stock in Stage 4.* Also promise yourself that you will never hold onto any of your stocks once they move into Stage 4. I'll show you in the chapter on stops how to make this last promise easier on yourself, so that it will be done automatically without your doubts and second and third guesses ever coming into the process. It will be mechanical and disciplined.

Don't get caught up in the macho game of riding out a decline. Hanging tough in Stage 4 is a masochistic and costly game. There is absolutely nothing ennobling or character-building about watching your hard-earned money go down the drain. All that you have to do to learn this incredibly important market lesson is to play the Kenny Rogers record "The Gambler." I'm not kidding. There's more solid market tactics in that short song than in all the fundamental clichés that bounce off the buildings on Broad and Wall streets. Think about these words of wisdom:

"You've got to know when to hold 'em, Know when to fold 'em, Know when to walk away, Know when to run."

Whether you are playing poker or the stock-market game, it's crucial to learn to play the odds and to use professional tactics.

If you change nothing else in your market operations after reading this book except to never buy or hold Stage 4 stocks, I can absolutely promise that you will improve your batting average so much over the next year that when you see your next year's income tax return, you'll think your accountant made an error. Don't get me wrong—there's much more you have to learn to really become a big winner; but this one tactic is so important that I want to stress it.

"Market analyst" Kenny Rogers goes on to tell us that "every gambler knows that the secret to surviving is knowing what to throw away, knowing what to keep, because every hand's a winner, every hand's a loser."

This point is also true. I've seen many portfolios over the years that had more winners than losers, yet they end up with major losses. The amateur investor creates a nightmare as he sells the winners too quickly with small profits while holding the losers that turn into Stage 4 disasters. The more sophisticated players, however, end up with super profits because they ride the Stage 2 winners all the way up while quickly getting out of their problem stocks. So it really is a matter of "knowing what to throw away and knowing what to keep."

Examine your own experience. How many times have you held a stock that should have been sold at 50, only to watch it drop down to 47, then 45, and then 40? How wonderful that your broker is there to hold your hand and reassure you it's still a $50 stock (unfortunately, the rest of the civilized world is misinformed). Ever the optimist, your broker probably offered this swell idea: If the stock was a good buy at 50, it's an even better buy at 40. So you didn't sell and, in fact, you compounded your error by engaging in that dangerous and destructive tactic of averaging down. You bought more at 40, telling yourself you'll now get out even when it gets back to 45. Months later, when that cheap stock at 40 became far cheaper at 25, the bad fundamental news that was really behind the drop belatedly became public. You ended up dumping the position for a huge loss as a Stage 1 base was just about to start forming.

Does this sound familiar? Never again will this nightmare be your destiny, because you will not be at the mercy of the stock as it plummets lower and lower and you keep hoping a bottom will form. Instead, you will be in control of the situation; you will take charge and get rid of any potentially crippling Stage 4 stock—whether you have a profit, are even, or have a loss. Remember, the market is a mechanical, non-thinking entity that doesn't know or care what price you paid for the stock. So if it's going to be a loser, say goodbye! Otherwise your profit will disappear, or your small loss will turn into a giant loss!

Now let's go back to the Chart 1–6, the XYZ stock. Note that it first broke down at 25⅞. It then had an initial drop to 23. There are almost always one or more rallies back to the breakdown point as bargain hunters feel that the stock is cheap compared to recent prices they've seen. Thereafter the downtrend gets going in earnest, and the MA starts to decline. From a reward/risk point of view, this is the most dangerous situation you will ever encounter in the marketplace. Think how exciting and profitable it is that you will never be in this situation again. When you pick up your daily newspaper, you'll see that plenty of trading took place in that stock—someone is buying. Just be glad that it won't be you.

In Stage 4, each decline drops to a new low while each reflexive oversold rally falls short of the prior peak. This is a textbook example of a downtrend. What's worse, all of this negative action takes place below the declining MA. Unfortunately, this is the stage where unsophisticated investors try to pick up a bargain because they think the stock has already fallen enough. But picking up fallen stars is a sure way to burn yourself!

Take a look at Chart 2–5 of Levitz Furniture from the early 1970s and you'll see just how destructive such amateur bottom-guessing in Stage 4 (shaded area) can be to your hard earned money. Instead of falling into this trap, learn to read the chart and use the perspective it gives you to remain unemotional and disciplined in your quest for big profits!

CHART 2–5

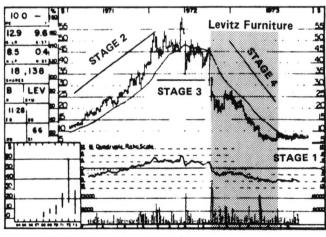

COURTESY OF MANSFIELD STOCK CHARTS

BUY THE NUMBERS

Now that you understand the concept of stage analysis, study these four charts and make sure you agree with the stage rating that each would get at this point in time. (An important hint to remember is

CHART 2–6

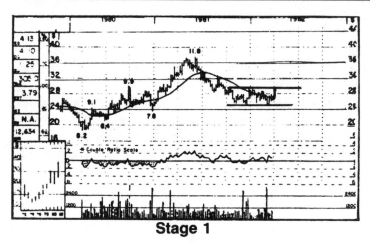

Stage 1

COURTESY OF MANSFIELD STOCK CHARTS

CHART 2–7

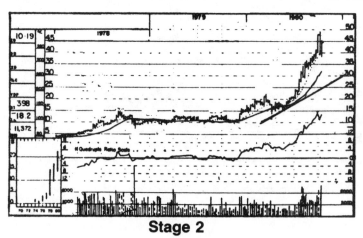

Stage 2

COURTESY OF MANSFIELD STOCK CHARTS

CHART 2–8

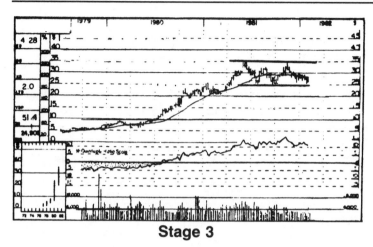

Stage 3

COURTESY OF MANSFIELD STOCK CHARTS

CHART 2–9

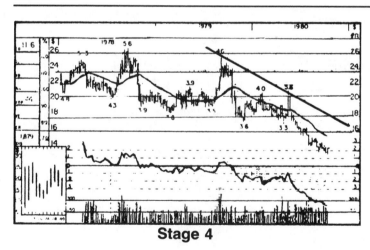

Stage 4

COURTESY OF MANSFIELD STOCK CHARTS

that the moving average is a great starting point for technically analyzing a stock.)

NOW IT'S YOUR TURN

Here's a little quiz for you. Go over these stock charts slowly and rate each one as of their latest entry. Study them until you agree with me on their respective stage ratings, because a clear understanding of my method now will most definitely help you score profits later. The answers will be found following the charts.

QUIZ

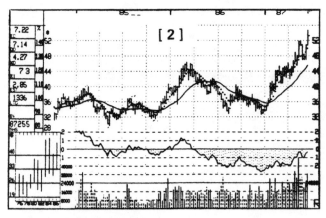

COURTESY OF MANSFIELD STOCK CHARTS

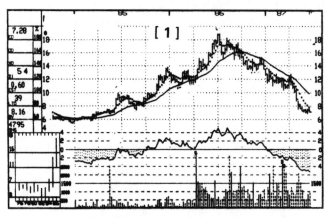

COURTESY OF MANSFIELD STOCK CHARTS

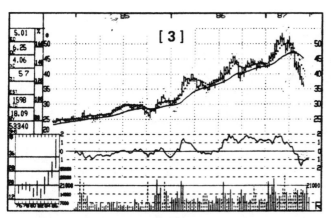

COURTESY OF MANSFIELD STOCK CHARTS

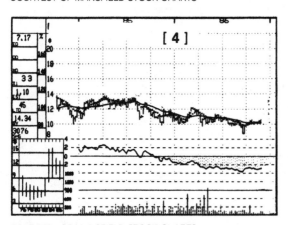

COURTESY OF MANSFIELD STOCK CHARTS

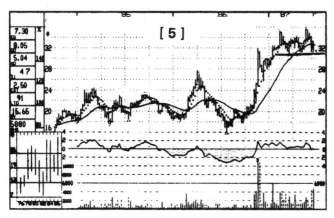

COURTESY OF MANSFIELD STOCK CHARTS

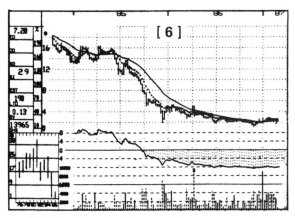

COURTESY OF MANSFIELD STOCK CHARTS

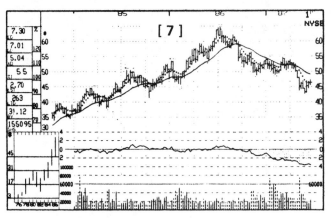

COURTESY OF MANSFIELD STOCK CHARTS

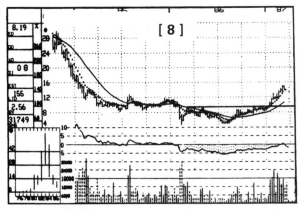

COURTESY OF MANSFIELD STOCK CHARTS

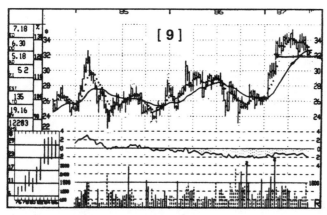

COURTESY OF MANSFIELD STOCK CHARTS

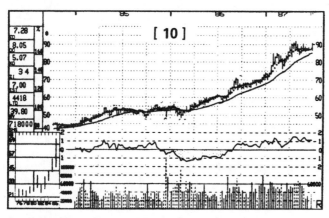

COURTESY OF MANSFIELD STOCK CHARTS

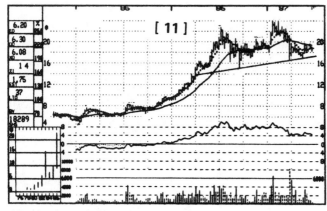

COURTESY OF MANSFIELD STOCK CHARTS

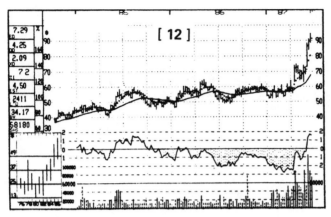

COURTESY OF MANSFIELD STOCK CHARTS

ANSWERS

1. Stage 4. MA declining and stock still below MA.
2. Stage 2. MA rising and stock still comfortably above MA.
3. Stage 4. MA declining and stock well below MA.
4. Stage 1. MA flat and stock price still in base area below resistance.
5. Stage 3. MA flat and stock price starting to whip back and forth through MA after big Stage 2 advance.
6. Stage 1. MA flat and stock price still in base area below resistance. All of this occurring after big Stage 4 decline.
7. Stage 4. MA declining and stock price still below MA.
8. Stage 2. Stock broke out above important resistance at 9, completing Stage 1 base. Stock now above rising MA.
9. Stage 3. After big Stage 2 advance, MA starting to flatten out while price whips back and forth through it.
10. Stage 2. Stock price still above MA (as it has consistently been for over one year) and MA rising.
11. Stage 3. This one is *very* tricky because the potential top is so large (forming for one year). MA, however, basically flat and stock price continues to whip back and forth through it. In

addition, stock is still above its major support so it's not yet Stage 4.

12. Stage 2. Stock price still far above rising MA.

THE REAL WORLD

Now that you're starting to get it, let's study some real-life examples of Stage 2 powerhouse advances and Stage 4 disasters to see that it isn't a case of "good in theory but not in practice." Nothing could be further from the truth! While no method of predicting the market is foolproof, the results are so startlingly good that you'll find it hard to believe!

In a future section I'll show you how to minimize the negative effect of those situations that don't work out according to plan. Take a look at the four stocks in Charts 2–10 through 2–13. All should have been bought when they moved into Stage 2 as recommended in *The Professional Tape Reader* (see arrow)—when they broke out of their Stage 1 bases.

Starrett Housing (2–10) completed an important Stage 1 base in early 1975 when it moved above 10. The MA then turned up,

CHART 2–10

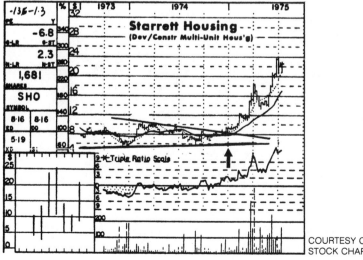

COURTESY OF MANSFIELD
STOCK CHARTS

CHART 2–11

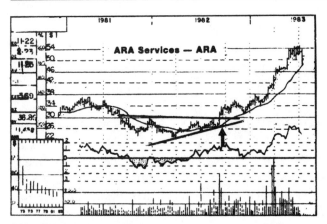

COURTESY OF MANSFIELD STOCK CHARTS

CHART 2–12

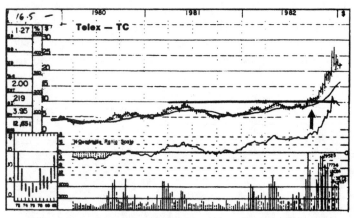

COURTESY OF MANSFIELD STOCK CHARTS

CHART 2–13

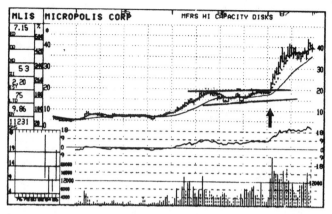

COURTESY OF MANSFIELD STOCK CHARTS

and it was a case of up, up, and away. Note how all corrections over the next six months held *above* the rising MA as the stock shot up to 24 within six months (a very healthy 280 percent annualized advance).

ARA Services (2–11) also demonstrated that same winning pattern when it broke out above 30 on especially heavy volume in 1982. It shot ahead to the mid–50s within the next nine months for a nice 100 percent annualized gain. Again all corrections stayed above the MA.

Telex (2–12) also broke out on extremely heavy volume when it moved above 10. It's no coincidence that the stock rocketed ahead for an incredible 680 percent gain annualized over the next three months! Once again, note how handily all corrections were dealt with above the rising 30-week MA.

Finally, of more recent vintage was our late-1986 recommendation of Micropolis (2–13) when it broke out above 19½ on *very* impressive volume for a fast 250 percent annualized gain. This is the only one of the four that was not an example of buying as the stock moved from Stage 1 into Stage 2. Instead, Micropolis was a buy when it first moved into Stage 2 in early 1986 as it broke out above resistance at 10. Then it formed what looked like a potential Stage 3 top (between resistance at 19½ and support near 15) before eventually breaking out a second time, when it moved above 19½ on very heavy volume. When this happens—which is relatively rare—the potential Stage 3 top bites the dust and the stock is put back into Stage 2. This is a powerful formation that is especially profitable for traders. So while longer-term investors want to do most of their buying near a base, when the risk is extremely low, traders should be alert for these continuation moves as they are usually very powerful and fast!

Now here are some stocks (Charts 2–14 through 2–17) that would have crippled your portfolio if you hadn't gotten out of them once they completed their Stage 3 tops and moved into Stage 4. Happily, all four were recommended for sale in *PTR* once they entered Stage 4.

Back in 1973, Avon was one of many so-called one-decision stocks of that era. Many intellectually lazy money managers convinced themselves that the only decision they needed to make for these growth stocks was when to buy. Don't ever believe in such fairy tales. There is never an investment—whether it be stocks, gold, real estate, gems, or Naugahyde futures—that is a "buy it and forget it" situation. All investments go through cycles, and when you hold through the down part of the cycle (Stage 4) you suffer both financially and emotionally. When Avon completed its

CHART 2–14

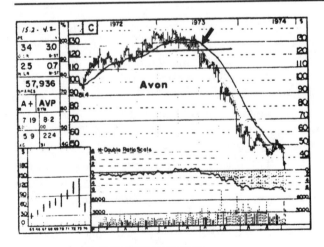

COURTESY OF MANSFIELD STOCK CHARTS

CHART 2–15

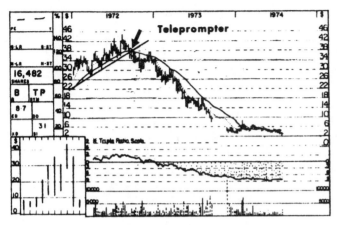

COURTESY OF MANSFIELD STOCK CHARTS

CHART 2–16

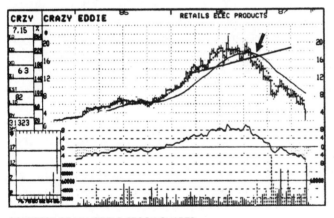

COURTESY OF MANSFIELD STOCK CHARTS

top and moved into Stage 4, it was earning $2.26 per share; yet when it was trading at $80 per share less, the earnings were $2.30 per share (for the trailing 12 months). If you fell into the trap of holding and rationalizing that it would eventually come back, then you should realize that, as I write (in late 1987), it's 14 years later

CHART 2–17

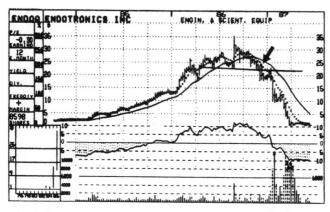

COURTESY OF MANSFIELD STOCK CHARTS

and Avon isn't anywhere close to its high of 140 or the breakdown near 120. It's still struggling in the mid-30's.

Look at Chart 2–14 of Avon and see how perfectly it followed the script with which you should be getting familiar. It broke support and sold off to 110. Then it staged one pullback rally back to the low 120s, where it originally had broken down. Thereafter, it was bombs away as Stage 4 took over. Every rally over the next year failed under the declining MA, so all of the millions of shares bought (because it was "cheap" at 80, and then 70, and then 60) in Stage 4 were motivated by the destructive bottom-guessing syndrome. Never again will this be your fate if you learn my method and follow it in a disciplined way.

Teleprompter (2–15) was another glittering favorite of that era as cable TV burst onto the scene. Despite the exciting fundamentals, Teleprompter clearly completed a major top when it broke below its MA and its important trendline. Once again there was a sharp initial decline (to 30) followed by a sucker (pullback) rally back to the breakdown level. Thereafter Teleprompter headed south with a vengeance. All rallies failed at or below the MA as the stock lost over 90 percent of its value.

Confirming the old cliché, "the more things change, the more they remain the same," the same dangerous pattern showed up in late 1986. This time two new junior high flyers—Crazy Eddie (2–

16) and Endotronics (2–17)—were shot out of the sky during a super bull market. As if to prove the limitations of fundamental analysis, a major brokerage firm issued a "buy" recommendation on Endotronics just days before its collapse! Once again things unfolded exactly as you'd expect. In both cases there were important sell signals registered as Stage 3 tops were completed. Again, after an initial decline, there was a pullback rally and then the selloffs really got rolling with all oversold rallies failing to move back above the respective MAs. I can guarantee you that similar situations will happen time and again in the future. The darling stocks of Wall Street will go down in flames and the bargain hunters and other scavengers will crow about the great opportunities they represent. Your strategy should be clear: Sell and then avoid the Stage 4 decline. In some cases even sell them short—which we'll go over later—while the crowd builds up losses and then rationalizes that they are unlucky.

Do you get the picture? By letting the market digest all of the relevant fundamentals (known and anticipated) and going with its judgment rather than what you read in the media and brokerage reports, your market batting average will improve considerably.

The question that usually pops up at this point during my seminars is "Can you apply this method to other areas, such as commodities or mutual funds?" The answer is simple—absolutely! Anything that trades on a supply/demand basis can be charted and interpreted in exactly the same manner. Just be aware that when dealing with commodities or stock index futures that the time frame is speeded up considerably, and a Stage 2 advance may unfold in a matter of weeks instead of months. So you'll need to use a much shorter-term MA.

Now look at the chart of weekly spot gold prices (Chart 2–18) versus its 30-week MA. Back in 1983, gold broke down from a Stage 3 top formation (down arrow) and moved into Stage 4 amid talk of eternal inflation and a $1,000 to $2,000 price. It crashed below $300 in the following months. In 1985, when inflation figures dropped to microscopic levels and the crowd's expectations should have brought about a further drop to $150 to $200, a base formed and the MA stopped declining. When it broke out above its gently downsloping trendline (see up arrow), a new bull move was launched that took gold close to $500!

CHART 2–18

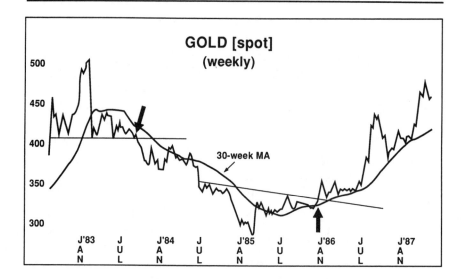

Finally, this method is very helpful when you want to do mutual-fund switching. It is particularly useful with both no-load and low-load sector fund trading. The sector fund is an investment vehicle that you should learn how to use. We'll go into detail about this later. For now, look at Chart 2–19 and see how easy and profitable it would have been to have bought Janus Fund when it moved into Stage 2. In September 1982 it was near 3½ (see arrow) after completing its Stage 1 base, as it moved above its downsloping trendline.

By now, no matter how addicted you are to fundamental analysis, I hope that you see the value of my technical method. As the chapters go on, you'll become more confident and proficient in applying it. So keep reading, digesting, and reflecting. And the next time you hear someone quickly dismiss technical analysis as voodoo or worse, smile to yourself, but don't argue. It's important that investors disagree. If everyone used the technical method and had the same bullish or bearish opinion, they wouldn't be able to open the market tomorrow. Also, we need an uninformed majority if we are to realize outstanding profits in the market.

CHART 2–19

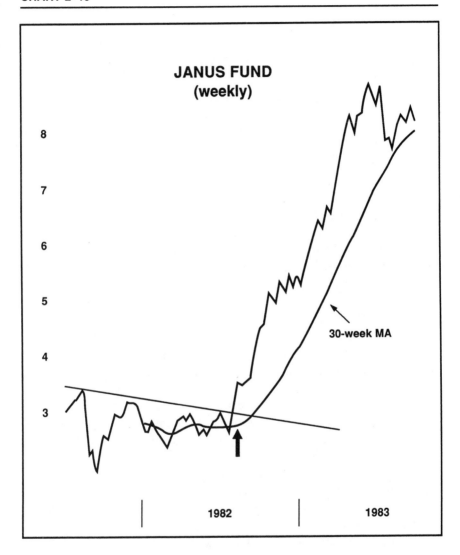

JANUS FUND
(weekly)

30-week MA

1982   1983

CHAPTER 3

THE IDEAL TIME TO BUY

HOW, WHEN, AND WHAT

In the past two chapters, you've already come a lot further than you realize. You can now take your portfolio and a chart book and go to work separating the good from the bad. Rather than blindly depending on your broker's advice you can now quickly see which of your stocks have a high probability of success and which ones are very likely to give you an ulcer. Knowledge is power and you are well on the way to becoming Hercules. But you still have some important learning to do. Now that the foundation is in place, you can easily differentiate between a bullish Stage 2 stock and a bearish Stage 4 situation.

The next step, however, is to construct the rest of the building and to learn the perfect time to buy. In addition, it's vital to understand how you should go about purchasing your stocks as well as knowing what to purchase. This is extremely important since when you glance through a chart book, especially during a rip-roaring bull market, you'll see hundreds of stocks that look buyable. Therefore it's absolutely crucial to learn how to cull out those few A+ stocks with super upside potential while taking a pass on the lesser lights.

Later in this chapter, we'll deal with the what-to-buy question, which is actually much more difficult than knowing when to buy. But first you have to master the next basic, which is knowing exactly where to enter a stock. When you see a chart of a stock that has had a major advance, there was one point that was the perfect time to have bought. This ideal entry point is what we are now going to focus on.

THE INVESTOR'S WAY

There are two great times for an investor to do new buying and both center around the breakout point. The first is when a stock initially moves out of its Stage 1 base and enters Stage 2. The second and safer time is when a stock pulls back toward the breakout point after the initial Stage 1 buying frenzy burns out. The advantage of purchasing on a pullback is that you can play movie critic and judge what you've seen. Did volume pick up impressively? Did the stock move far above the breakout point? Did volume then contract on the pullback? Or did XYZ just nudge above the critical resistance level and then fall back below it, which always signals a red flag warning? Once you've watched the action, you know whether you're dealing with a potential A + or C − .

So which tactic is best? Should you wait and only buy on a pullback? No! If you wait to do only such low-risk buying, you are going to miss out on some of the biggest winners. Those few stocks that never pull back are demonstrating the strongest rocket propulsion. These are going to be giant winners, so we most definitely do not want to be left on the launching pad. If you're a long-term investor, compromise and buy half of your intended position on the initial breakout, and the other half if the stock pulls back close to the breakout price and you like the post-breakout action.[1]

Chart 3 – 1 shows graphically what the process looks like. Point A is an excellent time to do new buying. It's an especially good entry point for investors. At this juncture the risk is extremely low since the base of support is just underneath your purchase price. Equally important, the upside potential is tremendous since the entire Stage 2 advance lies ahead of it. The only drawback is that it can take time for solid Stage 2 momentum to build. As with everything else in life, there are no free lunches, so it's a tradeoff. You are getting a terrific reward/risk ratio but must often pay the price of patience.[2] That's no big deal for an investor, but it can

---

[1]If, however, you are a trader and want to buy the stock, purchase your entire intended position on the breakout. That first move can be a home run for a trader. After taking a fast profit, you can repurchase it on a pullback for a second good play.

[2]In about 25 percent of the cases, the advance is immediate.

CHART 3-1

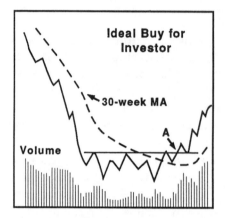

CHART 3-2

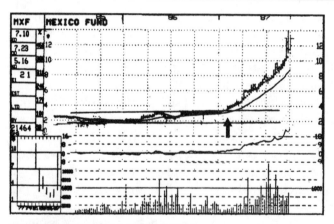

COURTESY OF MANSFIELD STOCK CHARTS

drive a trader crazy. So investors will do much more of this early Stage 2 buying than will traders.

That's the theory. Now let's look at a real life example. Mexico Fund broke out at 3¼ (see arrow on Chart 3-2) in early 1987. Volume started to increase as the stock promptly jumped 35 percent in a matter of days. Once the initial burst of buying had run its course, it temporarily peaked at 4⅜. Two weeks later, it pulled back to 3⅜—very close to the initial breakout. Volume favorably contracted on the pullback, so then is when you should have bought your remaining half of the position. Thereafter volume increased sharply as it gathered momentum and in the next nine months chalked up a fast 330 percent gain as it rallied to 14.

THE TRADER'S WAY

There is one other very profitable time to do new buying. It occurs after a Stage 2 advance is well underway, when the stock drops back close to its MA and consolidates. It then breaks out anew above the top of its resistance zone (point A on Chart 3–3). This is called a *continuation* buy. Again there is a tradeoff involved. In this case the probabilities are overwhelmingly high that the advance will be rapid, but there is a greater risk factor.[3] This type of buy is more suited to traders than investors. But investors, too, should be willing to do some late Stage 2 buying when the overall market is very strong and there aren't many initial breakout opportunities left. Early in a major bull market, however, there is absolutely no need for investors to do continuation buying since so many stocks are breaking out of their bases for the first time.[4] On the other hand, later in a bull market—such as in 1986–1987—there are very few early Stage 2 buys left, but plenty of the continuation variety still occurring. At those times even investors should do some continuation buying.

Chart 3–3 shows what this type of buy looks like. The moving average should be clearly trending higher. This is important! Just as a marathon runner needs something left in reserve for the finish, so does a Stage 2 advancing stock. If the MA starts to roll over and flatten out, you don't want that stock. Even if it breaks out in a continuation move, it is not likely to have that tiger in its tank

---

[3]Since the stock is much further along in Stage 2, there is a greater chance of a false breakout.

[4]Such as in the third quarter of 1982 when literally thousands of stocks were breaking out of Stage 1 bases.

CHART 3–3

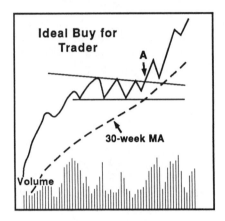

that we want. Instead, look for a stock that mimics the outline of this chart and has plenty of high octane power left.

Swift Energy provides a textbook example of what I'm talking about. After forming a multi-year Stage 1 base, it broke out at 2⅛ in early 1986 (arrow at point A on Chart 3–4). Over the next six months Swift advanced very nicely to 5⅜ for a better than 150 percent gain. The average investor—and unfortunately even some technicians—then started yelling that the stock was too high. Not true. In the following five-month period, SFY consolidated its huge gain while the 30-week MA continued its nonstop journey higher. Then, in February 1987, Swift broke out from this reconsolidation area at 5½ (arrow at point B) and promptly rocketed ahead 240 percent over the next four months. Not so surprisingly, it never pulled back close to its 5½ breakout point.[5] Although about 80 percent of initial breakouts from a Stage 1 base are followed by a handy pullback, this happens with less than 50 percent of continuation buys. This is especially true if the stock is going to be a

---

[5]It did, however, pull back close to its initial breakout point at 2⅛ when it first moved into Stage 2 in 1986.

CHART 3–4

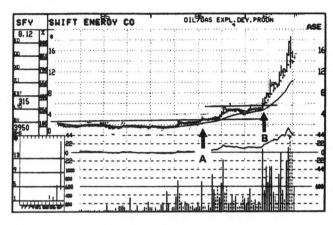

COURTESY OF MANSFIELD STOCK CHARTS

grand-slam home run. So the proper tactic when dealing with this type of breakout is to buy your entire position when it overcomes its significant resistance.

While there are no official rules, I would say as a rule of thumb investors over the years should do about 75 to 80 percent early Stage 2 buying with the remainder coming from continuation moves. Traders, on the other hand, should reverse the figures and do about 80 percent of their buying on breakouts that are already in Stage 2 and have consolidated near the MA before breaking out once again. The rest of a trader's buying should be of the early Stage 2 variety.

UNDER THE MICROSCOPE

Now let's slowly go through the process of how a stock completes its Stage 1 base and moves into Stage 2 so it will be absolutely clear exactly when you should do your buying. Look at Chart 3–5 and note how XYZ is moving between support near 8 and resistance at 12. The basing action is all taking place close to the 30–week MA which is no longer declining sharply but has instead started to

CHART 3–5

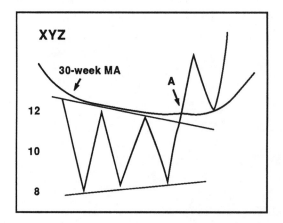

flatten out. When and if this stock breaks out above resistance at 12, that is the perfect time to enter the stock.[6]

But what if you are at work or on vacation when this exciting breakout occurs (point A on Chart 3–5)? When you pick up the evening paper, frustration sets in. XYZ, closed yesterday at 11½, closed tonight at 14, up 2½ points, and you've missed it. The answer isn't to call your broker and buy at any price. You also don't have to run out and buy a quote machine or have your broker call you a dozen times a day. In fact, such so-called solutions will very likely hurt you. First, they lead to emotional decisions, and that is a definite no-no. I've always found that my most profitable judgments are made late at night or on weekends. This is no accident. It's a time when you can calmly decipher the charts' message with no wild Dow swings or broker's calls to affect you. Second, it's obviously important to concentrate on your primary business during the day. There's a far better, more relaxing way that will put less stress on you and lead to much bigger profits. And don't underestimate the importance of staying mellow, because the market is stressful under the best of circumstances.

---

[6]Always remember—the bigger the base, the greater the upside potential.

USING BUY-STOP ORDERS

From now on whenever you want to buy a stock on a breakout, *use a buy-stop order.* Some of you already know what this order is but don't use it; a few of you more experienced players do utilize it. Most of you not only don't use it, but aren't even quite sure what it is. All of that is going to change right now. Learning to properly use this professional technique is the next secret of profitable investing that you are going to master. From now on you are going to use this order very often.[7]

What a buy-stop order does is tell the specialist that you want to buy stock XYZ. But—and this is an incredibly important but— *only* if the stock breaks out above a certain level. In the case of our ideal cycle chart (Chart 1–6 page 11), we want to buy only if the stock displays enough power to move above resistance at 12. By placing an order to buy 1,000 shares of XYZ at 12⅛ *stop,* the stock will not be purchased if XYZ fails to break out above 12. If it does catapult above the critical 12 level, it then becomes a market order to immediately buy 1,000 shares of XYZ. You don't have to be watching the stock. You probably won't even know when your order is executed. Be aware, however, that it doesn't *have* to be filled at 12⅛. The stock may be purchased at 12⅛ or 12¼ or even 12⅜; but, in the great majority of the cases, it will be very close to your ideal price.[8] If, however, the stock is traded over the counter, you aren't allowed to place buy-stop or sell-stop orders. In that case, you have to work with a broker who will put your OTC stock on his monitor and buy it for you as soon as it pops above resistance.

Using buy-stop orders is very important to your new market strategy. Before finishing up on this subject there are a few important refinements to learn. Nothing in the market or life is ever all one way. As profitable as this technique is, there are a few potential dangers to be aware of. One problem with this type of

---

[7]In a future chapter, I'll show you how to use its cousin, the sell-stop order, to protect your profits and minimize losses on an investment that doesn't work out.

[8]Especially if it's on the New York Stock Exchange rather than the American Exchange, which, in my opinion, has inferior liquidity to the NYSE and, in most cases, specialists that don't make as "tight" a market.

order is that you can get a very bad execution. While this may not happen once in fifty trades, one bad time is one too many.

Here's how to make sure that it never happens to you. Suppose stock XYZ closed last night at 11⅝. You look at your chart and decide that it's getting ready to break out above resistance at 12. You call your broker the next morning before the market opens and put in an order to buy 1,000 XYZ at 12⅛ stop. Unfortunately, right before the market opens good news is announced on the stock and it opens much higher at 15. Instead of getting in at your perfect entry price of 12⅛, you are now the proud owner of XYZ at 15. While the purchase may ultimately work out, it isn't where you wanted to enter the stock. In addition, the reward/risk ratio is now far less favorable than it was at 12⅛. Because of this potential negative, some traders and investors try to do an end run around the problem. They use what is called a buy-stop-limit order with just one specified price. This means that you can buy *only* at your ideal price (in this case, 12⅛) or not at all. I find this type of order an even bigger negative, as it creates more problems than it solves. Not once in fifty times, but more like one out of four, the stock will break out without your ever buying it because it runs past 12⅛ so quickly your order never gets filled.

BUYING WITHIN LIMITS

What's the answer? There's a variation of the buy-stop-limit order that very few market players know about. It combines the best of the stop concept, yet sets some higher limit to the price that you can pay. If we want to buy when crossing 12, we use a buy-stop at 12⅛, but also a limit of ¼ point above the breakout—in this case, 12⅜. We then enter the order as follows: Buy 1,000 XYZ at 12⅛ stop–12⅜ limit. You'll buy the stock with no problem at all, unless it trades very thinly, (in which case you'd stretch the limit to a half point above the breakout, and the order would read: Buy 1,000 XYZ at 12⅛ stop–12⅝ limit). Again, you've lessened the ulcer factor because you don't have to worry that you'll end up paying a horrible price.

Another potential problem is that you enter the order on Monday or Tuesday and the stock doesn't break out right away. Then you get busy and forget to enter it on Wednesday. Bingo. Murphy's Law—whatever can go wrong *will*—goes into effect and the stock makes its breakout. Your order isn't in and the stock ends up running away from you. Every market veteran has had this experience. There's an old market cliché that says the market will do what you expect, but not when you expect it to. It's absolutely true and, after playing the market game for years, I am now a firm believer in O'Toole's Law which states, "Murphy was an optimist!" So any tool that can reduce potential problems in the market should be considered valuable! That's why this next technique is so fabulous. It's simple yet very effective.

When you do your market homework and see two or three potentially exciting patterns that you want to buy—if they break out—simply do the following: Enter buy-stop orders for all three stocks on a *good-'til-canceled* (GTC) basis. This means that you have a standing order with the specialist until you either cancel the orders or they are actually executed. Just be careful to keep good records. It's your responsibility if you forget about the order. You may be surprised two or three weeks later when you find out that you bought 2,000 shares of Widget Technology. Here's how your buy order should now read: Buy 1,000 XYZ at 12⅛ stop–12⅜ limit–GTC.

Using GTC-stop orders will get you in the habit of doing several positive things. First of all, you won't have to watch the market closely during the day, which will allow you to concentrate your energies more clearly on your job. Second, you will make far better, less emotional decisions, since they will have nothing to do with that day's crazy market action. That's especially important with the ridiculous new-fangled buying and selling programs that now often move the Dow up or down 30 to 50 points in an hour. Wild intraday swings can upset and panic you out of a perfectly good position. Or sudden strength can cause you to scramble to buy something because it suddenly looks like the market is running away without you. Don't operate in this manner. It's crucial that you learn how to properly buy stocks in a disciplined, relaxed way. By using my method of stage analysis and combining it with GTC buy-stop orders, everything will be automatic, which is just what we want to accomplish. Over the years, it has become obvious to me that the more mechanical I've made my system and the less subject to judgments and emotions, the more profitable it has become. Interestingly enough, this subtle but important fact has been reinforced by dozens of Wall Street pros with whom I've talked who have learned the same lesson, often the hard way.

Why should this be so? Simple. Because we all are human and filled with an abundance of those twin demon emotions, fear and greed. Fear causes you to panic and sell at the bottom, while greed motivates you to buy right near the top. These are the driving factors behind the crowd's yo-yo mentality. In order not to get caught up in the fear-greed syndrome, set time aside each weekend to unemotionally scan your chart publication. You really only need an hour for this chore, but obviously the more time you can spare, the better. Make up a list of the few outstanding potential buys that you see among the many charts. Then, each night, chart and follow these few stocks plus any other issues in your portfolio. This simple exercise will help you develop a much more sensitive market feel. In addition, instead of being overwhelmed and continually whipsawed, you'll feel relaxed and confident as you follow your profitable game plan.

BUYING AND SELLING PATTERNS TO BE AWARE OF

Before getting into the specifics of what to buy, there are a few market patterns that occur with such unbelievable regularity that you must become aware of them. They will give you an extra edge in determining when to be more or less aggressive. It's especially important for traders to know these repetitious patterns, but even investors can raise their batting averages by being aware of these tendencies. While many of us technicians have done work in this area, no one to my knowledge has engaged in the in-depth research that Arthur Merrill and Yale Hirsch have. Merrill's book *Behavior of Prices on Wall Street* (Analysis Press, 1984) and Hirsch's book *Don't Sell Stocks on Monday* (Facts on File Publications, 1986) are excellent works on the subject. In the next few pages, with their permission, I am going to borrow heavily from their excellent data so you can better understand these important recurring patterns.

The first cycle that you should be aware of is the most important. This is one that both traders and investors alike should be thoroughly familiar with—the four-year presidential cycle.

Many investors mistakenly believe it is best to wait until after the election to buy. They reason that Wall Street prefers a Republican, business-oriented administration, and the market will decline if a Democrat is elected. This is wrong on two counts. First of all, the Dow Jones Industrial Average has actually racked up more

CHART 3–6

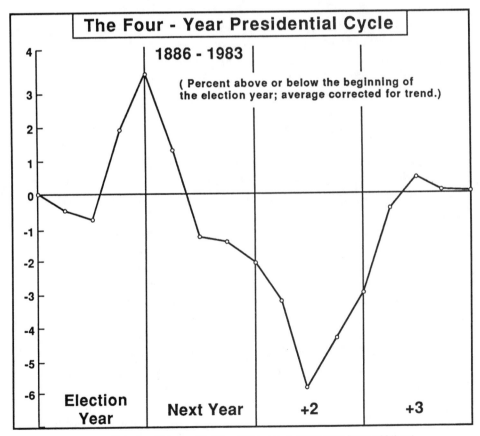

SOURCE: Arthur A. Merrill, *Behavior of Prices on Wall Street* (Chappaqua, NY:Analysis Press, 1984), p.4

points in this century under Democratic presidents than Republicans. Some of the gain, however, is due to greater inflation during the Democratic time in office. But even more important is the reality that no matter who is elected, the year following the election is usually a disaster. Bear markets have been as common as presidential candidates kissing babies. It's therefore not surprising that first years such as 1969, 1973, 1977, and 1981 all witnessed bear markets. (There are exceptions of course—1985 was a bullish year.) Historically, the probabilities are strong that in the second year the bear market will continue until a bottom is reached around mid-year (as occurred in August 1982). The rest of year two is bullish, and then the third year of the presidential term is the best one of the cycle (1987 until late August was no exception). The fourth year, which is the election year, is a choppy one, with weakness usually occurring in the first half and strength in the second half.

Over the past 100 years, this four-year cycle has unfolded with such unbelievable regularity that it almost seems as if the politicians are writing the script. After all any president wants to be reelected, so it makes sense to stimulate the economy in the two years before the election. Conversely, they usually deal with whatever negatives there are immediately following the election. Then there's plenty of time for the economy to strengthen before they have to run again. So while you should always keep a close eye on the market indicators, it's especially important to do so in the period following an election.

Another historical pattern is the market's behavior month by month through a typical year. According to Merrill's data, over the past 80–plus years, December has been the best performing month. He based his results simply on whether or not the DJ Industrial Average posted a gain for each given month. December was a winner 68 percent of the time.

In addition, Chart 3–7 shows that the three–month period of November, December, and January has the strongest bullish bias of any ninety days in the market year. This demonstrates that the year-end rally is no myth. July and August are also positive, which supports the idea that there really is a summer-rally syndrome. At the same time February, May, June, and September have a horrible

CHART 3-7

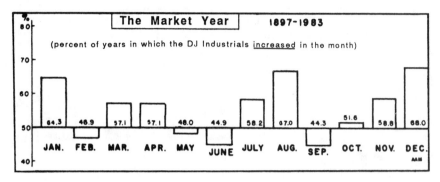

The Market Year | 1897-1983

(percent of years in which the DJ Industrials <u>increased</u> in the month)

JAN.	FEB.	MAR.	APR.	MAY	JUNE	JULY	AUG.	SEP.	OCT.	NOV.	DEC.
64.3	46.9	57.1	57.1	48.0	44.9	58.2	67.0	44.3	51.6	58.8	68.0

SOURCE: Arthur A. Merrill, *Behavior of Prices on Wall Street* (Chappaqua, NY:Analysis Press, 1984), p. 7

record and are times to go easy unless the charts and indicators are strongly positive.[9]

In his book, Yale Hirsch did some interesting studies based on the percentage gain or decline of the Standard and Poor's composite index since 1950. Overall his conclusions closely parallel Merrill's, but there are a few noteworthy differences. While he too showed the November-January period to be highly bullish, November actually nosed out December for first place. In addition, April scored quite well, as recent years have benefited from IRA buying. The poor months, however, still turn out to be February, May, June, and September.

Now let's look even closer under our microscope at the days of the week. Once again, reality and myth collide. The average investor believes that after a weekend of fun and sun, the market is ready to run higher on Monday. Then, since they've heard it repeated so often, they expect the market to sell off on Friday. The rationale is that traders are supposed to dump stocks before the weekend so they don't have to worry about weekend news events.

---

[9]All of this refutes the wisdom of Mark Twain, who said: October. This is one of the peculiarly dangerous months to speculate in stocks. The others are July, January, September, April, November, May, March, June, December, August, and February.

CHART 3–8

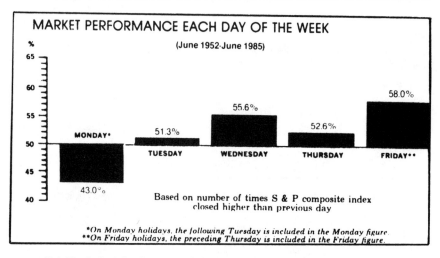

MARKET PERFORMANCE EACH DAY OF THE WEEK

(June 1952-June 1985)

Based on number of times S & P composite index
closed higher than previous day

*On Monday holidays, the following Tuesday is included in the Monday figure.
**On Friday holidays, the preceding Thursday is included in the Friday figure.

SOURCE: Yale Hirsch, *Don't Sell Stocks on Monday* (New York: Facts on File Publications, 1986), p. 17

This is absolutely wrong! (See Chart 3–8) As Yale Hirsch's figures indicate, Monday is the worst day of the week while Friday is the strongest. In a bear market, Monday is especially horrible, which is why it has been dubbed "blue Monday."[10] But even in a bull market it's sure not anything to get excited about.

Finally, there's one more misconception to clear up concerning the holidays. As Arthur Merrill states in his book, newspaper headlines often read something like, "Market rallies despite holiday—advance runs contrary to the usual pattern of selling before a long weekend!" This too is wrong! The facts are quite the opposite. The day preceding a holiday is usually a bullish one. Overall the market rises about 68 percent of the time on such days.

Obviously, if a favorable breakout occurs on a Monday, or in May, it should still be bought. Nevertheless, it's worthwhile when fine tuning your portfolio to learn these significant patterns that I've condensed for you. It will be beneficial to know when to be just a bit more or less aggressive, and it can help you develop pin-

[10]It's not surprising that the historic 508 point October 1987 crash occurred on a Monday. It's also very important for traders to know that in a declining market Monday is usually a disaster, but Tuesday often witnesses a trading low, especially if the first 60 to 90 minutes on Tuesday continue Monday's selloff.

point precision in your buying and selling. Take the time to become familiar with these patterns—it will be time spent profitably.

WHAT NOT TO BUY

Before moving on to the next very important topic—what to buy— I want to make sure that you know what *not* to buy. A very common mistake made by amateur technicians (and, surprisingly, even by some professionals who should know better) is to buy when a stock breaks out above its base even though it is still below its declining 30-week MA. This is not a stock that you want to purchase, since it is not yet ready to start a sustainable advance. In most cases, there will be a temporary rally for a few weeks, then the stock will falter. On a best-case basis, the stock will undergo additional basing as the MA flattens out. On a worst-case basis, it will break below the bottom of the trading range and start a severe new downleg.

Here are two examples from the 1973–74 bear market that illustrate exactly what I mean. Western Union got smashed badly in 1972 as it dropped from 68 down to 44. Then the bargain hunters came in and did their thing. Over the next several weeks a possible base started to take shape (Chart 3–9). The foreshadowing that it was doomed to failure was given by the 30-week MA which con-

CHART 3–9

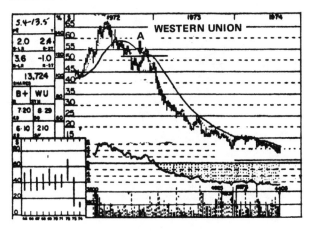

COURTESY OF MANSFIELD STOCK CHARTS

tinued to decline throughout the potential base formation. Also critical was the fact that the breakout (point A) from the trading range occurred below the MA. Even though WU later edged above its MA, the fact that the initial breakout took place below the MA was an additional warning sign. It was an even more serious red alert that the MA never stopped heading south. Never buy a stock in this position no matter how cheap it looks.

Now look closer at the chart. Over the next year and a half the stock that looked cheap near 45 became far cheaper as it fell to 8½!

Study Cannon Group and you'll notice that the same sucker pattern unfolded. Again, the stock looked cheap after dropping in a hurry from 45 to 22. A trading range then took place in 1986 between 27 and 22. Throughout all of the trading range gyrations, note that the MA continued to head south (Chart 3–10). When Cannon Group broke out above 27 (point A), you should not have considered buying it for even a moment because the breakout was below the MA and Cannon never even edged above the MA. In addition the MA continued to decline relentlessly. The predictable result was that Cannon Group turned out to be no bargain at either 27 or 22. Six months later it was trading at 4⅛!

CHART 3–10

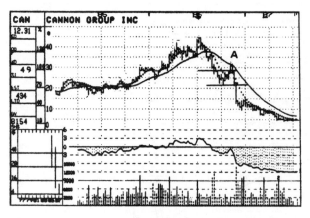

COURTESY OF MANSFIELD STOCK CHARTS

WHAT TO BUY

My "Forest to the Trees" Approach

Just as important as *when* to do new buying is *what* to buy. This is actually a far more complicated decision to reach. Once you digest the ideas in this section, it too will become routine.

It is really a three-part equation that I call my "Forest to the Trees" approach. What I mean is that you should work from the large question—how's the overall market—down to the smaller component—which stock looks best to buy. In between those two extremes is the middle part of the equation—which group is acting best technically. So the process unfolds in the following manner:

1. What's the trend of the market? If it's negative, you'll want to do very little if any buying, even if you see some stocks breaking out. Your probabilities of success are quite low when the market trend is going against you.

2. Which few groups look the very best technically? The importance of this question can't be overemphasized since my studies have consistently shown that two equally bullish charts will perform far differently if one is from a bullish sector while the other breakout is in a bearish group. The favorable chart in the bullish group will often quickly advance 50 to 75 percent while the equally bullish chart in a bearish group may struggle to a 5 to 10 percent gain.

3. Once you determine that the market trend is bullish and Group A acts the very best technically, the final step in the process is to zero in on the one or two best individual chart patterns in that sector.

If you follow this three-step process, you will find yourself heavily invested in the best acting stocks when the market is powering ahead, and sitting on large cash reserves when the overall trend turns bearish.

HOW TO IMPLEMENT THE STRATEGY

That's the theory, and it's a profitable one. But now you must learn how to execute it. As usual, the starting point is the market itself.

To determine if the market is technically strong or weak, you can't just tune into the six o'clock news and hear if the Dow was up 30 points or down 40. Unfortunately, many investors do just that. Such a surface approach will lead to whipsaws and guaranteed losses in the market for two very important reasons. First, the day to day action often disguises the market's real trend. You'll often end up mistaking a short term move for the major trend. Second, even if you luck out and identify the trend of the Dow Jones Industrial Average, the subsurface condition of the market is often moving in an opposite direction.

A perfect example of what I mean can be seen by looking at Chart 3–11 of the Dow Jones Industrial Average in 1982. From the beginning of the year through the mid-August low, the overall market trend was lower. At the same time, however, the percentage of bullish charts[11] on the New York Stock Exchange was slowly but surely improving. This was just one of many key indicators that caused me to turn bullish in July 1982, one month before the Dow launched one of the great bull markets in history. While the market averages were forecasting lower prices, the majority of my technical gauges were signaling that a new bull market lay ahead. Did the market *have* to turn? Of course not. The market, as we all know, is perverse and doesn't have to do any given thing. However, if you play the winning percentages, you'll be right better than 8 out of 10 times. That is a fine batting average when dealing with the future!

The way to gauge the market is by letting the trusted indicators unemotionally decide for you. I'm not going to teach you the indicators now since I want to cover them in detail later on. For now we'll assume that the trend is bullish. After you read Chapter 8, you'll be able to spot the next important market top and bottom!

---

[11]Each week I calculate the percentage of stocks on the New York Stock Exchange in Stages 1 and 2—this is the total that is charted versus the DJI. A quick shortcut that produces an excellent "Gallup Poll" for all 1500–plus NYSE stocks, however, is to simply do this exercise for the Standard and Poor's groups. This is just one of 50 technical indicators that make up my "Weight of the Evidence" in *The Professional Tape Reader*.

CHART 3–11

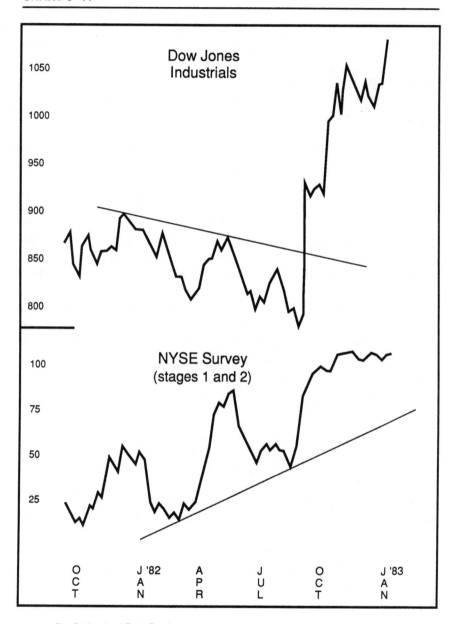

SOURCE: *The Professional Tape Reader*

SELECTING THE SECTOR

After reviewing the market indicators and confirming that the over-all market trend is bullish, it's time to move on to the next step. Zero in on the one or two groups that contain the most exciting upside potential with minimum downside risk over the next several months. This exercise isn't just important—it's *crucial*! After years of observing and studying market cycles, there is absolutely no doubt in my mind that sector analysis is just as important as overall market timing. In fact, in certain markets it is even more important (for example, in the 1977 two-tier market, which saw the blue chips undergo a bear market while the secondary stocks advanced).

So where do we start when analyzing groups? Most definitely not by reading the fundamentals. Back in 1982 when I turned bullish on the Mobile Home group (see Chart 3–18), the earnings were lackluster, yet they led the 1982–1983 hit parade on the upside. About the same time, in early 1981, oil stocks were being touted to the moon as the price of oil zoomed to $38 per barrel. There were reports that it was going to reach $100 amid horrible short-ages. The charts, however, told a very different story. Major Stage 3 tops were forming on the majority of oil charts and on the group chart itself (Chart 3–12). So rather than listening to the optimistic fundamentalists, the proper strategy was to start locking in profits. The rest is history, as the group crashed over the next several years.

CHART 3–12

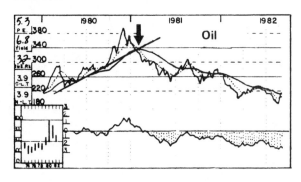

COURTESY OF MANSFIELD STOCK CHARTS

CHART 3–13

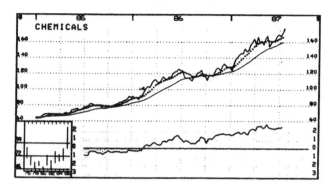

COURTESY OF MANSFIELD STOCK CHARTS

CHART 3–14

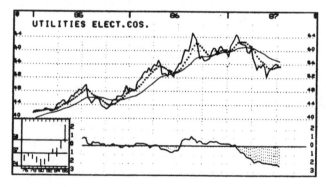

COURTESY OF MANSFIELD STOCK CHARTS

The place to start this next level of learning is the charts themselves. To do this, we are going to scan the Standard & Poor's weekly industry charts. This important input is also covered in the Mansfield chart service. The only difference when studying an industry rather than a stock chart is that the group graph doesn't have volume plotted on it. Other than that, everything else is exactly the same, as you can see from Charts 3–13 and 3–14.

First, check what stage the group is in. Chart 3–13 shows that, in 1987, chemicals were in a powerfully bullish Stage 2 uptrend while electric utilities were in a Stage 4 downtrend at the same time. Therefore, no matter how bearish an individual stock pattern appeared in the chemical sector in the first half of 1987, I wouldn't consider selling it short.[12] In the same manner, no matter how bullish a stock appeared in the electric-utility group in March 1987, I wouldn't consider buying it. One other reality this makes very clear is that you can easily lose money if you're in the wrong groups, even when the averages rocket ahead as they did in the first half of 1987.

When dealing with groups, use the same criteria that you do with stocks. Investors should concentrate their buying in those market areas breaking out of Stage 1 base patterns, while traders should lean toward continuation moves in already existing Stage 2 uptrends. There is one difference, though. If the group is already in a well established Stage 2 uptrend and is far above support, an investor wouldn't normally be in a big hurry to buy that pattern if it was a stock. But if the group is already well into Stage 2 and you find a stock from that sector first breaking out of its Stage 1 base, then it's fine for an investor to buy that particular stock. In the same manner, if a trader saw a continuation-pattern buy that looked good in a group that had just moved into Stage 2, the trader can definitely buy that stock. The most important factor when dealing with groups is that the sector be healthy. (That is, not in Stages 3 or 4). All things being equal, however, the very best situation for an investor is a stock that is an early Stage 2 breakout in a group with the exact same pattern. For a trader, the ideal is a continuation breakout within a dynamic group exhibiting the very same sort of pattern.

A second group signal is available by scanning the charts themselves. When you go through your chart book, if you see several stocks from one group that are suddenly turning bullish (or bearish), that's a clear-cut signal.[13] Make a list of the very best chart patterns with the sector designation. If you have six groups that have bullish Standard & Poor's charts, but most of your potential big winners

---

[12]If you own a stock in the favorably rated sector and it breaks below support and turns negative, you should still dump it. *Just don't sell it short!*

[13]This process is especially easy when dealing with the Mansfield NYSE section since it is arranged by market sectors. The Amex and OTC sections, however, are alphabetical.

are from one or two industry groups, that, too, is telling you something important. While all six groups will very likely advance, the one with the several excellent chart patterns will turn out to be the A+ of the batch.

This approach also helps keep you on the track in another way. At times, the Standard & Poor's industry charts are distorted by one stock in a given group undergoing a powerful advance or decline. By using this cross check method, you won't be thrown off because one stock is a takeover candidate or is a special situation that is suffering.

HERE'S HOW IT WORKS

Back in the good old days of 1978, I noticed unusual strength appearing in the individual casino stock charts while the hotel-motel and the leisure time[14] groups also showed fabulous technical strength. In addition, their respective relative-strength lines were all extremely bullish. Furthermore there wasn't a casino stock that had a bearish chart pattern. With all the buyables to choose from, I felt like a kid in a candy store hardly knowing which to choose. It's unusual to see such incredibly broad strength or weakness touch every stock in a sector, but when it does, don't overlook the obvious message that the market is giving you. Starting in late March 1978, I went on a casino recommending spree. Over the next two weeks, I recommended Bally, Caesars World, Harrah's, Holiday Inns, and Playboy (see arrows for buy points). They scored a grand-slam home run by advancing between 105 percent and 560 percent over the next few months.

The mobile-homes sector also exhibited that bullish one-two punch in the summer of 1982. The industry chart broke out of a powerful Stage 1 base pattern. The relative-strength line was bullish and all of the mobile home stock charts looked great. So between early June and mid-August, eight mobile home stocks were recommended in *PTR*—Coachmen, Fleetwood, Oakwood Homes,

---

[14]Standard & Poor's doesn't keep up a separate casino group, so you have to monitor hotel-motel and leisure time.

CHART 3–15

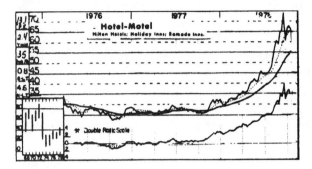

COURTESY OF MANSFIELD STOCK CHARTS

CHART 3–16

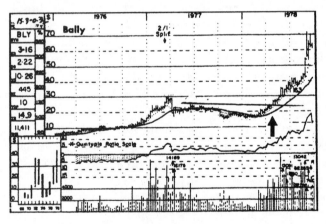

COURTESY OF MANSFIELD STOCK CHARTS

Philips Industries, Redman, Skyline, Winnebago, and Zimmer (see arrows on charts for buy points). This group was a bullish fantasy over the next year as it rocketed ahead for an average 260 percent gain.

Don't make the mistake of thinking that these stocks were great just because a new bull market was getting underway. Sure that helped, but if you didn't do your technical homework, you could have fallen into the fundamental trap of buying a low P/E

CHART 3–17

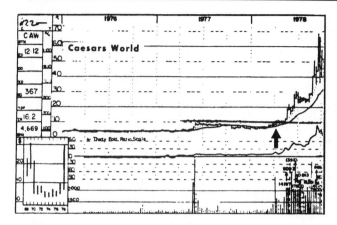

COURTESY OF MANSFIELD STOCK CHARTS

CHART 3–18

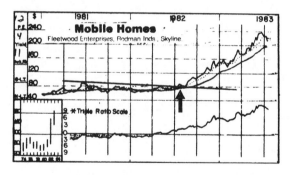

COURTESY OF MANSFIELD STOCK CHARTS

stock such as Warner Communications (3–22). It's a perfectly fine company and, in the summer of 1982 as the market was launching its new bull phase, the latest 12 months trailing earnings were a nifty $4.35. And WCI was only a little more than 11 times earnings. If you bought it in mid–1982 instead of the mobile—home stocks, one year later you'd have suffered a spanking 60 percent loss instead of a 260 percent gain!

Was there any technical foreshadowing which warned you to stay away? There sure was! Look at Chart 3–21 of the entertain-

CHART 3–19

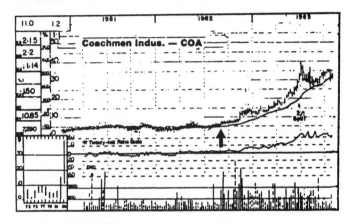

COURTESY OF MANSFIELD STOCK CHARTS

CHART 3–20

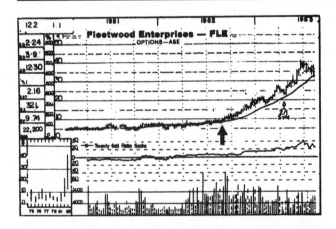

COURTESY OF MANSFIELD STOCK CHARTS

ment industry. It broke below its MA in the summer of 1982 while the mobile-home sector was breaking out on the upside. Furthermore, the relative-strength line was weak and actually dipped into negative territory that summer. Finally, its individual chart components were mixed, with some looking okay while others, such as Warner Communications, looking horrid. Note that Warner (Chart 3–22) broke down that summer into Stage 4 while most other stocks

CHART 3–21

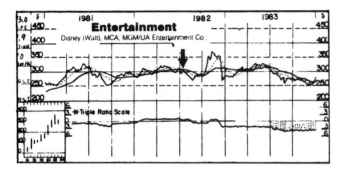

COURTESY OF MANSFIELD STOCK CHARTS

CHART 3–22

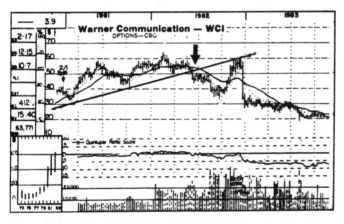

COURTESY OF MANSFIELD STOCK CHARTS

and groups were moving into Stage 2. Even after its first vicious crash in 1982, more trouble lay ahead. Its sharp oversold rally in late 1982 took the stock from the low 30s to 60. The rally, however, failed right at the bearish trendline.[15] Thereafter, the bargain-hunters were really punished as Warner plummeted to 20.

---

[15]Just as support, once broken, later becomes resistance on a rally, so too an uptrend line, once broken, is future resistance on rallies.

CHART 3–23

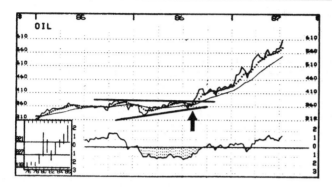

COURTESY OF MANSFIELD STOCK CHARTS

The game never changes. Charts 3–23 and 3–24 show a group and stock pattern of more recent vintage with similar results. Starting in August 1986, I turned bullish on the oil sector. The group broke out above significant resistance, and the relative-strength line shaped up nicely and moved into positive territory. Finally, the overwhelming majority of individual oil charts were screaming "buy." Interestingly enough, crude oil was near $10 a barrel, and there was worry that it was on the way to $6 to $8 per barrel.[16] This was the mirror image of early 1981 when oil had great headlines but poor technical underpinnings. It's also an outstanding example of contrary opinion in action. It was therefore no surprise that every one of the dozen-plus *PTR* oil-related recommendations (oil, oil drilling, and oil equipment) made in that period turned in winning performances, with several, such as American Oil & Gas (Chart 3–24), being spectacular.

Then, in December of that year, the computer stocks started popping their modems, and this was the next area in which to start doing aggressive buying. The industry group completed a Stage 2 consolidation near the 30-week MA (Chart 3–25) when it broke out above significant resistance. In addition, the relative-strength line was nice and peppy. It moved to a new high in addition to

---

[16]The charts have a way of discounting the future with uncanny precision. One year later, not only were oil stocks much higher, but crude oil was near $22 a barrel.

CHART 3–24

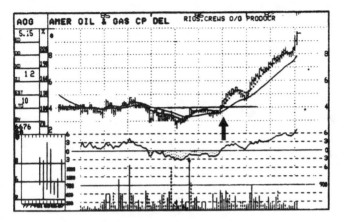

COURTESY OF MANSFIELD STOCK CHARTS

CHART 3–25

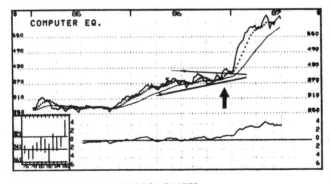

COURTESY OF MANSFIELD STOCK CHARTS

being in positive territory. Another added plus was given by the long-term background chart as the group registered a new all-time high. Finally, several individual stock patterns[17] in that group staged powerful upside breakouts (See Chart 3–26).

---

[17]Compaq Computer, Micropolis, and Tandem were three of several *PTR* recommendations from that sector at that time. The powerful group action helped every one become a big winner.

CHART 3–26

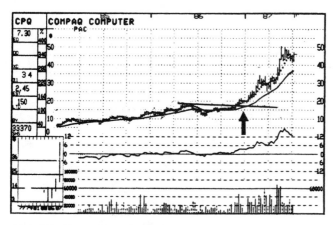

COURTESY OF MANSFIELD STOCK CHARTS

When all of these important factors check off positively, don't walk, *run* to your telephone and start giving your broker the buy orders as fast as you possibly can. Every year there are a few groups that far outpace all others on both the upside and downside. By following this step-by-step approach you will be able to position yourself in the few that lead the hit parade. At the same time, you'll avoid the downside disasters. And when the market climate is bearish, you will profit by selling short the weak sisters from the vulnerable groups. Don't underestimate the importance of group confirmation. I've seen countless examples of good-looking stock charts that turned in only ho-hum performances. When I checked out the group pattern, sure enough, it was usually in poor shape. On the other hand, I've seen many chart patterns that were good, but not great, that turned out to be super performers when they had the backing of a powerfully bullish market sector behind them. I've also witnessed many cases of stocks in weak groups that got bombed even when the overall market trend was bullish. Don't ever rationalize that it's a bull market so the stock will eventually work out.

Here's a perfect example of what I'm talking about. Despite a better than 600 point advance in the DJI from late 1986 until summer 1987, the real estate investment trust group acted just horrid (Chart 3–27). Lomas & Nettleton Mortgage, along with

CHART 3–27

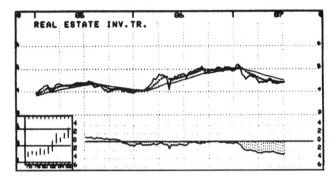

COURTESY OF MANSFIELD STOCK CHARTS

CHART 3–28

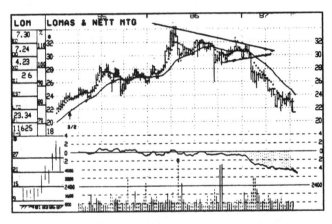

COURTESY OF MANSFIELD STOCK CHARTS

many others from the group, dropped significantly during the first six months of 1987 while the market averages rocketed higher (Chart 3–28). Here's that old fundamental trap in action, which will never again snare you. The P/E ratio was low and the company a good one, so how could it miss? Easy—because the group was negative, and the individual chart pattern was in the dangerous Stage 3 phase as the new year started. Then, once it broke below support at 29½, it moved into Stage 4 trouble. Finally, the relative-strength line was a disaster. With these negative ingredients it's easy to see why the

CHART 3–29

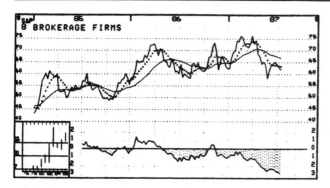

COURTESY OF MANSFIELD STOCK CHARTS

stock dropped over 30 percent while the Dow moved ahead spectacularly.

Another example of the negative group effect can be seen by studying the action of the brokerage group in 1987 (Chart 3–29). Whereas Lomas & Nettleton Mortgage was a bearish stock in a negative group, McDonald & Company Investment was a moderately favorable chart that staged a false upside breakout (point A) in early 1987 (Chart 3–30). Whipsaws such as these are quite com-

CHART 3–30

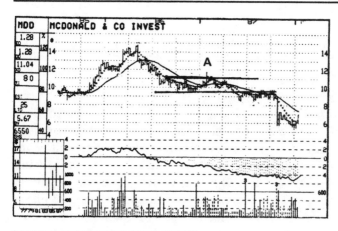

COURTESY OF MANSFIELD STOCK CHARTS

mon in a negative group. It wasn't a great surprise that the stock went nowhere fast on the upside, and then became another wrong-way Corrigan as it declined during one of the great bull-market rallies of history. The lesson is obvious. Don't try to be a whiz kid and attempt to find the one winner in a sick group. Don't try to prove you're a market genius. Let the so-called geniuses lose their money while you very simply find an A+ stock in an A+ group. Then just enjoy the ride, and the big profits!

QUIZ

1. Stock XYZ has excellent liquidity as it trades quite actively. It's currently trading at 23½. You decide it should be purchased if it breaks out above significant resistance at 25. How should the order for your broker read? (Pick one of the following.)
   A. Buy 1,000 XYZ at 25⅛ stop
   B. Buy 1,000 XYZ at 25 stop–25¼ limit–GTC.
   C. Buy 1,000 XYZ at 25⅛ stop–25⅜ limit–GTC.
   D. Buy 1,000 XYZ at 25⅛ stop–26 limit–GTC.

2.

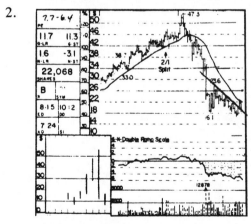

COURTESY OF MANSFIELD STOCK CHARTS

   Would you buy this stock as it broke above its trendline at 20? If not, why?

3. You should never buy stocks in the year following a   **T   F** presidential election.

4.

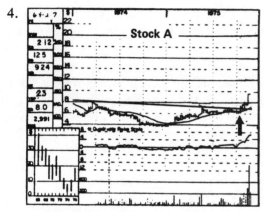

COURTESY OF MANSFIELD STOCK CHARTS

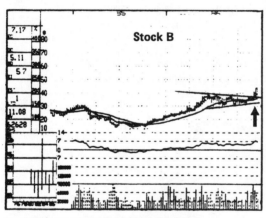

COURTESY OF MANSFIELD STOCK CHARTS

Which breakout is more suited for an investor? Which for a trader?

5. A GTC order is good for two weeks after you enter   **T F** it on the New York Stock Exchange.

6.

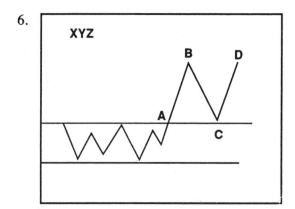

At what point in the cycle is stock XYZ the safest to buy? A, B, C, or D?

7. The third year of the presidential cycle has histori-   **T F**
cally been the most bullish part of the four-year cycle.

8. A trader should only buy on pullbacks.   **T F**

9. Late in a bull market, even investors should do some   **T F**
continuation buying.

10.

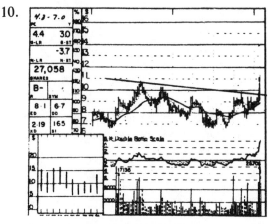

COURTESY OF MANSFIELD STOCK CHARTS

Even though this is a very bullish chart, you should   **T F**
not buy it if the overall market indicators are negative, and the group is unfavorable.

11. Breakouts from Stage 1 bases usually give you a sec-   **T   F**
ond chance to buy on a pullback toward the initial
breakout point.

12.

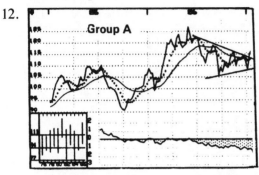

COURTESY OF MANSFIELD STOCK CHARTS

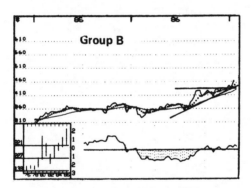

COURTESY OF MANSFIELD STOCK CHARTS

It's early 1987 and you correctly believe that the market is
ready to start a major advance. Which group would you do
aggressive buying in—A or B? Why?

ANSWERS

1. C. The stop should go in at the breakout; the limit should be
   ¼ of a point above the breakout since it is an actively traded
   stock; and it should be placed on a good-'til-canceled basis
   (GTC).
2. No, Because it is still below the 30-week average. In addition,
   the MA is declining, so stay away. This turned out to be the

proper decision not just in theory but in reality. The chart is of Clorox, and this breakout occurred in 1973 at 20½. One year later it was trading at 6.

3. False. The probabilities are *strongly* negative for that year, and if the major indicators turn bearish then stay away from stocks. But there are bullish exceptions such as 1965 and 1985.

4. Stock A is a better buy for an investor, as it's breaking out of a long-term Stage 1 base pattern. The chart is of Swank, and the breakout occurred in 1975 at 7⅛. One year later it was trading near 20. Stock B is better for traders. It had already advanced 300 percent before consolidating. The chart is Apple Computer, which broke out crossing 39 in 1986; six months later it was above 80!

5. False. A GTC order means just that—good-'til-canceled. But don't forget to keep records and cancel it if the pattern changes and you later change your mind.

6. C. The pullback toward the initial breakout point is the safest possible entry point.

7. True.

8. False. While even traders can do some pullback buying, they should do most of their buying on breakouts. If the initial advance is a good one, the trader can sell for a fast profit and then reenter on the pullback for a second good trade.

9. True. At that point, there will be very few Stage 1 bases left.

10. True. Don't ever fight the trend of the overall market and the group. This chart is of American Motors, and the breakout took place in early 1974 at 10. Both the indicator and group were negative, and less than a year later it was down close to 3.

11. True. But this is often *not* the case with continuation breakouts.

12. You should have chosen Group B. It was in a far stronger uptrend and, in addition, had no overhead resistance. Group A, on the other hand, had plenty of supply to contend with. Finally, the relative strength for A was terrible while B was fine. A is regional banks and seven months and 600 Dow points later, it was unchanged. Group B is oil, and it was one of the big winners in the first seven months of 1987.

CHAPTER 4

REFINING THE BUYING PROCESS

Now that we've learned to first check the market's major trend and uncover the few best groups, we are ready for the ultimate step. It's now time to narrow our choice down to a single buy candidate from the positive sector. How do we determine which one or two stocks from that group should be purchased? Is there really a way to predict which issues are likely both to go up *and* turn in an A+ performance?

There definitely is! While no system will ever be a perfect forecaster of the future, we can learn some simple rules that will put the probabilities of success strongly in our favor.

THE LESS RESISTANCE THE BETTER

I've already explained the concept of resistance, but let's quickly review it again and then delve deeper. This is going to be *very* important to your future batting average so we'll go over it carefully. On Chart 4–1, stock XYZ formed a trading range in the 18 to 20 zone after undergoing a severe decline. The area near 18 became a temporary floor of support while this trading range was in existence. On the upside, since rallies failed near the 20 level each time they attacked that price, 20 became resistance during the trading range. Then, after several weeks of zigs and zags within this neutral range, XYZ broke below the 18 support level. This, of course, was a negative indication and signaled the start of a new decline. After this new bout of weakness, XYZ stabilized at a low of 13. It then moved into a new trading range and built a solid base. New support

CHART 4–1

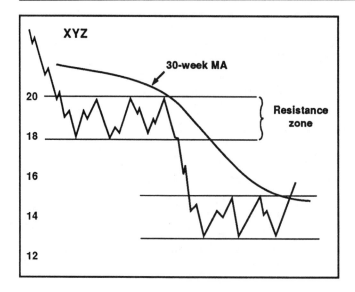

was now at 13 and resistance at 15. Finally it overcame the 15 resistance and, more importantly, also advanced above the MA.

You are now seasoned enough to know that this stock is a buy. But do you want to purchase it? Not necessarily. Even though the probabilities are very strong that this stock is going to advance and you'll make money, that isn't enough. At first this may sound crazy to you. I wouldn't be surprised to hear you say, "What is Stan talking about? I've bought a bunch of dogs that have gone down before I've gotten my confirmation slip. Now he's telling me that this stock is going to advance and I shouldn't buy it!"

Just think along with me one step further and you'll see that I haven't taken leave of my senses. It won't be a terrible thing if you buy stock XYZ—you'll make money in it. But I want to do more for you than just make money. We both want you to make big money!

There's a concept in economics called *opportunity costs* which applies perfectly here. Taking away all of the fancy ivory-tower jargon, it means that we all have limited resources, whether it be $25,000 or $25 million. So we must *maximize* our resources—which, in this case, is your market stake. If we buy stock XYZ and it advances 20 percent, but stock ABC in the same time period gains 200 percent, we have actually lost profit-making potential. Therefore, what we want to do is to uncover the A+ stocks and play those while leaving the Bs and Cs alone for others.

Now go back to Chart 4–1 and I'll show you why this is a B– buy. Once XYZ gives a positive signal by breaking out above 15 resistance, you must look at where the next area of resistance is. It's 18, which was the floor of support from the prior trading range. Remember that support, once broken, later becomes resistance when the stock rallies back to that level. If XYZ does overcome that resistance it will find the going very tough all the way up to 20. So the entire 18 to 20 area presents *significant* potential resistance. That doesn't mean the stock will never overcome that area. What it does mean is that it will use up a great amount of buying power to get through this zone. So it will most likely stall in that area for quite a while. Even in the unlikely event that it gets past the resistance in a hurry, it will be tired and need to regroup. It's no different from someone who has to climb six flights of stairs to get to their apartment versus another person who can simply take an elevator. Who is obviously going to have more energy left? It's the same with stocks. If stock XYZ and ABC both stage breakouts and then benefit from 500,000 shares of buying in the next several sessions, which one is going to go further? The one with little or no resistance in its path, or the one with plenty of overhead supply? The answer is obvious.

So now let's look at Chart 4–2 of stock ABC. It's in the same group as XYZ and is also breaking out above resistance and its MA. But whereas XYZ had a clear zone of resistance just a few points overhead, ABC has no overhead resistance on the chart. While it may have traded at higher prices, it hasn't done so in the past 2–plus years. (The Mansfield chart shows the history for about 2½ years.) While resistance is still in existence even from several years ago, my studies have shown that the older the resistance, the less potent it is. This makes sense since resistance is created by sellers who bought at higher prices and want to get out close to their purchase price after the stock declines. As time passes, more and more investors take their losses at the end of each trading year. So if it doesn't show up on the chart, it's no big deal.

CHART 4-2

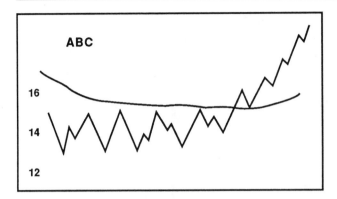

There is one last step to this exercise—check the long-range perspective on the Mansfield chart. This is a high-low bar chart of each of the past 10 years. If there is no resistance (it hasn't traded above this price in the past 10 years) on this chart, then you should really get excited because you are looking at an A+ situation.

Here are some real life examples that reinforce the theory. Look at Chart 4-3. When Allegis Corporation broke out above the top of its one-year trading range in 1987, there was no further resistance on the chart. Then when the long-range perspective was checked, the green lights really started to flash. There was no resistance (see arrow on long-range perspective) above that level in the past ten years.[1] It's no surprise that AEG rocketed ahead a fast 30 points because the buying met absolutely no resistance. Whenever a breakout occurs with a stock moving into virgin territory (it's never before traded there), this is the most bullish situation you can buy. Think about it. There isn't one person who is long and has a loss. Nobody wants to get out even one or two points higher. So the buying power can really have an explosive effect on prices.[2]

---

[1] Don't get confused. The latest yearly entry includes 1987. As it made new highs, the 1987 yearly high was updated.

[2] Two other bullish factors were also present: sharply increasing volume and dramatically improving relative strength.

CHART 4-3

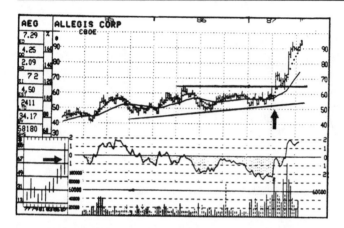

COURTESY OF MANSFIELD STOCK CHARTS

Now look at Chart 4-4 of Pan Am Corporation from the same bullish airline group in 1987. Even though it broke out of a base pattern and moved above its trendline and MA, it shouldn't have been mentioned in the same breath with Allegis. There was resistance near $6\frac{1}{2}$ where the rally failed in late 1986. Even worse, there was heavy supply near 7 where PN broke down in early 1986 as it then got smashed down to 4. Finally, when you check out the long-term perspective, it becomes obvious that there was *very* significant resistance just above 8. (Between 1983 and 1986 PN topped out above 8 in each of the four years.) Whereas Allegis was an A+, I'd grade Pan Am a C − .[3] Remember, if you had to do something with the stock, PN would be a better buy than a sale; but you don't have to bet every race. And you don't have to buy every Stage 2 stock—only the outstanding ones.

Are you starting to see what you should be looking for? It's not enough to find a Stage 2 stock, even in a good group. There are several other factors to check, which we'll get to in a moment;

---

[3]In addition to heavy overhead resistance, there are several other technical negatives: the base is relatively small, the relative strength line is mediocre, and the volume pattern is only fair.

CHART 4-4

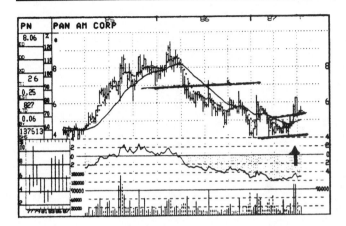

COURTESY OF MANSFIELD STOCK CHARTS

but one of the most important is where overhead resistance is situated.

Here's another case history that will reinforce the proper techniques to use. Reynolds Metals is in the aluminum group, which was in great shape in 1987. In early 1987, RLM flashed a very bullish signal as it broke out on the upside from a one-year trading range. One quick glance at Chart 4-5 shows that there was no resistance overhead for the past 2½ years. Then a bit more digging via the long-range perspective chart showed that this was a new ten-year high. Bingo! Your buy order should have been sent in a hurry, because the chart fulfilled all of the criteria that we've been stressing.[4] Within a few months the stock was a fast double as the heavy buying met no significant resistance along the way.

Now contrast that action with the breakout that occurred at almost the exact same moment in another member of the group—International Aluminum (Chart 4-6). IAL broke out when it moved above 20 in early 1987. But unlike RLM, International Aluminum had plenty of resistance just overhead, near 24½. Not only was

---

[4]In addition, the base pattern was a full year, the relative strength quite healthy, and volume impressive.

CHART 4–5

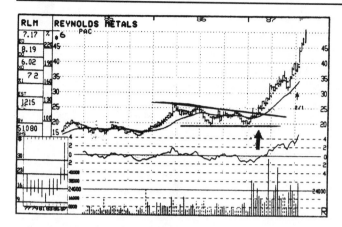

COURTESY OF MANSFIELD STOCK CHARTS

CHART 4–6

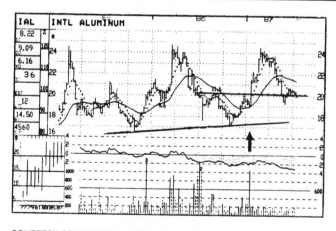

COURTESY OF MANSFIELD STOCK CHARTS

that the high early in 1987, but also in 1986, 1985, and 1983. So what happened? Instead of moving out with a bang as Reynolds did, it advanced with a whimper, and after a fast advance to 24½ it quickly fell back to 20. Other problems with the pattern were ho-hum volume after the first week, mediocre relative strength, and a relatively small base pattern. Six months later, you would have been even while Reynolds would have more than doubled your money, which is better than a 200 percent annualized gain.

The message is obvious: always check where and how much resistance is overhead on any stock before you pick up the phone to dial your broker with a buy order.

THE IMPORTANCE OF VOLUME

The next important factor to concentrate on is volume. Once you learn to spot this telltale clue, you'll be well on the way to separating the so-so buys from the explosive big winners. Even if we never were to discover the reason why volume is so important, a quick perusal of any chart book would convince you that volume confirmation on a breakout is crucial. There is, however, a very good reason why volume signals really work. Volume is a gauge of how powerful the buyers are. As I said earlier, stocks can fall of their own weight, but to advance it takes plenty of buying power. It's no different from pushing a boulder up a hill. It takes a tremendous expenditure of energy to move it up the hill, but once you let it go, it can build up plenty of downside momentum on its own.

The rule is very simple. *Never trust a breakout that isn't accompanied by a significant increase in volume.* Chart 4–7 shows exactly how a technically healthy pattern should unfold volume-wise. When the stock is in the base area, the volume pattern will be erratic. My studies have led me to a different conclusion than many technicians. Some believe there must first be a spike that shows the final panic dumping of the stock. They feel that volume should then contract—dry up—showing a lessening of selling pressure. While this is a nice theory, I've seen far too many charts with far different volume formations that turned out to be big winners. So to keep things simple yet profitable, I wouldn't worry what shape the volume pattern takes while it is forming a Stage 1 base. However, once XYZ breaks out above the top of its resistance area and moves above its 30-week MA, I want you to worry plenty about volume. As Chart 4–7 shows, volume should pick up significantly on the breakout. If it doesn't, the probabilities are very high, that at best, you've got a mediocre winner on your hands that will advance only a few points. At worst, the stock will turn

CHART 4–7

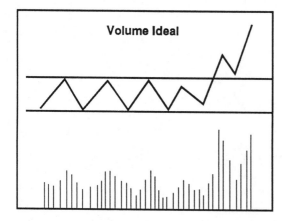

out to be a false breakout that will soon be back in the trading range.

Investors always want hard and fast rules, and too often we technicians are guilty of complying. I don't agree that there is a magic level of volume necessary for identifying a winner. Rather than looking for breakouts that have a randomly picked number such as 4.65 times the average volume of the past few weeks, I look for the following: either a one-week volume spike that is *at least* twice the average volume of the past month (preferably it is even higher), or a volume build-up over the past three to four weeks that is at least twice the average volume of the past several weeks coupled with at least some increase on the breakout week.[5] Whatever the exact number, if there is no significant increase in volume when the breakout occurs, then avoid that stock. If you have purchased it with a buy-stop order, then sell it for a fast profit when it advances after the breakout (which it will usually do).

Here are some real-life examples of volume, or the lack of it, in action. Chart 4–8 shows that when Allied Signal broke out there was no great increase in volume. The average volume for the past

---

[5]If you are using daily charts instead of weekly graphs, look for a volume increase on the breakout day of better than twice the average volume of the prior week.

CHART 4-8

COURTESY OF MANSFIELD STOCK CHARTS

four weeks had been under 20,000 on the chart. (Two zeroes are dropped, so its actual volume was about 2 million shares for the week.) On the week of the breakout, volume did not even reach the 40,000 level, let alone exceed it. This was a sign that buying in the stock wasn't powerful enough to take it past resistance near 50. Therefore, it wasn't any great surprise when ALD pooped out at 49¼. If you had bought it with a 43⅝ buy-stop a few weeks earlier, you should have taken your fast profit near 49 as it neared its 1986 high.

Now contrast this ho-hum action with the breakout that occurred in another area of the Dow 30 blue chips—Goodyear Tire and Rubber in late 1986. Chart 4-9 shows that exciting buying entered on the GT breakout. The average weekly volume for the prior four weeks was approximately 22,000, but on the breakout week it was almost triple that figure. And then it grew larger and larger over the next two weeks. That's A + action! GT then pulled back close to the MA near 40 a few weeks later. Note that there was another bullish signal given on the pullback. Volume contracted by over 75 percent from peak levels. If trading had remained at peak levels then you would not have done any further buying. However, this was not the case. With the tremendous increase of volume on the rally, followed by the very dramatic drying up of

CHART 4–9

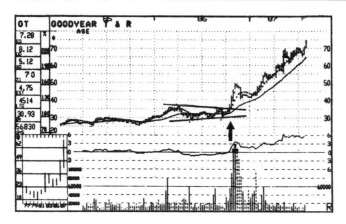

COURTESY OF MANSFIELD STOCK CHARTS

volume on the pullback, the stock was shouting as loud as it could to buy more. You then should have bought the other half of your position in the low 40s.

Here is one more case that will help you master this very important profit-producing concept. Both stocks in this pair (Charts 4–10 and 4–11) are from the same market cycle and the same group. Yet one racked up a 300–plus percent gain, while the other produced a loss. The answer wasn't in the stars—it was in the volume. Puerto Rican Cement (Chart 4–10) had an average volume of 120 for the four weeks prior to its breakout at 9 in early 1986. Volume then expanded tenfold, which showed that somebody was suddenly urgently wanting to buy. These somebodies were right, because the stock they grabbed at 9 sold at 38½ only 15 months later.

Texas Industries (Chart 4–11) was another cement stock that broke out in early 1986. But this stock fizzled rather than sizzled. Instead of expanding, volume actually contracted and stayed well below its high of the past few months. This was a good reason to pass on TXI and not buy when it moved above 31½. The volume signal would have saved you, because a few months later TXI was down to 22 while Puerto Rican Cement rocketed higher and higher.

There is much more to learn but let's stop for a minute and go over some of the key points that we now know to look for. First,

CHART 4–10

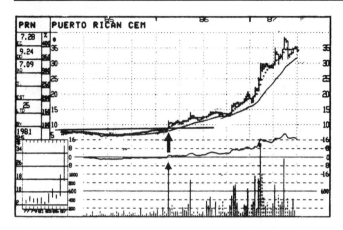

COURTESY OF MANSFIELD STOCK CHARTS

CHART 4–11

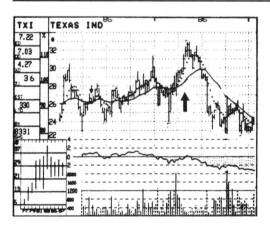

COURTESY OF MANSFIELD STOCK CHARTS

we want the market trend to be bullish. Second, the groups should be positive. In addition, the chart from that favorable group must be breaking out into Stage 2 with a minimum of resistance overhead. Finally, volume most definitely *must* confirm the breakout. Look at how many check lists we have and how you can separate the good from the bad and the ugly.

There's so much to learn when using technical analysis; yet so very often some academic economist will come along and tell you that charts don't work and the market is random in its trading. Years ago this used to upset me, but now I laugh to myself. Do all of these moves look random to you? And how can you crank 1,000 breakouts into a computer and treat them equally, as if they were all A+ moves? It would be comparable to averaging the distance that all quarterbacks can throw a pass, from a Dan Marino and a John Elway to a Little League player. But that's okay. These random walkers will be selling their stock to us on the breakout, so we'll let them think charts are akin to voodoo as they buy into Stage 4 stocks that drop lower and lower.

IT'S ALL RELATIVE

The next important factor to check out when narrowing down our list of potential buys is the *relative strength* (RS). This is a measure of how a stock is acting in relation to the overall market. Even if a stock is rising, it can show poor relative strength. Likewise, a declining issue can demonstrate positive relative strength. Think about it. If XYZ rises by 10 percent while the Standard and Poor's composite[6] advances by 20 percent, XYZ is lagging badly even though it is moving higher. Not only isn't it a leader, but it obviously is being pulled reluctantly higher. Therefore, the probabilities are very high that when the overall market turns down XYZ will get bombed. Conversely, if it drops by 10 percent while the market averages plummet by 20 percent then it is putting on a good show of relative strength. And once the market turns higher, this stock will likely lead the hit parade.

The formula for relative strength is a simple one:

$$\frac{\text{price of XYZ}}{\text{price of market average}}$$

If stock XYZ is currently at 50 and the S&P composite average is at 310, then its relative strength is .16 (50 ÷ 310). Some technicians calculate this figure every day, but I've found it to be unnecessary.

---

[6]You can use any market average as long as you are consistent, but the Standard and Poor's composite or Dow Jones Industrial Average are best.

CHART 4–12

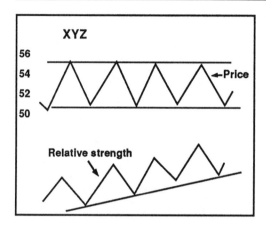

If you do it once a week[7] you'll see a clear-cut pattern forming over time, and that's what is important. One week the relative strength can be positive, while the next week it is negative. The true picture forms only over a period of time.

Chart 4–12 shows the price of XYZ on the top portion of the chart, with the corresponding relative strength for XYZ at the bottom of the graph. Note that while the price action of the stock is neutral—moving in a 51 to 55 trading range—the relative-strength line is telling a different story. It's favorable that the RS line is trending higher. The probabilities favor an upside breakout from this neutral range. On the other hand, even if the stock fools us and breaks out on the downside, we do *not* want to sell this stock short. Whenever an issue exhibits superior relative strength, it is telling you loud and clear that its downside action will be limited, so look elsewhere for a short sale. If you own the stock, however, you must still respect the breakdown and get out.

There's an alternative to keeping up your own RS graphs. Some chart services[8] include relative strength on the graphs. Look

---

[7]Always do it on the same day, whether it be every Wednesday, Thursday, etc. My preference is each Friday since that closes the chapter on the week's trading.

[8]Both Daily Graphs and Mansfield Charts provide a relative strength line on their respective charts. In addition, Mansfield uses a proprietary method for calculating a zero line which is also helpful, but the overall pattern is the most important factor to concentrate on.

CHART 4–13

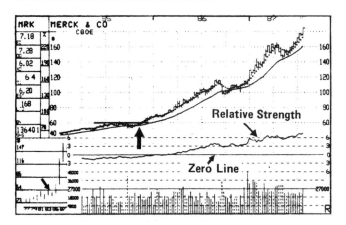

COURTESY OF MANSFIELD STOCK CHARTS

at Chart 4–13 (see arrow) and you'll see where the Mansfield Chart service plots relative strength. They use a complex weighted formula, but the results are the same. When you see inferior action in the RS line compared to the price performance, don't ever buy that stock. Conversely, when you see a very positive relative-strength trend, do not consider shorting it.

Mansfield's relative strength also has a zero line (see Chart 4–13) on it. Above zero is a long-term positive, while below zero is a long-term negative. While it happens rarely, it's an important long-term plus if all of the positives on our check list (group confirmation, minimum resistance, heavy volume, and so on) are met and, at the same time, the RS line moves from negative to positive territory. For short selling (which we'll cover later), the opposite is true. A break below the zero line is an important negative when all of the shorting criteria are present. Don't think, however, that you can never buy a stock below the zero RS line, or that you can never short a stock above the zero line. If the relative strength is in good shape and improving and *all* other criteria are positive, then go for it. But absolutely *never* buy a stock, no matter how good the other factors, if the relative strength is in negative territory and it remains in poor shape.

Now let's look at some real-world examples of relative strength in action. First, go back to Chart 4–13 of Merck. Once it broke out above 60 in late 1985[9] the relative strength really did its thing. In fact, even before the breakout relative strength was trending higher, which was a positive sign. Then, after MRK broke out above 60, it moved into positive territory and continued to strengthen throughout 1986 and the first half of 1987. It's no surprise that Merck's price tripled, making it one of the biggest of the blue chip winners of that period.

Charts 4–14 and 4–15 demonstrate the merits of relative-strength charting. Adams-Russell (Chart 4–14) staged a major breakout in early 1986 as it broke out above resistance at 15. The volume was impressive, and once it moved above 16 there was no further overhead supply on the long-range perspective. Prior to the breakout, relative strength had only been so-so. But in the few weeks before it broke out, it started advancing nicely. When the breakout occurred, the RS graph moved above the zero line. With all of our buy criteria fulfilled, it was not shocking that AAR came close to tripling in the next year and a half.

Alpine Group (4–15) broke out above 5½ in early 1986. Volume expanded sharply; resistance was nonexistent on the long-range perspective and the RS line was in good shape. Even though it was below the zero line before the breakout, the RS line was trending higher for 90 days prior to the breakout. When the stock moved above 5, the RS line moved above the zero line—a second favorable relative-strength signal. The stock followed the game plan very nicely as it quadrupled over the next year and a half.

Now let's look at the reverse side of the coin—those breakouts which are *not* accompanied by positive relative strength. Once in a while such mediocre breakouts will turn into big winners, but don't worry about that. Our game plan is to look for the 80 to 90 percent favorable probabilities, not the longshots. We'll leave them to the horse players.

Chart 4–16 shows what inferior relative strength looks like. Even though XYZ is trending sideways in a 50 to 55 trading range, the RS line is telling us to look out below. It is trending lower, showing that the stock is acting far weaker than the overall market. It's therefore very likely that the eventual breakout from this neu-

---

[9]It also moved to a new high on the long-range perspective, so there was no overhead resistance.

CHART 4–14

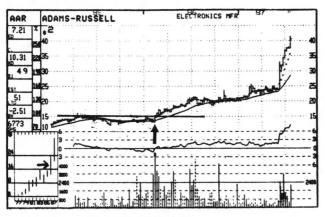

COURTESY OF MANSFIELD STOCK CHARTS

CHART 4–15

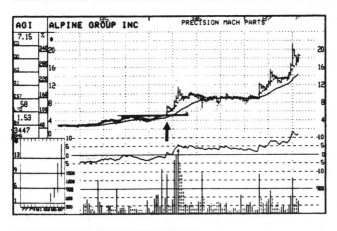

COURTESY OF MANSFIELD STOCK CHARTS

tral range will be on the downside. Even in the rare case where the stock ends up popping out on the upside, it's not worth buying since its advancing action will very likely be only mediocre.

Here's what I'm talking about. Acme United Corporation on Chart 4–17 broke out on the upside in early 1987 at 8½ (point B). The RS line, however, was warning you not to buy the breakout. Here's why. First, the RS line was deep in negative territory, well

CHART 4–16

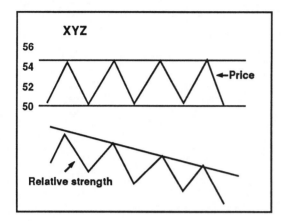

CHART 4–17

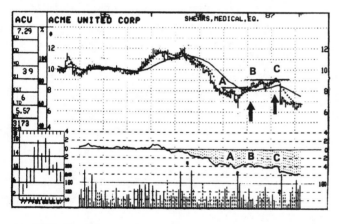

below the zero line. That doesn't automatically exclude the stock from buying considerations, but it's a red flag. The stock's RS line had better be putting on a decent show of strength, or forget it. This was a case of forget it—ACU already had two strikes against it. Strike two was the RS line, which was in a major 12-month downtrend since its early 1986 peak. Strike three was signaled when ACU broke out at point B and the RS line was lower than it was

CHART 4-18

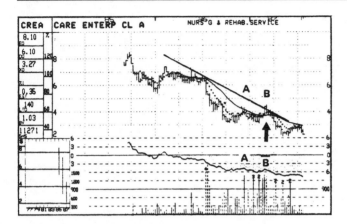

COURTESY OF MANSFIELD STOCK CHARTS

at point A, even though the price line was higher. That should have been the end of any consideration about buying it. But to further tempt the unwary, the stock broke out again a few months later at 9⅛ (point C). Again, the RS line was lower than at its prior peak (C was lower than B on the RS line). The end result was that instead of moving higher with the rapidly rising Dow, Acme actually declined.

This same losing pattern showed up in Care Enterprises (4–18). In early 1987, Care broke out at 4¼ (point B). Once again, the RS line was in poor shape. It was in a major downtrend, in negative territory and lower at point B in the breakout than at point A. It's not surprising that the stock then fell by 50 percent even though the market averages moved higher.

Finally, Chart 4–19 cinches the case. Grand Auto had a relative-strength line that needed Geritol. The breakout (point B) had very poor relative strength (point B below A); the RS line was below the zero line and the stock was in a downtrend. (Another warning to pass on this breakout was the lack of volume confirmation.) Grand Auto then reversed and dropped 40 percent in a rising market.

So the lesson is clear. Overlook the message of relative strength at your own peril. We want the very best buy candidates, not the also-rans. Relative strength helps you zero in on tomorrow's big winners today!

CHART 4-19

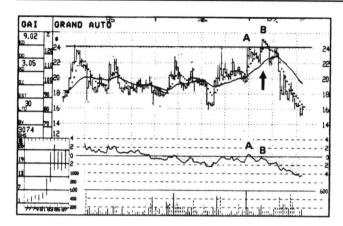

COURTESY OF MANSFIELD STOCK CHARTS

QUICK REFERENCE GUIDE ON BUYING

Before going further, here's a handy checklist that will do two things for you. First, it will act as a quick review of the very important steps we've covered in the buying section. Second, it will serve as a future reference guide to the proper sequence to use when looking for new buy candidates.

- Check the major trend of the overall market.
- Uncover the few groups that look best technically.
- Make a list of those stocks in the favorable groups that have bullish patterns but are now in trading ranges. Write down the price that each would need to break out.
- Narrow down the list. Discard those that have overhead resistance nearby.
- Narrow the list further by checking relative strength.
- Put in your buy-stop orders for half of your position for those few stocks that meet our buying criteria. Use buy-stop orders on a good-'til-canceled (GTC) basis.
- If volume is favorable on the breakout and contracts on the decline, buy your other half position on a pullback toward the initial breakout.

- If the volume pattern is negative (not high enough on breakout), sell the stock on the first rally. If it fails to rally and falls back below the breakout point, *immediately* dump it.

FURTHER TIPS FOR BUYING

The steps that I've already covered in the buying process are crucial. On a scale of 1 to 10, with 10 being the most important, they are 10s! If you follow them faithfully, you are going to be very pleasantly surprised. I now want to teach you a few more refinements. They aren't as important, but they can raise your profits to an even higher level.

When you read most books on technical analysis, you are quickly introduced to all sorts of exotic and confusing formations. Suddenly you are thrust into a world of triangles, pennants, and flags. I'm not saying there isn't merit to these fancy formations, but they aren't crucial to your scoring big profits in the market. I promised you at the beginning of this book that I'd only deal with the most important technical indicators. So forget about saucer bottoms and flying wedges and what-have-you. Nevertheless, there are a few formations you should be familiar with; these are both easy to spot and very profitable.

The first one is the head-and-shoulder bottom formation. This is the most powerful and reliable of all bottom formations. Most investors have heard of it, but few really know one when they see it. In fact, novice technicians usually imagine them on every other page of a chart book, just as a first-year medical student often worries that he has contracted every disease that he studies.

This dynamic pattern appears after a stock has suffered a major decline and is ready to reverse sharply to the upside. Chart 4–20 shows what to expect as this pattern unfolds. First there is a decline that drops XYZ to a new low, followed by an oversold rally (point A). The left shoulder has just formed but it is too early for you to know that at this time.

Next there is a smash that drops the stock to yet another new Stage 4 low. But now comes the first sign of budding strength. Once the urgent selling pressure runs its course, XYZ surprisingly rallies very close to the same resistance level as last time (point B). The

CHART 4–20

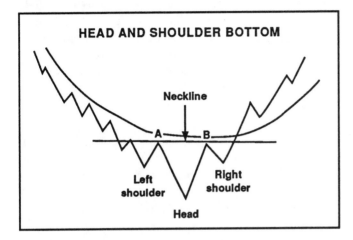

head has just formed on what is very unusual and bullish action. (Up until now, rallies that started after a new low was registered failed far below prior peaks.) So although it's still too early to buy, you get the feeling that something is going on.

Next there is another decline that gets underway, but it doesn't drop the stock to a new low. In fact, it doesn't even take XYZ all the way back to the last low, which is another subtle sign of strength. Ideally, the rally peaks (points A and B) will be at the same approximate price, and the two selloffs—on each side of the reverse head—will be approximately equal. But don't be a fanatic; both the peaks and the two selloffs can be off a bit. Just be sure that there is some semblance of symmetry.

After this selloff ends and the stock starts to rally once again, the right shoulder is completed. One other thing to be aware of is that points A and B on the chart (the first two peaks) should be connected with a trendline that is called the *neckline*. Keep a close eye on the neckline, because if the stock breaks out above it a bullish signal will be given.[10]

---

[10]Don't ever jump the gun. In a significant number of cases, the head-and-shoulder bottom formation will never be completed and instead will break out on the downside.

As for volume, on the head-and-shoulder bottom there are all sorts of fancy theories. Most theories view this scenario as bullish: volume heaviest on the left shoulder, somewhat lighter as the head forms, and contracting as the right shoulder forms. But forget about volume in the formation. After studying literally thousands of such reversal patterns, I've come to the conclusion that volume is not a good indicator of future upside potential for head-and-shoulder bottoms.

There are two signals that are important and very reliable. Both are from our system, and neither must ever be ignored. First, make sure that the 30-week MA is in fine shape. It should no longer be declining and the stock should not still be below it after it breaks out above resistance. If the MA is declining, don't buy the stock even if it breaks above the neckline, and even if it moves above the MA. If the MA later stops declining, you can buy the stock on a pullback toward it. If the stock is still below the MA after it moves above the neckline, don't buy it until it also clears the MA.

The second important signal is volume *after* the stock breaks out above the neckline and the MA. While you shouldn't spend a lot of time worrying about volume as the head-and-shoulder bottom is forming, you should worry plenty about what happens afterwards. The same volume rules that we went over earlier still hold.

CHART 4–21

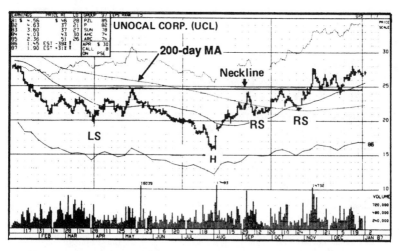

COURTESY OF DAILY GRAPHS AND LONG TERM VALUES

CHART 4–22

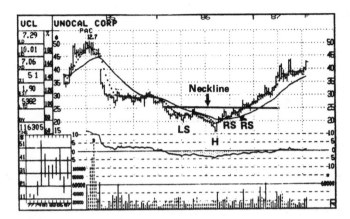

COURTESY OF MANSFIELD STOCK CHARTS

There must be a significant increase in volume on the breakout or it isn't trustworthy.

Head-and-shoulder bottom patterns are definitely easier to spot on a daily chart than on a weekly graph. Look at Unocal first on the Daily Graphs Chart (4–21), then on the Mansfield weekly Chart (4–22) and you'll see what I mean. Nevertheless, the really powerful patterns can be picked up even on the weekly chart. Let's start practicing so you'll soon be sharp enough to spot them. First look at Unocal on Weekly Chart 4–22. Once it moved above the neckline at 24 7/8, it was a solid buy. Volume confirmed and relative strength was improving, so the big advance in the coming months was predictable.

Now look at Chart 4–23, which shows a head-and-shoulder bottom pattern forming over a one-year period. Usually they will take shape much faster, but this makes it no less valid. Let's follow the zigs and zags closely because they are instructive. First, ASA dropped to a low at 32 in late 1985 before rallying back close to 41. The reverse left shoulder was now in place.[11] Now another more

---

[11]Note that a small potential bottom formation took place within that left shoulder with a minor breakout occurring at 41. You should not have considered buying at that point, as the MA was still declining and nearby overhead resistance starting at 45 was only a few months old.

CHART 4–23

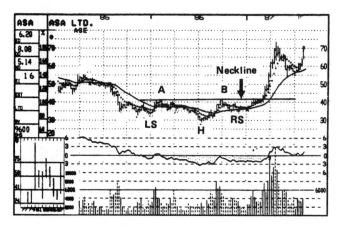

COURTESY OF MANSFIELD STOCK CHARTS

powerful decline set in that took ASA all the way down to 28. However, instead of staging a mediocre rally, the stock took off sharply on the upside. Where did it rally to? Right to the vicinity of the last peak, as this push failed at 41½. The reverse head was now in place. The fact that ASA could break to a new low and then power back slightly above its last rally peak was an important signal that aggressive buyers were starting to return to the stock.

But there was still a bit more work to do. The ensuing decline took ASA to 34⅜, which was about 2 points higher than the bottom registered on the left shoulder. Once the next rally started, the right shoulder was set. Next, the two rally peaks (points A and B) are connected to form the neckline. Now it's time to wait and watch. When ASA moved above the neckline at 42½, your buy-stop order was executed. Volume picked up on the breakout, which was encouraging. Relative strength improved sharply within the few weeks before and right after the breakout, which was an added plus. And, finally, although resistance still started in the mid–40s, it was close to two years old, which made it far less potent. With all of our fail-safe systems in place it was okay to buy your other half position. While you can't easily see it on the weekly chart, ASA quickly moved above 44, then pulled back close to 42 where additional buying should have been done. The stock then moved up to 49

CHART 4–24

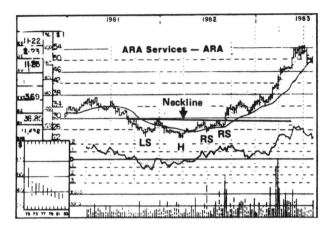

COURTESY OF MANSFIELD STOCK CHARTS

before dropping back to 46, which was the last chance to buy ASA before it rocketed up to 73½.

ARA Services (4–24) provides additional insight into the wonders of the head-and-shoulder bottom. Study it for a moment and you'll see the same favorable picture taking shape. First there was a drop to a new reaction low near 24. The left shoulder formed as ARA rallied back to 30. Then in early 1982 the stock plunged to a new Stage 4 low near 22. Thereafter, the buyers moved in, once again taking prices back up close to the prior peak. The head took shape and the neckline formed. ARA then dove to 25 as it held well above the prior low. Now an interesting phenomenon occurred that you should be aware of. The stock again rallied back close to 29 but didn't break out. After that it quickly dropped below 26 before starting another rally. Thus there were two right shoulders.[12] This is not unusual and in no way diminished the bullish implications of the pattern. Technical purists demand two shoulders on the left side if there are two on the right side. I disagree. Such symmetry isn't important as long as the necessary criteria are met. Anyway, ARA was an excellent buy at 30 once it broke above its

---

[12]This same phenomenon also occurred on the Unocal head-and-shoulder bottom—see Charts 4–21 and 4–22.

CHART 4–25

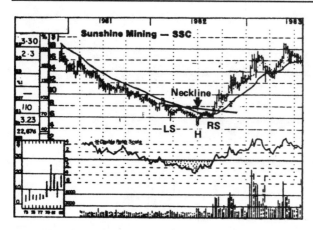

COURTESY OF MANSFIELD STOCK CHARTS

neckline. It was also helped out by impressive volume and excellent relative strength.

Are you starting to see what to look for? It's important to get used to spotting valid Stage 1 head-and-shoulder bottoms because these are powerful patterns. They don't form nearly as often as amateur technicians believe, but when they do occur you should definitely ride them.

Now study Charts 4–25 and 4–26 of Sunshine Mining and TRW. They will help you train your eyes for this profitable formation.

One last thing you should be aware of is that the head-and-shoulders bottom can also be an indicator for the general market or for a group. Here's what I mean. While an isolated formation or two doesn't have any significance for the market, several such patterns forming in the same time span does. For instance, in late 1974 and again in mid–1982 there were plenty such formations. This was a bullish indicator for the overall market. Those of you who remember your market history know that in both instances major bull markets began. In the same vein, several such patterns forming in one group is a very bullish signal for that sector. A perfect example of this was seen in 1986. Several oil-related stocks— oils, drillers, and oil-service stocks—completed head-and-shoulder bottoms before the group turned out to be one of the big winners in 1987.

CHART 4–26

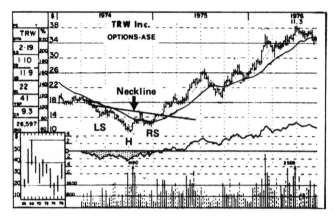

COURTESY OF MANSFIELD STOCK CHARTS

DOUBLE-BARRELED ACTION

While the next formation that I'm going to teach isn't as dynamic as the head-and-shoulder bottom pattern, it is a very profitable one. This is especially true when it occurs in conjunction with impressive volume, favorable relative strength, and minimal overhead resistance.

As you can see from Chart 4–27, stock XYZ should first hit a low (point A), then bounce higher once the selling pressure lessens. Then a second wave of selling develops which brings XYZ all

CHART 4–27

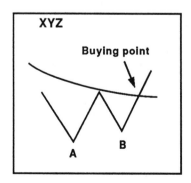

the way back down to its prior low (point B). It's a favorable sign if the renewed selling pressure cannot ignite a significant new down-leg in the stock. It doesn't matter if there is a marginal new low with B dropping slightly below point A. The important thing to watch for is that on the next rally the stock snaps back toward the recent peak. The breakout can occur immediately thereafter; or, in some cases, the stock may consolidate for several weeks before breaking out above resistance and moving into Stage 2. Whatever shape the bottom takes, *do not* anticipate. Don't buy prematurely. In some cases the breakout never occurs and the stock plummets to a new low. At other times, the breakout may come many months later, and by then you'll have become frustrated and sold the stock. It's common for this pattern to form within a matter of weeks, as it did with Anchor Glass Container (Chart 4–28) and Sun Micro-systems (Chart 4–29). However, in a smaller percentage of cases, it can form over a very long period of time, as Harvard Industries did (Chart 4–30). Take a moment to look at each of these three case histories.

In the case of Anchor Glass Container (4–28), the stock dropped close to 10 (point A) before rallying to 14⅛. A second wave of selling then took the stock back to 10½ late in 1986. A slow rally then got underway, with volume starting to increase (a favorable sign). However, after reaching 13½ that rally also failed to clear the important 14⅛ resistance, and a further consolidation took place during the following weeks. Then, once the stock had moved both above its trendline and above the 14⅛ resistance, the Stage 2 advance was underway.

In the case of Sun Microsystems (4–29), the double bottom formed very quickly. Once it moved above resistance at 15¼, it was ready to go into orbit. Note that the relative strength increased nicely at that point as the stock moved into positive territory. In addition, volume was very impressive. Finally, once the 20 level was overcome there was no further overhead resistance.

As for Harvard Industries (4–30), the double bottom formed over a 15-month period; but once the bottom formation was com-pleted and the stock moved above resistance at 8, the results were the same as with Anchor Glass and Sun Microsystems.

You should also be on the lookout for these formations in the market averages. In late 1974 (Chart 4–31), after the worst bear market since 1929–32, a powerful double bottom appeared in the

CHART 4–28

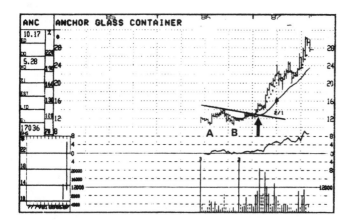

COURTESY OF MANSFIELD STOCK CHARTS

CHART 4–29

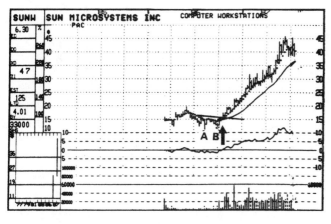

COURTESY OF MANSFIELD STOCK CHARTS

Dow Jones Industrial Average. After declining to point B, the next rally moved the blue-chip average above the downtrend line and the 30-week MA. The 1975–76 bull market was underway.

Be very careful when dealing with double bottoms because they form frequently, whereas valid head-and-shoulder bottoms are few and far between. Be very demanding and make sure all of the

CHART 4–30

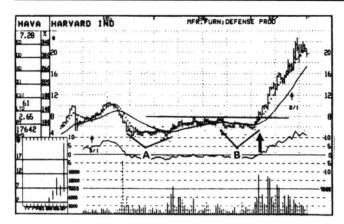

COURTESY OF MANSFIELD STOCK CHARTS

CHART 4–31

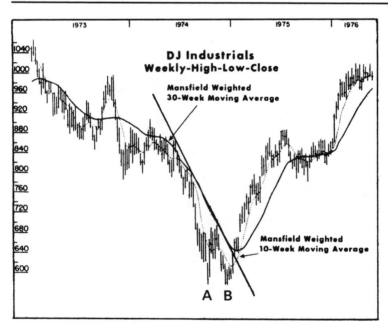

COURTESY OF MANSFIELD STOCK CHARTS

criteria we've gone over in the past few sections are met so you don't end up buying B – and C – double bottoms.

BIGGER IS BETTER

There's an old saying among technicians—"the bigger the base, the bigger the move" (the corollary being, "the bigger the top, the bigger the drop"). I heartily subscribe to that statement. While there are plenty of cases where short-term bases, when mixed with all the other winning ingredients, produce excellent results, always be on the lookout for a breakout from a very large base formation. This is especially important since these formations usually lead to very extensive and long-running advances. Intuitively, this theory makes a lot of sense. Just as a big house needs a very strong foundation, so, too, a large base can propel a stock higher over an extended period of time. It also makes sense in technical terms. What a big base really means is that a lot of stock has changed hands during the Stage 1 formation. Many disenchanted sellers who were holding the stock as it plummeted, hoping to get out even, finally sold the stock in disgust to a new group of buyers at this low price. This cuts down the amount of resistance that is overhead. Many of the former potential sellers who were disgusted and wanted to get out even have now dumped their stock. The new holders are willing to be far more patient and wait for the stock to advance significantly before selling.

Here are two examples of what you should be looking for. American Barrick Resources (4–32) broke out above resistance near 4 in early 1986 and advanced almost 400 percent over the next 15 months. All of the factors I've been stressing were in place. There was a long base pattern that was completed when ABX moved above resistance. Volume was not only impressive on the breakout, but had been building up in the prior several weeks. In addition, there was no nearby resistance and the RS line moved into positive territory on the breakout.

The same winning combination was evident in Korea Fund (4–33) in 1986. When KF moved above resistance at 18, it signaled that it had completed its long-term base and was ready for a sub-

CHART 4–32

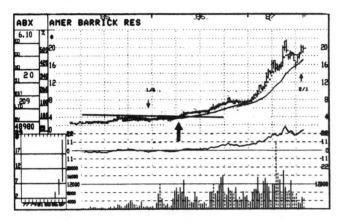

COURTESY OF MANSFIELD STOCK CHARTS

CHART 4–33

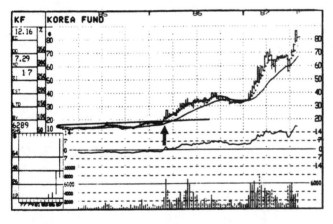

COURTESY OF MANSFIELD STOCK CHARTS

stantial advance. The move up to 86 over the next year and a half was that substantial advance. Once again, volume, relative strength, and the lack of nearby resistance were all textbook perfect.

We've come a long way in the past few chapters, so let's stop and reflect on what we've learned. By now you should realize that winning in the market is a matter of discipline and being able to spot patterns which time and again have correlated with big winners. You should also realize that the more of these favorable patterns we tie together, the more likely we are to win, and the bigger our gain will be.

STAN'S DON'T COMMANDMENTS

Now that you are familiar with when and what to buy, here's a checklist of when and what *not* to buy. Although the list is short, it is *very* deep in wisdom. If you thoroughly learn it and make sure to never violate any of these rules in the future, you are going to find your experiences in the market much more fun and profitable.

- Don't buy when the overall market trend is bearish.
- Don't buy a stock in a negative group.
- Don't buy a stock below its 30-week MA.
- Don't buy a stock that has a declining 30-week MA (even if the stock is above the MA).
- No matter how bullish a stock is, don't buy it too late in an advance, when it is far above the ideal entry point.
- Don't buy a stock that has poor volume characteristics on the breakout. If you bought it because you had a buy-stop order in, sell it quickly.
- Don't buy a stock showing poor relative strength.
- Don't buy a stock that has heavy nearby overhead resistance.
- Don't guess a bottom. What looks like a bargain can turn out to be a very expensive Stage 4 disaster. Instead, buy on breakouts above resistance.

QUIZ

1. It is a *very* favorable factor when a stock breaks out   **T** **F** above resistance and moves into virgin territory.
2. Relative strength measures how a stock performs in   **T** **F** relation to its volume pattern.
3. If all other factors are positive when a stock breaks   **T** **F** out (market trend is positive, group is strong, there is minimal resistance, etc.), then a lack of volume confirmation can be overlooked.

4. The volume pattern within the base area is even more   **T   F**
   important than the volume characteristics on the
   breakout.
5. The older the resistance, the less potent it is.   **T   F**
6. Even if a stock is declining, it can demonstrate fa-   **T   F**
   vorable relative strength.
7. The most powerful and reliable reversal pattern to   **T   F**
   look for after a major decline is a double bottom that
   then moves above its MA.
8. This chart is an example of a head-and-shoulder bot-   **T   F**
   tom reversal.

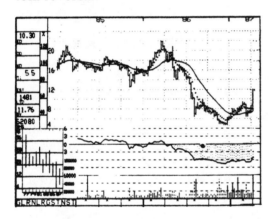

COURTESY OF MANSFIELD
STOCK CHARTS

9. Which one of these two stocks would you buy? (Assume that
   in both cases the overall market and group action is positive.)

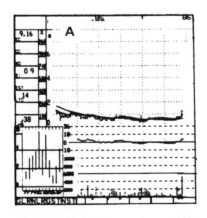

COURTESY OF MANSFIELD STOCK CHARTS

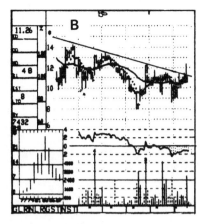

10. Which one of these two stocks would you buy? (Again assume that in both cases the overall market and group action is positive.)

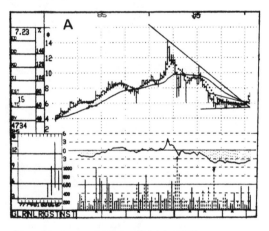

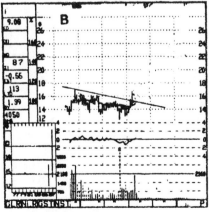

11. Which one of these two stocks would you buy?

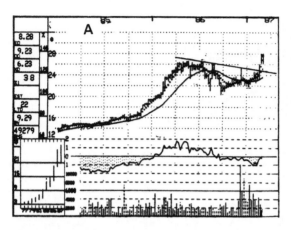

COURTESY OF MANSFIELD STOCK CHARTS

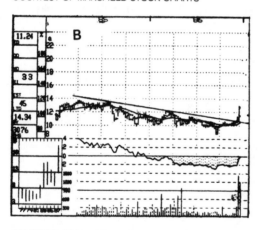

COURTESY OF MANSFIELD STOCK CHARTS

12. Which one of these three stocks would you buy? (Again assume that in all cases the overall market and group action is positive.)

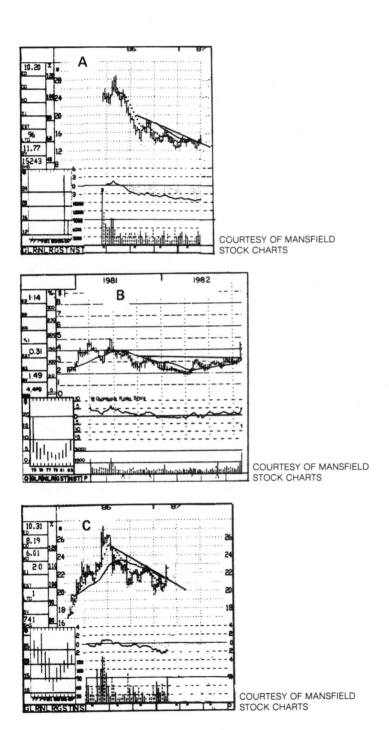

COURTESY OF MANSFIELD
STOCK CHARTS

COURTESY OF MANSFIELD
STOCK CHARTS

COURTESY OF MANSFIELD
STOCK CHARTS

ANSWERS

1. True. There is no further resistance to slow down the advance.

2. False. Relative strength measures how a stock performs in relation to the overall market.

3. False. Never overlook poor volume on a breakout. It is a *very* important danger signal that the breakout lacks staying power.

4. False. The volume pattern within the Stage 1 base isn't all that important, but it is very important on the breakout.

5. True.

6. True. If a stock declines, but declines *less* than the overall market over the same time span, it is demonstrating positive relative strength.

7. False. The most powerful and reliable bottom reversal pattern is a head-and-shoulders formation that rallies above its MA.

8. True.

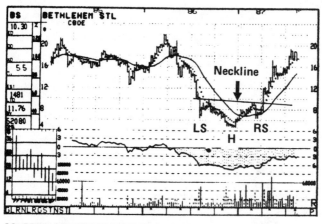

COURTESY OF MANSFIELD STOCK CHARTS

9. A. In the case of A, there was no nearby resistance, while B had plenty of nearby resistance just overhead. In addition, A had a large base pattern (18 months) while B had a smaller base (6 months). Also, stock A had excellent volume confirmation while B's was only fair (it was double the previous four weeks but below two other weeks in the base pattern). Furthermore, A had improving relative strength while B had poor

relative strength (in negative territory and lower on the break-out than at the start of the base). The end result is that stock A (which is Marcade Group) broke out at 1⅛ in mid–1986 and one year later was up to 7⅝. At the same time, stock B (Alpha Industries), which broke out at 11½ in 1986, was down to 6⅜ one year later.

10. B. (American Cablesystems) The relative strength was im-proving at the time of the breakout in the case of American Cablesystems, while it was mediocre for IRT Corporation (stock A). In addition, IRT had heavy resistance near 8½ (which was a prior support before being broken). At the same time, Amer-ican Cablesystems had some (but not overwhelming) resistance in the 16 to 17 zone, then no more! The end result was that IRT broke out at 6¼ in early 1987. Eight months later, it was down over 35 percent. American Cablesystems broke out at the same time at 15⅛ and seven months later was up 85 percent.

11. B. (Facet Enterprise) The most important negative factor with National Services (stock A) was the *very* poor volume on the breakout from the continuation pattern. At the same time, the volume confirmation was excellent on the Facet breakout. In addition, Facet had sharply improving relative strength while National Services, RS was only so-so. The only negative on the Facet chart was the resistance at 14, but it was 18 months old and the base was large enough to attack it. Finally, the volume was so exceptional it was worth going with. Facet broke out at 10½ and eight months later was more than double that price at 23⅛. On the other hand, National Service broke out at 25¾ and six months later was only up to 26¼!

12. You should have bought stock B (Mobile Homes) when it broke out at 3¼ in 1982. Relative strength was excellent on the Mobile Home breakout and mediocre on A (Rothschild) and C (Chi-cago Rivet & Machine) in early 1987. In addition, Mobile Home had the largest Stage 1 base pattern and broke above a hori-zontal trendline, while the other two issues broke above de-clining trendlines. It's not surprising that Rothschild broke out at 14¼ and five months later was still 14¼, while Chicago Rivet broke out at 22 and six months later was at 21. Mobile Homes, on the other hand, advanced 300 percent over the next year.

DON'T PUT ALL YOUR EGGS IN ONE BASKET

Now that you know what to buy and what not to buy, there is one last topic to cover: diversification. No matter how expert you become with my system, don't ever expect to achieve perfection. The future is too uncertain. It is feasible to be right a very high percentage of the time. But that implies being wrong now and then. Prudence dictates that you spread your risks over a number of stocks. That prevents one unfortunate choice from dealing you a crippling blow.

Even when protecting your long positions with sell-stops (which I'll teach you how to do in Chapter 6), you can get hurt badly if you don't diversify. If you lose 15 percent on a position to which you have committed your entire market stake, that puts quite a crimp in your wallet. And if you're unlucky and hit a second 15 percent whipsaw, your capital is badly depleted. But if you have your money equally distributed in 15 positions and one loses 15 percent, that loss represents only 1 percent of your market capital.

A perfect example of the market law of averages was exhibited in early 1987 in *The Professional Tape Reader*. Three of the buy recommendations I made in early January of that year were Dravo (Chart 4–34), Tandem Computers (Chart 4–35), and Texas Instruments.

CHART 4–34

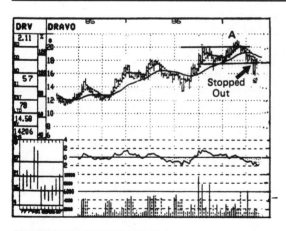

COURTESY OF MANSFIELD STOCK CHARTS

CHART 4-35

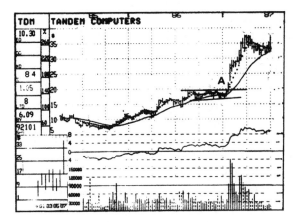

COURTESY OF MANSFIELD STOCK CHARTS

Dravo moved to a new multi-year high when it broke out above resistance at 20 (point A). Unfortunately, it made little headway and was stopped out when it broke below major support at 18. At the same time, Tandem Computers quickly came close to doubling from our recommended price of 19⅞ (point A). Texas Instruments also turned in an A+ performance, although it took a bit longer to almost double from our recommended price of 41⅞.

If all of your capital had been in Dravo, the powerful market advance that started in early 1987 would have been a disappointment to you. By diversifying your money among these three holdings, you would have walked away smiling.

Many who attend my seminars ask, "What is the right number of stocks to hold in my portfolio? Is it 8, 10, or 12?" The answer? There is no single magic number! But there is an approximate area which makes sense to me. I know that one or two stocks is far too dangerous an allocation of capital. I also believe that 40 to 50 stocks are far too many issues to keep track of. Keeping a watchful eye properly focused on your portfolio is a lot like being a parent. The more children you are responsible for, the harder it is to keep close tabs on them. So too with stocks. If your market assets are allocated among 50 stocks, it is very difficult to get a feel for how each one is acting. In addition, there is the tendency to concentrate on the issues that are acting well and put aside your concern about the laggards, figuring they will come to life later. What happens is that you let the good stocks subsidize the bad ones.

The proper way to look at your stocks is to make believe that each position is the only one you have. If it's acting fine, great, ride with it. But if it's lagging badly and acting poorly, lighten up on that position even if the sell-stop isn't hit. Move the proceeds into a new Stage 2 stock with greater promise. To be more specific, for a small portfolio that's investing a modest amount ($10,000 to $25,000), I'd diversify into no more than five or six stocks. But as you move up the ladder into six-digit or higher portfolios, 10 to 20 stocks are the most that I'd invest in at any one time. Also, use approximately equal dollar amounts when constructing your portfolio. Don't do as so many investors do who think in terms of the number of shares they can purchase. They buy 1,000 shares of everything, whether it's a $5 or $40 stock. To use a nice round number, if we were investing $100,000 in 10 stocks, each position should be approximately $10,000 in value. So if you are buying a $50 stock, you will purchase only 200 shares. If a second position is a $10 stock, you'll enter a buy order for 1,000 shares. Common sense should be applied when constructing your portfolio. *Don't put all your eggs in one basket.* But don't go to the other extreme of using too many baskets!

There is one other form of diversification to be aware of and practice. Don't do all of your buying from just one group. If three or four sectors exhibit great technical action, buy Stage 2 breakouts from all of them rather than from only group A. If one group suddenly reverses, your portfolio will still do well. If you practice these two forms of diversification and properly utilize my system, you should do very well in the market year in and year out!

CHAPTER 5

UNCOVERING EXCEPTIONAL WINNERS

Have you ever dreamt of buying a stock today, then going to sleep and waking up tomorrow to the exhilarating news that the company is being taken over at a substantially higher price? In this chapter I'm going to show you how to make this dream come true at least occasionally. In addition, you'll learn about a little-known technical method I've developed that can produce profits as startling as takeovers.

First, let's examine the takeover dream which, for most investors, leads to financial nightmares. I've seen investors buy on rumor after rumor and have not one deal pan out. Some terrible losses can pile up while they wait for the announcement that never comes. Why do so many investors chase these rainbows? It's a simple study in psychology. First, there's greed. We all want to hit that big gusher in a hurry, so we dream that maybe this time our ship will come in. Second, there's a theory in psychology called intermittent reinforcement. It says that if an animal gets what it wants, even in a small percentage of the cases, it will keep coming back for more. It's been demonstrated time and again that if a mouse gets cheese just once when going through a maze, it will try to navigate that maze over and over again, even when the cheese is no longer there. People aren't that different from animals. Why else would we play the slot machines in Las Vegas or try to win a lottery? All it takes is one jackpot going off in the casino, or one lottery winner in the headlines, and we start dreaming again.

As long as you keep this longshot syndrome in control and do no more than put a few coins in a slot machine, or buy an occasional lottery ticket, this all-too-human trait is no big deal. But if it drives you to continually buy rumor stocks, then it's a very serious problem. It will cost you dearly, because for every one rumor that turns out to be true, hundreds end in Stage 4 downtrends. Those aren't winning odds.

And yet more and more stocks are being gobbled up as take-over mania becomes ever more popular. Is there a way to intelligently play this game? Yes, and once again the disciplined answer is in the charts. Simply do the following. First, only play this game with a small percentage of your capital. The great majority of your buys should come from your studies. Second, if you hear a rumor, judge the source. If it's your stockbroker, and a few of his prior recommendations have actually worked out, that's a better source than if your broker has never had a bullseye in his life.

But don't stop there. Now comes the discipline. Get out your charts and study the stock carefully. If the stock looks like Beverly Enterprises did in mid-1987 (Chart 5–1), then forget it, even though there were takeover rumors surrounding it. If the stock is in Stage 4 and the relative strength is a horror show, walk away from that slot machine right then and there. Or if the chart is bullish but so far above its ideal entry point, as Anchor Glass Container (Chart 5–2) was in mid–1987 near 28, then forget it.[1] I'd rather miss out on a potential profit any day than buy a stock with a poor reward/risk ratio. All you've lost when you miss a winner is a potential profit. Like buses, another one will come along. But what you've lost when you get broadsided by a losing situation is a portion of your very precious capital. Here a bit of mathematics comes into play. If you have $50,000 invested and you lose 20 percent, you are now reduced to a $40,000 market stake. To get back to even you now need a 25 percent gain on your next trade. And if this trade is a loser, then the percentages move even further against you. So *discipline* and *selectivity* are operative words to always keep in mind. Remember, we can make really big money in the market even if we pass up 100 winners and buy only 10 stocks during the year, with 7 or 8 turning out to be winners.

But what if the chart of the rumored stock looks bullish and it hasn't broken out yet? Or if it has already moved above resistance

---

[1]Anchor Glass should have been purchased in early 1987 near 14. But never buy a stock when it is overextended and has a poor reward/risk ratio, which was the case with Anchor later in the year.

CHART 5–1

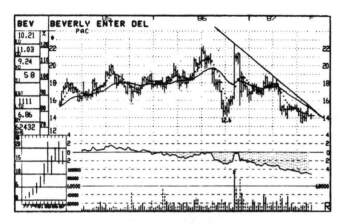

COURTESY OF MANSFIELD STOCK CHARTS

CHART 5–2

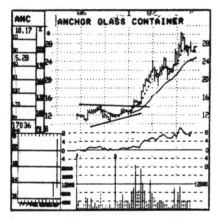

COURTESY OF MANSFIELD STOCK CHARTS

but is still close to the ideal entry point? If all the factors are favorable and you would honestly consider buying it even without the rumor, then it's worth a shot—the takeover possibility is simply icing on the cake. This was the case with Kidde (Chart 5–3) in mid–1987. The stock was a valid buy as it moved above 37 on huge vol-

CHART 5-3

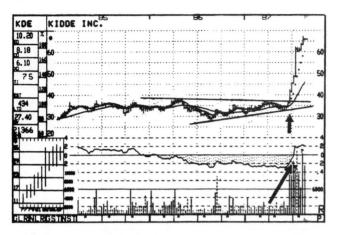

COURTESY OF MANSFIELD STOCK CHARTS

ume, rumor or no rumor. Volume was impressive, relative strength was improving, and there was no further overhead resistance. A few weeks later, that buy looked even better as the stock hit 67¼ on the news that Hanson Industries was taking over KDE.

Just remember that the same chart rules still apply. If the volume or any other important factor is negative, then pass on it. When it comes to spotting takeovers, there is one telltale clue to always look for, and that's volume. This is especially true if the takeover is going to be announced within the next few weeks. In almost every case where a merger is imminent, volume builds to an incredible crescendo. This makes sense, since more and more people find out about a takeover as it nears completion. Even though nobody is ever supposed to pass along inside information, it does happen. The charts show time after time that some people do know and are buying on that knowledge. So *never* believe in any potential takeover that doesn't show a *very* significant increase in volume.

Now let's examine several other real-life examples of stocks that were taken over, so that you'll know exactly what to look for.

Study Chart 5-4 of Hammermill Paper. Back in mid-1986 there were rumors that it was a possible takeover target. But what if you had never heard any stories about the stock? Simply based on the rules I've taught you, this was a solid buy candidate as it moved

CHART 5–4

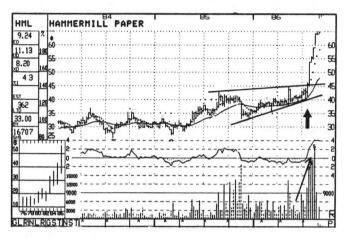

COURTESY OF MANSFIELD STOCK CHARTS

above 45. The market trend was in fine shape. In addition, the group was positive, with several other stocks in the sector also bullish. Furthermore, relative strength was positive and improving rapidly. Another favorable factor was that once it broke out above resistance at 45, there was no further overhead supply. And, most important, the volume pattern looked great! Carefully scrutinize the volume for a moment, because it's the key to spotting takeovers. Not only was it high on the breakout, which is a bullish sign, but there was also a steady increase in volume in the prior eight weeks. That was the real clincher! Even if you hadn't heard any stories about HML, it was a continuation buy that you should have strongly considered. HML zoomed from 45⅛ to 65 during the next five weeks following the breakout and was then taken over by International Paper.

Chesebrough Ponds (Chart 5–5) displayed the same winning pattern in early 1987. Again, all of the technical factors were in place for a big winner whether or not your broker had any tales to tell you. The market trend was bullish, the group positive, there was no significant overhead resistance, and the relative strength was excellent. The coup de grace was the volume buildup. When the stock broke out, volume registered its highest one-week reading on the chart. Therefore, whether or not you heard anybody whispering

CHART 5–5

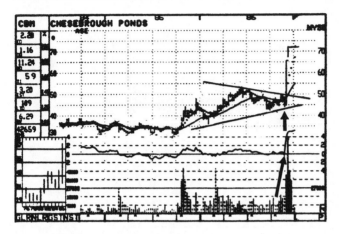

COURTESY OF MANSFIELD STOCK CHARTS

about the stock, Chesebrough should have been bought. Every technical sign that you could ask for was flashing buy, and the stock complied nicely by racing quickly from 50 to over 72.

Is the pattern starting to become clearer to you? Even if you'd heard nothing about the stock, the chart would have been the tipster that something was brewing. And if no takeover was in the works, then something else positive was happening, and the probabilities were great that it would have rocketed higher anyway.

Let's put another case history under the microscope and follow it step by step. In late 1986, Burlington Industries (Chart 5–6) was already in a powerful Stage 2 uptrend when it broke out above resistance near 40. All factors were positive and the stock merited buying as a continuation breakout. Volume, however, was not spectacular. It merely fulfilled its two-times criteria, and the stock worked its way higher in the following weeks. In early April 1987, however, something exciting was beginning to take shape. Rumors about BUR were making the rounds, and the stock broke out above resistance at 50 on unbelievably heavy volume. If you already had purchased Burlington, this was a reason to buy more; if you didn't own any, this action warranted some buying. The stock jumped from 50 to 77½ over the next few months. Again the heavy volume was the tip-off that a merger was in the works.

CHART 5–6

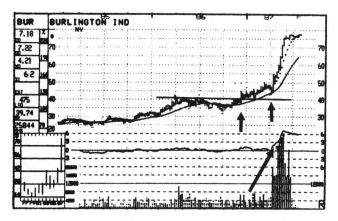

COURTESY OF MANSFIELD STOCK CHARTS

If, after studying these case histories, you really believe that no insiders act upon their knowledge before merger news is announced, then you are far less cynical than I.

Here are two more case histories of stocks that had a takeover pattern before the merger news was publicly announced. In the case of Fruehauf (Chart 5–7), the Stage 1 base was very large, resistance wasn't heavy, and relative strength was improving nicely. Most important of all, the trading activity showed the classic pattern of increasing volume that we want to see. Therefore, when it broke out above 27 in early 1986 it should have been bought, whether or not you heard any stories. Such buying paid off as FTR quickly ran up close to 50.

In the same manner, Purolator Courier (Chart 5–8) was an exciting purchase that paid off handsomely if you followed the technical rules for uncovering a big winner. When it broke above its downtrend line at 20⅛ in late 1986, relative strength was improving nicely as it moved above the zero line. In addition, dramatically increased volume indicated there was a good chance that resistance near 24 would be taken out. This turned out to be the case as the stock zoomed toward the 40 level.

By now it should be obvious what things you must be alert to when looking for takeover targets. No amount of gossip or rumor

CHART 5–7

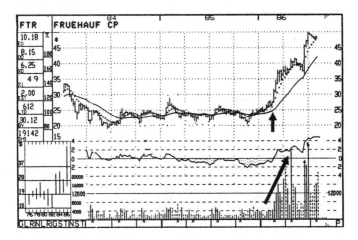

COURTESY OF MANSFIELD STOCK CHARTS

CHART 5–8

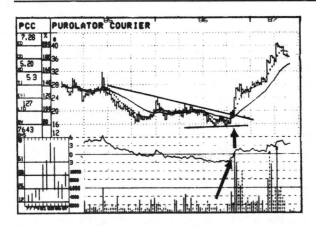

COURTESY OF MANSFIELD STOCK CHARTS

can make up for a negative Stage 4 pattern such as Financial Corp. of America (Chart 5–9) in 1987. Yet if I had heard a good story on a stock with a strong technical pattern—such as Safeway Stores (Chart 5–10) in 1986 — I would most definitely have put it down on my potential shopping list of buys. Then when it broke out above

CHART 5-9

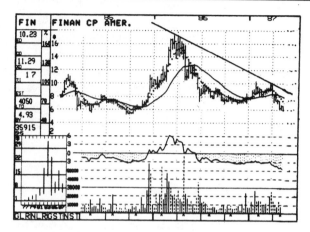

COURTESY OF MANSFIELD STOCK CHARTS

CHART 5-10

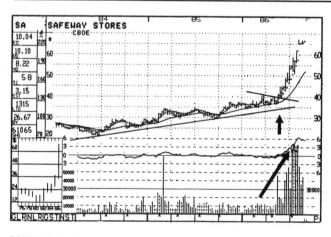

COURTESY OF MANSFIELD STOCK CHARTS

40 with positive relative strength, no further overhead supply, and a sharp volume increase, I would have rated the stock a strong buy candidate—takeover or not. As it turned out, it was taken over, as was every stock that I've shown you so far in this chapter, except for the two negative charts of Beverly Enterprises and Financial Corporation.

So follow these rules and you'll be amazed how often you end up buying what the insiders buy, without knowing the information that they are privy to. This is exactly what occurred when I recommended stocks such as Caesars World, Owens-Illinois, Piedmont Aviation, and Spectradyne (Charts 5–11 through 5–14) in *The Professional Tape Reader.* All became takeover targets, along with several other recommendations, and moved substantially higher in the months ahead. While I'm sure some *PTR* readers thought I had heard a good story on these stocks, the simple reality is that I read the message of the tape. From now on, you will be able to do the same.

THE TRIPLE CONFIRMATION PATTERN

There is a second pattern to look for that also produces outstanding profits. It has nothing to do with takeover candidates, unless by coincidence. The results, however, are equally spectacular and, in some cases, *even more profitable* than a merger stock.

I discovered this technique long ago and introduced it in *The Professional Tape Reader* back in the mid–1970s. Be aware that while this formation produces some unbelievable winners, it is *not* for short-term trading. Rather it is a method whereby aggressive investors can uncover potential big winners to ride for a major advance.

CHART 5–11

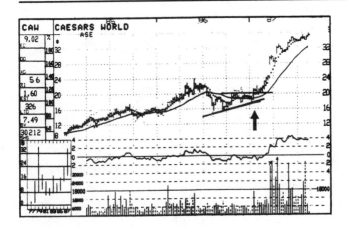

COURTESY OF MANSFIELD STOCK CHARTS

CHART 5-12

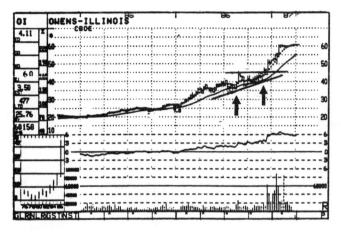

COURTESY OF MANSFIELD STOCK CHARTS

CHART 5-13

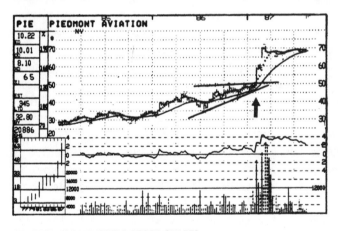

COURTESY OF MANSFIELD STOCK CHARTS

In football, a player who is a triple threat can run, pass, and kick. It is very rare to find someone who is outstanding at all three. This pattern also occurs only occasionally with stocks, as it requires the unlikely to happen—three different favorable signals must be flashed in close proximity to each other.

CHART 5–14

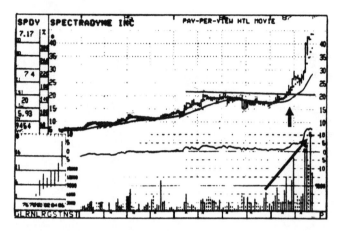

COURTESY OF MANSFIELD STOCK CHARTS

In addition to the basic requirements of the stock being above the MA, the following three events must take place. First, there must be a *volume signal*. This is vital! The market champs almost always have substantially larger volume on the breakout than during any point in the Stage 1 base area. For this type of big winner we want to see volume of even more than twice the average trading of the past four weeks. In addition, the heavy volume should *not* be short-lived. The initial volume surge should be followed by several more weeks of heavy trading. This signal indicates a sudden tremendous interest in the stock, as well as additional future demand. Since the stock is starting to run away on the upside, buyers will be fast to add to positions on any corrections. When the dips are too shallow to accommodate their buying, these buyers will often get into a buying panic.

Once again, very impressive volume (A on Chart 5–15) is the key ingredient to a super winner, but it's not the only one. The second factor to focus on is *relative strength* (B on Chart 5–15). This is a very important tool to use in distinguishing good from great buys. For this triple-threat pattern, the RS line must be in a certain position. It should either be in negative territory or hugging the zero line in a neutral manner. Then, as the Stage 2 breakout occurs, the RS line should move decisively into positive territory. This is very im-

CHART 5-15

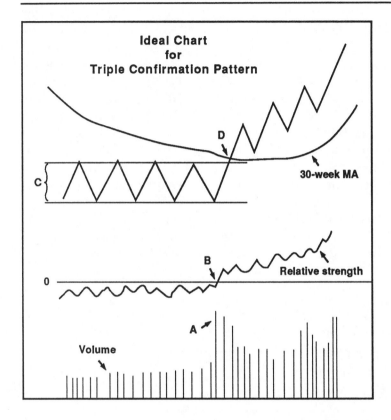

Ideal Chart
for
Triple Confirmation Pattern

30-week MA

Relative strength

Volume

portant! I've shown that you can buy stocks which have an RS line in negative territory as long as it is improving and *all* of the other technical factors are positive. But when looking for this very special big-winner pattern, there can be no compromises. If relative strength remains in negative territory, it doesn't fulfill this special criteria, even though the stock can still be a good buy and can chalk up a fine gain.

The third clue to look for is a *big move before the stock breaks out*. I know it sounds strange since we all want to buy as cheaply as possible; but this is an important element of this aggressive big-payoff pattern. If a stock has wide swings while still in its Stage 1 base pattern, then it's far more likely to be a ball of fire once it breaks out. Just as a high jumper gets into a low crouch before taking off upward, a stock that first dips and then gets up a good head of steam will be far more powerful once it leaves the starting gate. As a rule of thumb, stocks that have risen some 40 to 50 percent or more *before* breaking out do the best in the months ahead. But this does add some near-term risk to the breakout, which is why I stressed earlier that this kind of buying is strictly for investors rather than traders.

Back in 1971, Anthony Industries fufilled all of the necessary criteria perfectly. Volume expanded by about four times normal levels—a definite sign of important buying interest (A on Chart 5–16). Furthermore, volume remained heavy in the following weeks. The RS line also moved decisively into positive territory (B on Chart 5–16). The third significant clue that a big payday was shaping up was the volatile action that Anthony Industries displayed while it was still in its Stage 1 base. It swung back and forth between support at 5 and resistance at 10. Therefore, when it first broke out at 10⅛ in late 1971 (point D on Chart 5–16) it had already advanced 100 percent! To many investors this was a time to do

CHART 5–16

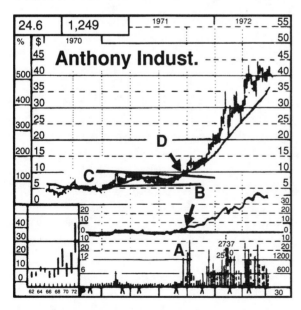

CHART 5–17

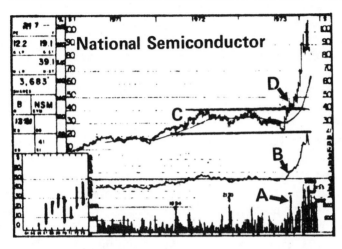

National Semiconductor

COURTESY OF MANSFIELD STOCK CHARTS

selling since the stock was overbought.[2] But now that I've trained your eye and you are starting to develop a feel for charts, you should view the situation differently from the average investor. At point D, Anthony was first moving into Stage 2 on heavy volume. So instead of joining the crowd with conventional terms such as overbought and overvalued, you should have said only one word— buy! Over the next eight months, our big-winner theory became reality as Anthony advanced over 300 percent.

National Semiconductor (Chart 5–17) demonstrated this same big-winner potential back in 1973. Since the overall market averages had already turned negative, you should not have been looking to do much buying. Rather you should have had plenty of short sales working for you during that bear market. If, however, you came across one outstanding buy pattern such as National Semiconductor you could have hedged your shorts with one excellent buy candidate such as this. But you better have made sure it was an A+, because there is no room for anything less when the overall market

---

[2]*Overbought* is a technical term which means that on a short-term basis the stock has advanced too rapidly and is due for a temporary correction before moving higher.

trend is negative. National Semiconductor was such an A+. It was a three-way winner as volume increased impressively by almost three times the average of the prior few weeks (A on Chart 5–17). In addition, volume remained at a very heavy level in the following weeks after the breakout. Relative strength was close to the zero line before the Stage 2 breakout. Thereafter it moved quickly and strongly into positive territory.

The third important signal that a big advance was shaping up was the big move National Semiconductor staged before the Stage 2 breakout took place. The stock came close to doubling as it moved from near 20 to 40 before breaking out at point D at 40½ . Again, many thought the stock was too high after such a sharp advance, but you know better. To see how powerful this triple confirmation pattern can be, National Semiconductor rocketed ahead over 150 percent within the next three months—an incredible 600 percent annualized advance. This is a fabulous move anytime, but it's especially impressive coming in the midst of the 1973–74 bear market. So always be alert for this formation, because when you spot it you want to fully exploit it.

To make sure you've got this important concept down pat, let's look at a few more examples of this very profitable phenomenon. In early 1987, volume increased sharply in Blocker Energy (Chart 5–18) as it broke out of its Stage 1 base pattern at 1⅛ . Not only did volume easily exceed the average of the prior weeks by more than twice, it was more than five times heavier. Such a sharp increase in volume shows that big money is becoming interested in a situation, and it almost always forecasts a significant advance. Blocker was no exception. Again, it was as easy as A-B-C to uncover this big winner. While the fundamentals were none too enticing and the red ink was plentiful, the telltale technical clues were there.[3] In addition to the group being very bullish, there was only limited overhead supply to worry about, and that resistance was about a year and a half old. Furthermore, the Stage 1 base was very large. On top of all these bullish signs, all three of our big-winner factors were in place. Volume was excellent on the Stage 2 breakout, showing that there was plenty of propulsion behind

---

[3]Blocker reported deficits in six of the eight quarters before it broke out.

CHART 5–18

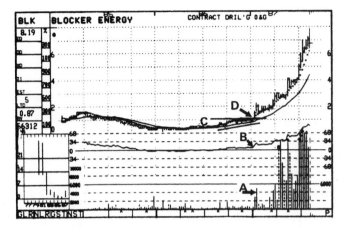

COURTESY OF MANSFIELD STOCK CHARTS

this potential winner. Second, relative strength had been hovering near the zero line slightly in positive territory. Once the breakout took place, there was no more. The RS line took off like a shot from the neutral zero line. Finally, although the low price disguises it, there was one heck of an advance before the breakout occurred. Blocker moved from its low at ⅜ to 1⅛ as it broke out—a hefty 200 percent advance. But the predictable fun was just getting underway, as Blocker chalked up a 600 percent gain in the following 11 months.

Are these just a few lucky shots in the dark? No way! While these patterns don't pop up every day, or even every week, they do form periodically. As you become more skilled in reading the charts, you will pick out these patterns and ride them for all they are worth—which will be plenty.

Both Keystone Consolidated and Philippine Long Distance Telephone (Charts 5–19 and 5–20) fulfilled all three requirements of my big-winner technique. Again, the results were fabulous! Interestingly enough, when the upmove in Keystone started at 4⅝ the latest 12-month trailing earnings were a *deficit* of $3.70 per share, with many P/E watchers worrying that the company was on the road to bankruptcy. And after the jet-propelled advance up to 30, what do you think the earnings had improved to? As of mid-

CHART 5–19

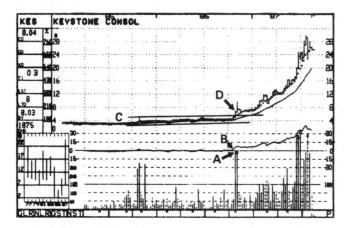

COURTESY OF MANSFIELD STOCK CHARTS

CHART 5–20

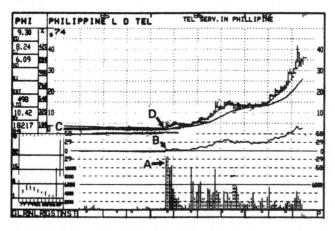

COURTESY OF MANSFIELD STOCK CHARTS

1987, with the stock up to 30, the cumulative earnings for the prior 12 months were a rousing deficit of $1.16. The earnings still hadn't moved into the black! So much for fundamental analysis and price/ earnings ratios! As for the activity within the base, it met our 40 percent-or-more criterion, although it is hard to tell from this chart.

One of the few weaknesses of the Mansfield chart is that it is an arithmetic scale rather than a logarithmic, or percentage, scale. When a low-priced stock advances sharply, the low-priced action looks miniscule even though the percentages are large. When you find one of these special big-winner patterns, invest much more heavily in it because the probabilities are great that you have a grand-slam home run on your hands.

Once you've mastered the concepts of this very important chapter, you'll know how to uncover those special situations that make investing so much more rewarding than savings bonds. And you'll know the right time to hop aboard.

QUIZ

To help you hone your skills, here are a few actual case histories of stocks that broke out. But in each group of three charts, only one turned out to be a big winner. By applying the rules of this chapter for uncovering big winners, see if you can pick the home run in each group.

(Pick the best stock out in each group of three.)

1. A. B. C.

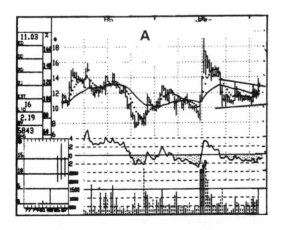

COURTESY OF MANSFIELD STOCK CHARTS

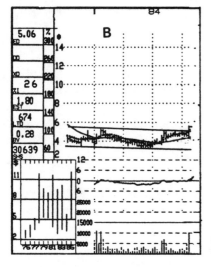

84

B

COURTESY OF MANSFIELD
STOCK CHARTS

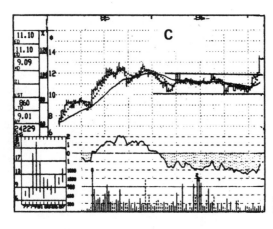

C

COURTESY OF MANSFIELD
STOCK CHARTS

2. A. B. C.

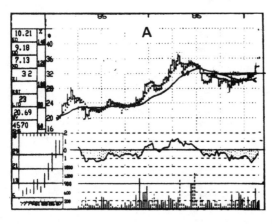

A

COURTESY OF MANSFIELD
STOCK CHARTS

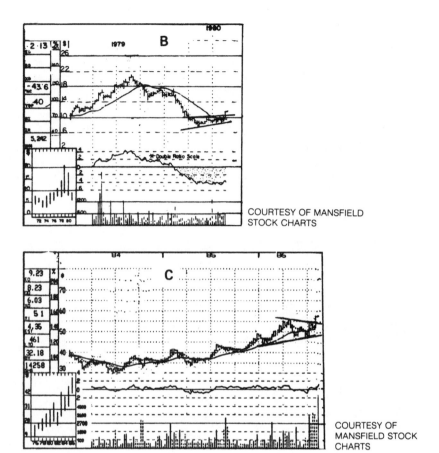

COURTESY OF MANSFIELD
STOCK CHARTS

COURTESY OF
MANSFIELD STOCK
CHARTS

3. Which *two* stocks would you buy in this group? A. B. C.

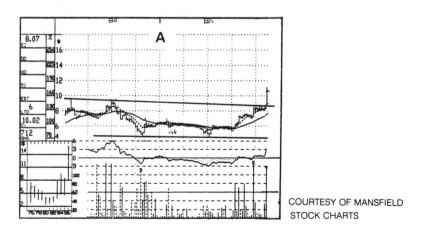

COURTESY OF MANSFIELD
STOCK CHARTS

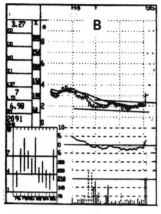

COURTESY OF MANSFIELD STOCK CHARTS

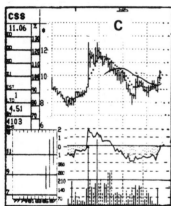

COURTESY OF MANSFIELD STOCK CHARTS

4. All three of the following stocks are good buys.   **T** **F**
   A. B. C.

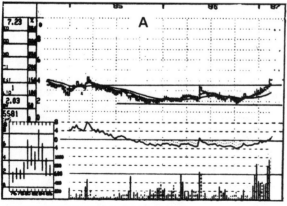

COURTESY OF MANSFIELD STOCK CHARTS

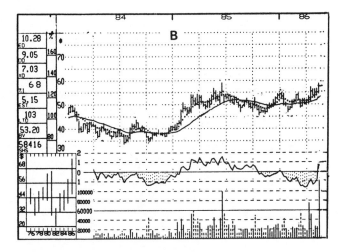

COURTESY OF MANSFIELD STOCK CHARTS

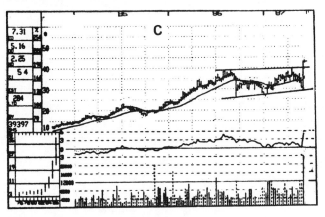

COURTESY OF MANSFIELD STOCK CHARTS

ANSWERS

1. The proper pick is stock B, Republic Airlines. It had that triple-winning pattern, as volume increased by over three times on the breakout, the stock had advanced by over 50 percent when it broke out, and the relative strength moved above the zero line. As confirmation, the volume increased further in the following months, and Republic was taken over by Northwest Airlines in early 1986 at 17 for a fabulous gain. As for stock A

(MacGregor Sporting Goods), the relative strength wasn't impressive; but even more important, volume wasn't twice the average of the prior four weeks. The end result was that it moved up a few points to 15½, then crashed down to 8 by mid–1987. Finally, as for stock C (Inter-City Gas), the volume was very poor on the breakout, so it should not have been considered. It broke out at 12¼ and eight months later had managed to reach 15.

2. In this case, you should have purchased stock C (Ex-Cell-O). The volume buildup was impressive and the relative strength healthy. It should have been bought breaking out above 55. A few weeks later it was taken over by Textron at 77½.

    Stock A (Van Dorn) had fair volume and only okay relative strength. The stock broke out moving above 32 and eight months later had edged up to 40.

    Finally, stock B (Lamson & Sessions) had horrid relative strength and even worse volume. It was the worst of the three and ended up performing that way. It broke out at 10¼ and moved only fractionally higher before dropping to 4 one and a half years later.

3. Both stocks A (Crown Crafts) and B (International Proteins) were excellent buys. Crown Crafts was a triple winner as it increased close to 100 percent before breaking out, had a very impressive volume increase on the breakout, and also saw the RS line move into positive territory. The stock broke out at 9 and 18 months later was up to 87½.

    International Proteins was also a three-way winner as it increased by over 50 percent before it broke out, had a sharp volume increase, and also saw the RS line turn positive. Not surprisingly, less than two years later the stock was up to 20¾.

    As for stock C (CSS Industry), volume was only fair. Even though it was more than twice the average, volume on the breakout was less than several weeks in the base pattern. It broke out at 10⅛ and six months later was only up to 12.

4. True. All three were great buys. Stock A (GTI) was a three-way winner which broke out at 3½. Four months later it was up to 10. Stock B (Sperry Corporation) was also a three-way winner that showed a very impressive volume buildup. It should

have been bought moving above 57. Just a few weeks later it was taken over by Burroughs Corporation at 76½. Finally, Harcourt Brace (stock C) was a great buy coming through 40 as volume increased sharply, relative strength was positive, and there was no further overhead supply above 40. All of these positive factors paid off in a fast move that sent the stock up to almost 60 within a matter of weeks.

CHAPTER 6

WHEN TO SELL

You are now more than halfway down the road to successful investing. To complete the journey, there is one more very important step to master—learning when to sell. The sell decision is crucial if you are going to really win big in the market. Unfortunately, few market players ever master this important step.

Carrying just one Avon from 140 down to 19, or a Floating Point from 45 to 8½, can put you out of action fast, with no chance of a comeback. (See Charts 6–1 and 6–2.) It's hard to believe how many times I've seen portfolios filled with stocks that were once winners but are now disasters. You know the story. XYZ was bought properly at 40 and then it quickly ran up to 60. But the word was out that it would soon run to 100, so why sell? When it dropped to 20, you discovered only too well why it should have been sold.

Alfin and VM Software (Charts 6–3 and 6–4) illustrate clearly how important it is to learn how to sell properly. In both cases, buy signals were registered (point A on the charts). In the following months, these stocks made advances that are the stuff of a buyer's dream. But if you had stayed married to them, that dream would have turned into a nightmare. After an exciting advance, each gave back its entire gain. Even worse, they actually turned into losses! Once you perfect the techniques of this very important chapter, you'll *never again* experience this gut-wrenching roller-coaster action.

Also damaging to portfolio results is the tendency to sell too soon. How often have you bought a stock just right, then seen it triple in 12 to 18 months—but without you still in it? Instead of riding it from 40 all the way up to 120, you took a fast profit at 50,

CHART 6–1

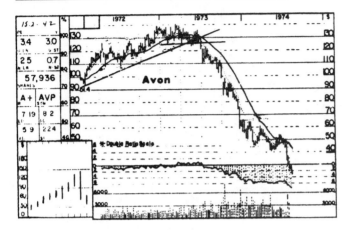

COURTESY OF MANSFIELD STOCK CHARTS

CHART 6–2

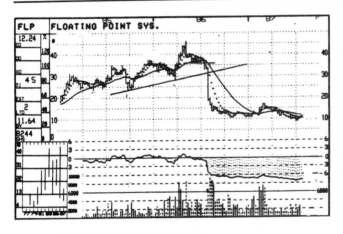

COURTESY OF MANSFIELD STOCK CHARTS

wrongly believing that you can't go broke taking a profit. The truth is that in the long run, you need to capture these giant advances to offset the losses from occasional mistakes. By doing this, you'll have big net profits left over.

The problem is that an investor or trader often sells for no other reason than his feeling that the stock is too high. He then

CHART 6–3

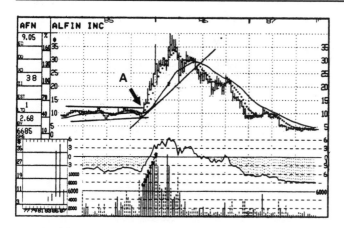

COURTESY OF MANSFIELD STOCK CHARTS

CHART 6–4

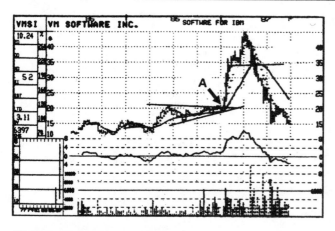

COURTESY OF MANSFIELD STOCK CHARTS

watches it go much higher without him. Is there really a way to make an intelligent judgment that a particular stock has had it and is about to stagger? There most certainly is, and it centers around my method of stage analysis. Before getting into the proper techniques of selling, it's useful to analyze the incorrect approach followed by most investors.

DON'TS FOR SELLING

1. *Don't base your selling decision on tax considerations.* This is truly a case of letting the tail wag the dog. Too often an investor will decide that he can't sell a given stock because there is too big a tax bite. Then in the following months the stock plummets and wipes out a good portion of the profit. This decline, if avoided, could have paid for the taxes and still have left a good gain. Furthermore, you then could have moved into a new Stage 2 situation that had the potential to rack up an additional gain.

The following true story will show you exactly what I mean. Back in 1978 when I was speaking at an investment seminar, I said that after having been bullish on the casino stocks, I was now issuing a sell signal.[1] After my speech, a distraught investor (we'll call him Jim) came over and said that he had a serious problem. He was holding several thousand shares of Resorts International Class A (see Chart 6–5). The stock was around 65 at the time and the high was 70, so I figured at worst he had a five-point loss. I therefore told him, "Don't be so upset. Just take your small loss and you'll make it up in another issue." He then shocked me by saying, "Oh, I don't have a loss. I bought the stock around 20. My problem is that I have too big a profit and will have to pay too much in taxes." I told him that everyone should have such problems, and that I would sell the stock and simply consider the tax consequences as a cost of doing business. One year later, when I again addressed that same conference, I saw Jim again. When he came over to say hello, he reminded me about our talk the prior year. I asked how his problem had turned out. "Oh, I don't have a problem anymore," he said, "Resorts is now back down to 20 and I no longer have a gain to worry about."

Don't ever fall into this trap. When a stock turns negative, it's a sale whether you have a profit or a loss or have to pay taxes. The bloodless verdict of the marketplace doesn't know what you paid for the stock and doesn't care. You have to learn to be objective and dispassionate.

---

[1]Although they hadn't yet officially moved into Stage 3, casino stocks were exhibiting classic signs of a blow-off. Both volume and price movement were excessive.

CHART 6–5

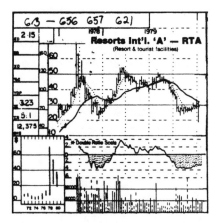

COURTESY OF MANSFIELD STOCK CHARTS

2. *Don't base your selling decision on how much the stock is yielding.* Far too often, investors decide to hold onto a stock that is weakening because it pays a great dividend. This is silly because after the stock drops a few points, as in the case of Rochester Gas & Electric in 1987 (Chart 6–6), the selloff wipes out the whole year's worth of dividends plus more. This type of thinking is especially common when dealing with utility stocks, which typically offer a generous yield. It's great to hold onto these stocks while they are in Stage 2. Even though they won't usually rocket ahead, they are good total-return situations (price appreciation plus yield) that certainly beat the 5½ percent yield of the bank. But once these stocks move into Stage 4 and start heading south, it's ridiculous to hold onto them any more than you would hold any other Stage 4 loser. Remember, if you get a 10 percent yield but lose 20 percent because of price depreciation, that's not winning mathematics. And that's the good news. It could be worse. There's always the distinct possibility that the plunge in stock price is a signal of future bad economic news for the firm. The news may be so negative that the company may not even have the ability to pay future dividends at all. Many investors in Continental Illinois and other falling angels learned this lesson the hard way.

CHART 6–6

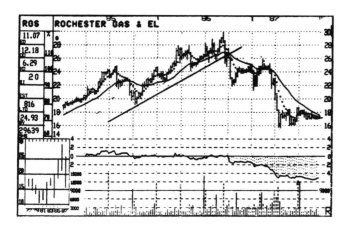

COURTESY OF MANSFIELD STOCK CHARTS

3. *Don't hold onto a stock because the price/earnings (P/E) ratio is low.* This ratio often appears to be at a bargain level even though your stock is topping out. The stock often declines and only months later reports disappointing earnings. By this time the P/E ratio no longer appears low at all, but at that point it is too late to sell profitably. In addition, there are many cases where the P/E ratio is low—and stays low—and the stock gets bashed anyway. Chart 6–7 of Chase Manhattan illustrates exactly what I'm talking about. When CMB neared 50 in 1986, the P/E was a very low 7. Interestingly, 13 months later the P/E was an even bigger bargain at 6. Unfortunately, the stock had moved into Stage 4 and dropped from close to 50 down to 34. So much for low P/Es as a reason to hold on!

4. *Don't sell a stock simply because the P/E is too high.* The converse of the prior example is also a serious problem. There's an old Wall Street joke that has an investor ask his broker why a given stock went up. For lack of a better explanation, the broker quips "more buyers than sellers." There's more truth than fiction to the message behind that joke, but few investors ever learn it. They always want rational answers why a stock moves. They are really getting either excuses or conjecture. Few market participants

CHART 6–7

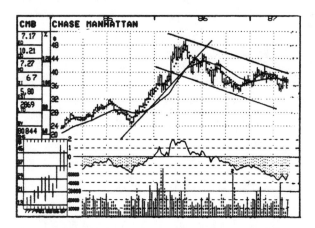

COURTESY OF MANSFIELD STOCK CHARTS

ever learn that the market isn't always rational. All it does is reflect the prevailing psychology or mood of investors. If investors become overly bullish and lapse into optimistic dreams, then high P/Es can go much higher. Tandem Computers (Chart 6–8) illustrates this point clearly. The P/E ratio of 32 was no bargain in late 1985 when TDM moved above resistance at 10 (point A). Fifteen months later, it was an even higher 44 as the stock price neared the 38 level.

Investors are like manic-depressives: when they become optimistic, they'll find excuses to buy stocks no matter how high the P/E gets. On the other hand, when they become bearish and worried, they will shy away from buying no matter how cheap the P/E appears. So the secret is to accept that too high can become much higher when a stock is in Stage 2, and hold back on your selling until you see the whites of their eyes and Stage 3 starts to form. This is far more important than too high a P/E, because it objectively shows that the very powerful buying which catapulted your stock higher is now finally meeting equally powerful selling. It is not the fuzzy concept of being overvalued that causes a stock to top out, but the measurable reality that supply finally equals demand.

Chart 6–9 of Maxtor says it all. When MXTR moved above 8 resistance in early 1986, the stock was a solid Stage 2 buy even

CHART 6–8

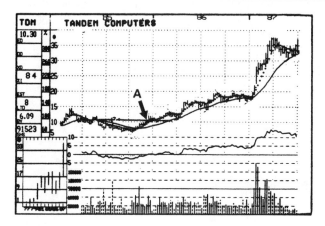

COURTESY OF MANSFIELD STOCK CHARTS

CHART 6–9

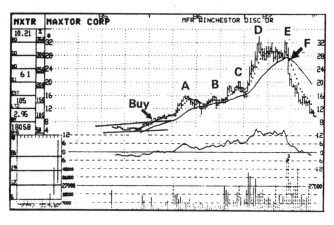

COURTESY OF MANSFIELD STOCK CHARTS

though the P/E was far from cheap at 16. Then at point A the P/E was a very high 28. Later at B it was still a fundamentally dangerous 24. At point C it was still on the high side at 20. Yet, since the MA was still rising, our method of stage analysis argued strongly to ignore the P/E danger and hold. Months later the stock zoomed up close to 34 and the P/E reached a very high 33 (point D). Still later at point E, the P/E was a worrisome 28. If you had based your sell decision on this ratio, you would have sold at a price of 16 (point A). But MXTR didn't flash a *real* sell signal until point F, when it broke down from an important top formation as the MA leveled out. A few months later, the stock crashed to 9⅝. Note that the P/E was on the high side for 18 months while the stock advanced. Only after supply moved into equilibrium with demand and a dangerous Stage 3 top formed did Maxtor finally decline. This clearly illustrates why our technical method is so much more helpful and precise than the subjective theory of P/E overvaluation.

    5. *Don't average down in a negative situation.* Whether it's watching Polaroid (Chart 6–10) drop from close to 150 down to 16 in 1974, or seeing Western Health Plans (Chart 6–11) drop from 15⅞ in 1985 down to 3 two years later, the details are always the same. These are stocks that had moved into Stage 4 and should have been sold. Unfortunately, many investors fell into the fundamentals trap. First they held on because it was a good company— or so they thought. When they realized they were in trouble, they determined to get out even on the next rally. This is market masochism at its worst. In so many Stage 4 bombings, the stock never gives you the opportunity to come close to getting out even. Then panic takes over and these ill-starred investors shoot themselves in the foot by averaging down.[2] This technique is great in theory, but suicidal in practice. Those who practice this dangerous technique are courting financial disaster. Anacomp in 1983–84 (Chart 6–12) and Halliburton in 1981–82 (Chart 6–13) are just two more examples out of several hundred that show how you could have been wiped out by employing this foolish tactic. Anacomp gave a clear sell signal when it broke below 18 on its downward trek to 2. Halliburton also flashed sell when it broke below the MA and support at 70 on its way to 21.

    Don't ever fall into the seductive trap of thinking that by buying more at a lower price, the stock will only have to rally half as much before you get out even. Do as professionals do—average up, not

---

[2]*Averaging down* is buying more stock at lower prices to produce a better average cost price.

CHART 6–10

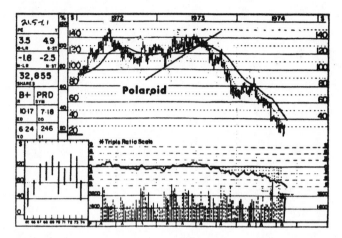

COURTESY OF MANSFIELD STOCK CHARTS

CHART 6–11

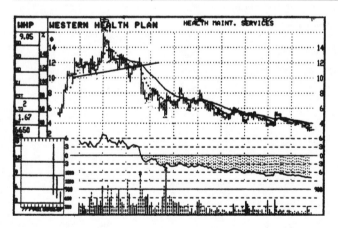

COURTESY OF MANSFIELD STOCK CHARTS

down. When market action starts to show them they are right, the pros pile on further—not when they've been proven wrong. Instead of sitting on a problem stock, they get out promptly. Learning how to handle a losing situation and keeping losses to a minimum is one of the most important secrets of successful investing. It is so im-

CHART 6–12

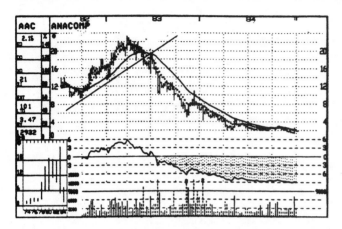

COURTESY OF MANSFIELD STOCK CHARTS

CHART 6–13

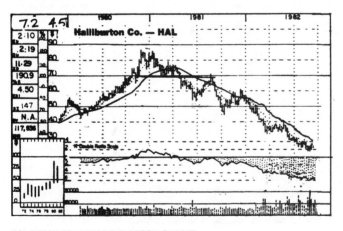

COURTESY OF MANSFIELD STOCK CHARTS

portant that I devote an entire section later in this chapter to this very important topic.

The averager is thrown off the profitable track since he is buying more rather than getting out. Even if the stock rallies a bit he runs into further trouble because he has a target price in mind where he'll get out even. When the advance fails to reach that price, he grimly continues to hold because of his mathematical goal.

As you can see from these few examples, averaging down can be particularly crippling if you hold through a real Stage 4 debacle. Every time you average in the hope of hitting the bottom, you simply add more shares and more losses to your portfolio. The result is that you throw good money after bad. Instead of being a conservative portfolio device, it's actually highly speculative. Trying to guess the bottom in a weak stock is like fishing in the ocean with your fingers. Hope is a foolish reason for holding on, and it's an even worse reason for buying more! So learn to lock in your profits using protective sell-stops, and cut your losses short by recognizing when your stock is running into trouble. If you follow this winning discipline, you'll still have the capital to make up your loss on future purchases.

6. *Don't refuse to sell because the overall market trend is bullish.* While it's true that a powerful bull market will often bail you out of some of your less brilliant judgments, don't think it's a panacea for every market problem. Sure, the major uptrend will usually add points to your Stage 2 winners. It's also true that a raging bull market will often limit the downside on problem stocks. This is why there is an old Wall Street saying: "Don't confuse brains with a bull market." Nevertheless, if a stock really starts to flash technical danger, don't think twice—get out. Just the fact that a stock is showing weakness in the face of a soaring market is a warning that disaster is getting ready to strike. McLean Industries (Chart 6–14) and Sunbelt Nursery (Chart 6–15) exemplify this point. While the Dow Jones Industrial Average rallied from 1,250 to 2,746, McLean dropped from 15 to 75 cents. In the same manner Sunbelt sold off from 15½ to 5½ while the Dow raced ahead from 1,500 to 2,746. Holding these, as well as dozens of other stage 4 disasters, because the overall market was bullish proved very costly. Don't ever fall into that trap.

7. *Don't wait for the next rally to sell.* When the chart pattern signals that a stock is running into trouble, get out immediately. Don't wait around trying to recoup an extra point or two on a rally. Chances are this tactic will cost you a lot of your market capital. The cases of River Oaks and Savin (Charts 6–16 and 6–17) demonstrate this situation. River Oaks should have been sold breaking

CHART 6–14

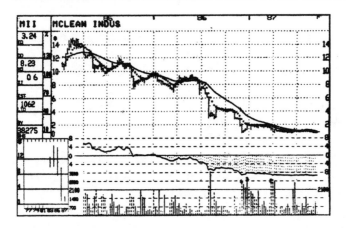

COURTESY OF MANSFIELD STOCK CHARTS

CHART 6–15

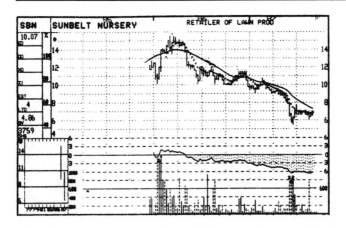

COURTESY OF MANSFIELD STOCK CHARTS

below 6. It never rallied back to that level on the way down to a low of 25 cents! Savin gave a strong sell signal breaking below 7¼. It never rallied back to that level as it headed south with a vengeance, bottoming at 1⅛. So once you spot the telltale signs of danger and realize that your stock is a sale, do just that—sell it and don't worry about getting a fractionally better price.

CHART 6–16

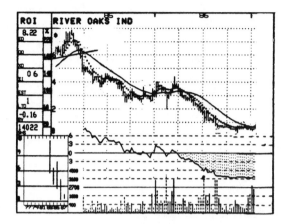

COURTESY OF MANSFIELD STOCK CHARTS

CHART 6–17

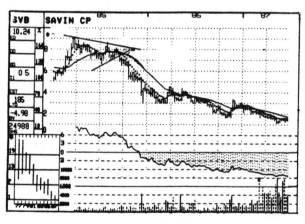

COURTESY OF MANSFIELD STOCK CHARTS

8. *Don't hold onto a stock simply because it is of high quality.* So-called quality stocks have cycles too, and once they turn negative will cause you just as much financial heartache. IBM is considered to be the epitome of quality. But its chart (6–18) should convince you that quality is no shelter from severe loss. In early 1973, as the stock reached its peak above 360, the trailing 12-month

CHART 6–18

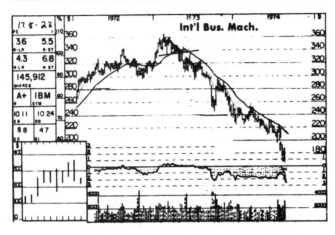

Int'l Bus. Mach.

COURTESY OF MANSFIELD STOCK CHARTS

earnings were $8.82 per share. Twenty months later the earnings were up to $12.24. Unfortunately, the stock price showed that the market didn't care. It had entered a stage 4 pattern that carried it down to 155! So much for quality.

Central Hudson Gas & Electric (Chart 6–19) also teaches this important message. It turned negative in 1986, breaking below 35, and dropped close to 23 while one of the great bull markets in history unfolded. Every dog has its day in the market. When a low-quality stock moves into Stage 2, that's its day; and it's a better buy at that point than a high-quality company that has entered Stage 4.

SELLING PROPERLY—THE INVESTOR'S WAY

Now that we know what *not* to do, let's zero in on the correct way to determine when to sell. While the theory is similar for both investors and traders, there are different guidelines and parameters for each. First let's deal with the investor's way; we'll examine how a trader should operate in the next section.

The first thing any good trader or investor should do is realize that they must never hold any position without a protective sell-

CHART 6–19

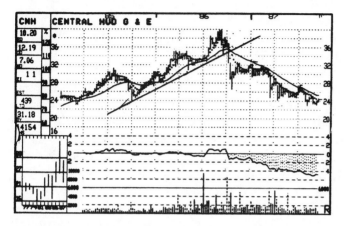

COURTESY OF MANSFIELD STOCK CHARTS

stop. Any futures trader worth his salt knows that this is a crucial technique for success. The stock market isn't all that different. The moves are just slower. And with the advent of stock index futures and programmed trading, the distinction is narrowing quickly. Cycles that used to take years to unfold in the 1950s and 60s are now occurring in a matter of months.

This increased volatility in the stock market is a two-edged sword. On the positive side, it gives us a chance to make money even faster. The downside is that when a reversal occurs, your stock can move from Stage 2 into Stage 3 far more quickly. This is especially true if it's one of the overly loved institutional favorites. These issues can really change direction in a hurry when bad news comes out and the institutional herd starts to panic. The way to protect yourself is by using a sell-stop order. It is the mirror image of the buy-stop order that I taught you in Chapter 3.

SELL-STOP ORDERS

A sell-stop order will be executed only if a predetermined level is hit. For example, if stock XYZ is currently trading at 30 and you put in a sell-stop order at 26⅞, it will go into effect only if XYZ breaks below 27. It then becomes a market order to sell. In most cases the transaction will take place very close to 26⅞. As with the buy-stop order, you should enter it on a good-'til-canceled (GTC) basis. One difference from our buy-stop technique is that if the stock is on the New York Stock Exchange, I suggest that you place a straight *sell-stop* rather than a sell-stop limit order. On the NYSE you can use either, but selling is far different from buying. When trying to purchase, we can be very choosy about how much we are willing to pay for a given stock. If it breaks out at 20⅛, and we had placed a 20⅛ stop-20⅜ limit order that isn't filled, so be it. But when selling, you already own the stock and it doesn't pay to fool around. If it turns negative, you want out.

On the American Stock Exchange, you aren't allowed to use a straight stop order. They only accept stop-limit orders. But the Amex has almost joined the 20th century. Previously the stop-limit had to be at one price (e.g., stop 26⅞-limit 26⅞). If the stock dropped quickly below your sell level without your receiving an execution, you were out of luck. Now, however, they allow the price to be spread out so you can say, for example, sell XYZ 26⅞-stop-26 limit. Therefore, if you enter the order with a wide spread, there should be no problem. Again, be sure to enter it on a GTC basis.

As for over-the-counter stocks, we must deal with the same problem we encountered on the buy side. No stop orders, either sell or buy, are allowed. You must work closely with your broker on these stocks and have him follow them on his monitor. If they break their danger levels, they should be sold *immediately*—at the market—which should pose no problem since this is all you are really asking of your stockbroker. From now on you are going to make your own buy-and-sell decisions. All you want from your broker is service. Most will be happy to comply, especially since you are going to be a far more active account than the buy-and-hold clients. If you come across a broker who isn't cooperative, get a new broker!

While on the subject of stockbrokers, I want to stress that you should make sure that you do not pay full commissions! It's obvious that you can save substantial commissions at a discount broker, and there are many excellent ones. But what is not so obvious, and many investors don't realize, is that you can get a substantial discount from most full-service brokers. It's simply a matter of asking; doing a bit of shopping around and negotiating. Again, since you are going to be a fairly active account, you should have no problem negotiating a healthy discount. Don't underestimate how important the savings will be to you over the years. Dealing with either a discount or full-service broker (or both) is fine as long as you get a good commission rate.[3]

The proper use of protective sell-stops is going to be a central part of your selling strategy. It will keep your decision-making simple, objective, and unemotional. You also won't have to constantly rethink whether it's time to lock in your profit or cut short your loss. This simplification of the selling process is more important than ever with the market becoming increasingly volatile. You don't want to suddenly sell a perfectly fine Stage 2 stock simply because you see that the Dow has dropped 60 or 70 points that day, and your stock has dropped sharply because it's gotten caught in the cross-fire of several sell programs.[4]

The overwhelming majority of market professionals use protective sell-stops, but the public does not. The reason is simple. Very few market players truly understand how to properly use them. This incredibly profitable tool has gotten an undeserved bad reputation because many investors hear about them and then use them in the following ridiculous manner. They read about and embrace the notion that sell-stops should be placed 10 to 12 or 15 percent below current prices to protect their positions. This is bad advice that leads to even worse results. There is no magic level that is the right percentage. You can't consistently make money in the market following such shallow thinking. How can 10 percent or any other given percentage be the right level? Does the market know or care what price you paid?

---

[3]Discount brokers are fine for your New York and Amex order, but they aren't great for your over-the-counter orders. These trades need to be monitored since you can't use stops. So use a full-service broker for OTC orders. For that reason, it makes sense to have accounts at both.

[4]When the premium between the Standard & Poor's stock index futures and the S&P composite narrows to a certain mathematical point, it becomes profitable for index arbitrageurs to lock in a sure small profit. They do this by selling the 500 stocks in the S&P composite and buying the S&P stock index futures. This process puts short-term pressure on the market averages. Buy programs are the other side of the coin and are initiated when the premium becomes large.

Chart 6–20 shows what I mean. USX Corporation broke out
at 22⅜ (point A) in 1986. If you had arbitrarily protected it with a
10 percent sell-stop set at 20⅛, you would have sold the stock on
the dip to 19⅝ (point B). Unfortunately, this would have been right
before the stock was taking off and getting ready to double. Again,
if after it ran up to 33¼ (point C) you decided to move the protective
sell-stop up to 10 percent below current levels (point D) for the
second time, it would have been stopped out needlessly as it dropped
to 29½ (assuming you had repurchased the stock after getting
stopped out at point A). USX then started another powerful upleg.
Instead of reaping the rewards of a powerful Stage 2 uptrend, you
would have been whipsawed all over the chart and paid needless
trading commissions. Horror stories like this are far too common
and are the reason that those few investors who do experiment
with sell-stops usually abandon them in a hurry.

The protective sell-stop is an incredibly helpful and profitable
technique *when properly used.* That's what you are now going to
learn. The first thing to know is that you must be flexible when
you place your initial sell-stop. Sometimes it will be 8 percent below
your purchase price, other times 12 percent or more. The percentage will *not* be the determining factor. Instead, the prior support level and 30-week MA will be your two keys to focus on.

CHART 6–20

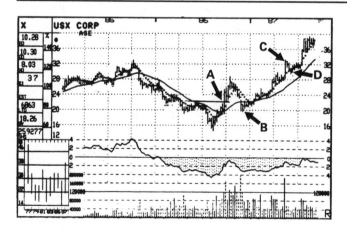

COURTESY OF MANSFIELD STOCK CHARTS

When you set your initial stop, pay less attention to the MA and more to the prior correction low. If stock XYZ is trading in an 18¼ to 20¼ zone, and you buy it when it breaks out at 20⅜, the stop should be placed right below the significant floor of support. You could set the stop at 18⅛ (below the 18¼ bottom). But here's a little secret that I've learned over the years which has served me well. If the sell-stop should be placed right above a round number, or on it, set it instead just *under* the round number. For instance, if the stop should be 18⅛ or 18, enter it at 17⅞. Psychology plays a very big part in market moves, and this is another example of herd instinct. Many investors like to buy at round numbers. If the stock is trading at 18½ or 18⅛, buy orders will often accumulate on the book at 18. Therefore, that level is a tough one to crack. If it's violated, then you really know your stock is running into trouble and you'd better exit quickly. I've seen it happen so often that the proper level for the sell-stop is right above the round number, say 18⅛. It hits that level and then only a few hundred shares trade at the round number without it being violated. Then a new rally gets going. To a somewhat lesser degree, this phenomenon also occurs at halves (18½, 19½, etc.). So if the sell-stop should be set at 18⅝, place it below the half at 18⅜.

From now on, never hold a stock without a protective sell-stop. As soon as you buy an issue, immediately enter a GTC sell-stop. This way you will never be left unprotected and end up with an unpleasant surprise staring you in the face when you open the evening newspaper. Also, never enter your order to buy until after you've calculated exactly where your protective stop should be placed. By getting into this habit, you will have an additional filter working for you when you narrow down your list of buy candidates. If all of the prior buy criteria that I've outlined for you are met, and you end up with three great buys, you should now check out the initial sell-stop levels. If stock A has a breakout at 20 and the sell-stop should be placed at 17⅞, then the downside risk is 11 percent. Stock B has its breakout at 40 with a sell-stop level of 33⅞. That's a downside risk of 15 percent. Finally, C has a breakout at 60 but a protective stop level of 56⅞. Since that translates into a potential worst-case loss of 5 percent, all other factors being equal, stock C is your best choice from a reward/risk point of view. While there are occasional exceptions because a chart pattern is so outstanding, try to limit your purchases to those cases where the initial stop isn't greater than 15 percent below your purchase price.

SELL-STOPS IN THE REAL WORLD

Now let's get to specifics so you will be sure to know exactly where your sell-stop should initially be placed, and when and to what level it should later be raised. Stock XYZ was in a trading range of 18¼ to 20¼ before it broke out and moved into Stage 2. You bought the stock at 20⅜ and the initial stop was set under the round number at 17⅞. Now all you have to do is sit back and wait. In the unlikely event that the stock breaks down, you will be sold out when the 17⅞ stop is hit.

In the more likely and happy circumstance that your stock starts to move higher, here's what to do. As long as the stock is above its rising 30-week MA, and the MA is rising in Stage 2 fashion, be sure to give it plenty of room to gyrate. We are going to trail the sell-stop behind the advancing price in the following manner. After the first substantial correction of at least 8 to 10 percent, you are now going to get set to raise the stop. But you don't actually change it until your stock ends its correction and moves back toward its prior high (point A on Chart 6–21). If a break below that correction low (point B) would also violate the 30-week MA, that is a valid point to which an investor should raise the sell-stop. If, as in this example, the correction low is *above* the rising 30-week MA, place the sell-stop below the MA (point C). Continue moving the sell-stop up as the MA advances (points E, G, I, etc.). In this case the correction low is 21, while the MA is up to 20. The sell-stop should therefore now be raised to point C at 19⅞ (under the round number of 20). One last point. Don't raise the stop to 19⅞ until *after* the stock rallies well off the low at point B back close to prior peak A.

Next, the stock rockets ahead in normal Stage 2 action after the first correction. After peaking near 35 (point D), it corrects back to the 28 level before resuming the advance. At this point the MA is up to 26. Therefore, when you raise the sell-stop place it at 25⅞ (point E). Again, don't raise the stop until XYZ rallies to point

CHART 6–21

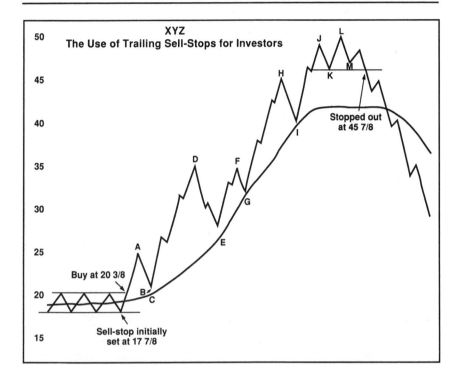

XYZ
The Use of Trailing Sell-Stops for Investors

Buy at 20 3/8

Stopped out
at 45 7/8

Sell-stop initially
set at 17 7/8

F, which is close to its prior peak. The next decline to point G terminates right at the MA at 32⅛. After the next rally gets underway and brings the stock close to point F, the stop should be raised to 31⅞—again, under the round number. In the same manner, the sell-stop should later be raised to point I at 38⅞. At this time, the last low is at 40, while the MA is up to 39¼.

Now comes an important change in tactics, so pay close attention! The MA has stopped rising and flattened out after point I. Once this occurs, the probabilities are high that a Stage 3 top is starting to form and the next serious violation of support and the MA can well bring on Stage 4 problems. Therefore, once a stock moves into this higher risk zone you should become more aggressive with your sell-stop. In the case of XYZ, that means moving the stop under the correction low at point K even though it is *above* the MA. Since K is at 46, raise the sell-stop to 45⅞. Then, in the following weeks, a potential head-and-shoulder top forms with the neckline near 46. Since point M is at 46½, which is so close to the 46 stop, you need not raise the stop for such a trivial change. Eventually 46 support is broken, and you are sold out of your position with an excellent profit before a new Stage 4 decline starts to take away a good portion of your gain. Using this technique, you won't end up selling at the very top eighth, which is fine, because we are dealing with the real world. But you will usually sell quite close to the high and with a substantial profit to show for your time and effort. Furthermore, you won't end up giving back the big profit as happened to those investors who failed to sell Alfin and V M Software (Charts 6–3 and 6–4). Instead you will move out of your position with surgical precision just as you entered it with your buy-stop. And since a stock usually drops very rapidly when it first moves into Stage 4, you'll get out before the pain begins.

Using sell-stops results in a minimum of emotion and misgivings. Your sell will often occur without you even knowing about it, while you are busy with your workday or even on vacation. Best of all, there will be no gut-wrenching decision-making. Should you hold despite the bad news? Should you sell because your broker heard a negative story on the stock? Is XYZ now too high or getting ready to tumble? It's all mechanical and disciplined. Most important of all, we let the market make the judgment for us. And since the market is the ultimate reality when dealing with the trend, its judgment is far more likely to be right than all of our balancing of pros and cons!

Enough theory. Let's look at some real-life examples so you will feel comfortable adjusting your sell-stops in the future. Chart 6–22 shows Skyline Corporation when it came to life in the early 1970s. It provides us with an excellent illustration of how an investor should implement my system of trailing a sell-stop beneath your stock. SKY should have been purchased in the low 20s in late 1970 when it moved above its 30-week MA and into Stage 2 (point B). Initially, the protective sell-stop should have been placed under the prior correction low before the breakout (point A). That would have kept you from taking too much of a loss if the bullish scenario didn't work out. In the following weeks, SKY first rallied up to

CHART 6–22

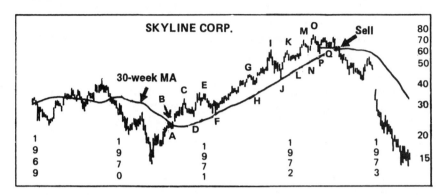

SOURCE: Data Graph

point C before correcting. Then the next rally took the stock up to a new recovery high (point E). You should have raised the stop to point D when SKY rallied close to its prior high point (C). Note that D was below both the prior correction low and also the 30-week MA. After the next selloff dropped the stock down to the MA and then took it back close to peak E, it was time to take further action. The sell-stop should have been raised to point F (below the previous bottom and 30-week MA) as the stock neared its prior peak. After a sharp rally to peak G and then another dip, followed by yet another move to new highs, the sell-stop should have been raised to point H. This was well below the prior low but right beneath the rising 30-week MA. After yet another new up-move that ended at point I, SKY dropped substantially. Not co-incidentally, the sharp selloff once again halted right at the 30-week MA. Once the stock rallied sharply off that low, the sell-stop then should have been raised to point J. This again was below *both* the MA and prior correction low.

Following this disciplined method would have locked in a great profit, even if the stock had gone no higher. But Skyline wasn't done with its Stage 2 advance. It next rallied up to point K, dropped a bit, and then advanced to point M. Now the sell-stop could be raised to L. Note that point L was well below the bottom, but was also below the rising MA. (As long as the MA is sloping upward at a sharp angle of ascent, *investors* should be sure to give a stock plenty of room when placing the stop.) Next you should have raised the sell-stop to N, then to P. But once the MA starts to level out and a potential Stage 3 top begins to unfold, it is time to pull the sell-stop up tighter. Now you should have pressed the stop up to point Q even though it was *above* the MA.

Finally, in late 1972, close to two years after purchase, SKY set off its sell-stop at point Q as it broke below its horizontal trendline. It soon broke below the 30-week MA and Stage 4 trouble was ready to set in. Note that you didn't sell at the exact top, but you did catch the lion's share of the two-year rally and almost tripled your money.

While it looks like a lot of attention was needed for these sell-stop changes, just the opposite is true. Only a few adjustments had to be made over a two-year period. The rest of the time, you just relaxed while the cycle unfolded. Furthermore, you didn't constantly worry about the news headlines and each weekend have a debate with yourself about whether you should hold or sell. Finally, and most important of all, you sold when the market flashed its clear-cut message that the supply/demand equation was turning negative. If you didn't sell, it would have been another case of up, down, profit turned to loss. Not surprisingly, the tremendous gain that took over two years to create vanished in a matter of months once destructive Stage 4 appeared. Just as it takes more time and energy to push a boulder up a hill than for it to fall, so it is with stocks. Both gravity and fear bring things down in a hurry.

Chart 6–23 of Goodyear Tire and Rubber again illustrates how investors should go about achieving relaxed, disciplined profits. GT should have been bought when it moved above 35 in 1986 (point A). The initial protective sell-stop should have been placed at 29⅞ (point B), right beneath the prior low before GT broke out and moved into Stage 2. Once the stock rallied up to 50 (point C) and then dropped back close to 40, it was time to get ready to raise your stop. After GT rallied substantially above that low, the sell-stop should have been raised to 39⅞ (point D). This placed it beneath the last significant low, and also below the 30-week MA. It also was below the psychological round number of 40. In the months ahead, it should have been raised to points E, F, G, H, I, and J. Then in the October 1987 massacre, Goodyear broke below 67 as it entered Stage 4. In the meantime, you should have exited at 66⅞ with no questions asked and a fabulous profit in hand.

CHART 6–23

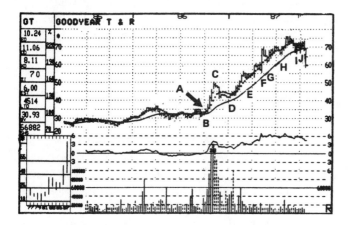

COURTESY OF MANSFIELD STOCK CHARTS

CHART 6–24

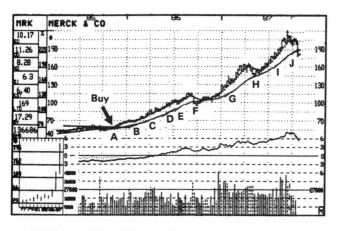

COURTESY OF MANSFIELD STOCK CHARTS

Chart 6–24 of Merck illustrates that even if the stock slightly penetrates the MA along the way, you can still stay with it. However, this is only true if two important criteria are met. First, the MA must still be rising. And second, the prior correction low must not be violated. If you bought Merck back in 1985 when it moved above resistance in the low 60s, your initial stop should have been set at point A. Then, as it rallied after correcting along the way, the protective stop should have been raised to B, C, D, and so forth. As you can see, the sell-stop was *always* kept below the MA even if the correction low held above it. This is an important point for investors to keep firmly in mind, because the trader's way is quite different.

After you raised the sell-stop to point E, Merck rallied to a new high before selling off sharply and temporarily nudging below the 30-week MA. But it didn't break down far enough to set off the stop at point E. After a lengthy consolidation that took place as Merck moved between support in the high 90s and resistance near 115, the stock broke out on the upside once again. The stop then should have been raised to point F. In the following months, after each correction the protective stop should have been raised further to points H, I, and J. Then, in October 1987, MRK finally hit its sell-stop when it broke below 190. While you didn't get the exact high, you came darned close and, in the process, tripled your money, which is nice work when you can get it.

This method of protecting your profits and limiting your losses is really fabulous. It will add immeasurably to your market success over the years. But don't expect it or any other technique that I teach you to be perfect. There will always be a few failures and whipsaws along the way, which is simply a cost of doing business. This lack of perfection is a small price to pay for the disciplined approach to scoring big profits that you are going to utilize.

Chart 6–25 of Wal-Mart Stores provides us with one of the whipsaw cases that come along now and then. If you had bought Wal-Mart near 15 back in 1985, you should have initially protected it with a sell-stop set at point A. In the following months, the stop should have progressively been raised to B, C, D, and E. Unfortunately, in late 1986, the stock broke down below support at 22. Even worse, it clearly broke below the 30-week MA, which was no longer rising. It certainly appeared that WMT had completed a Stage 3 top and was starting a Stage 4 decline as the protective stop at 21⅞ was set off. True, you had locked in a decent profit, but in the following months Wal-Mart reconsolidated and broke out on the upside again, as it moved above resistance at 25. It was now clear that the breakdown was a false one and the probabilities favored the start of a new advance.

CHART 6-25

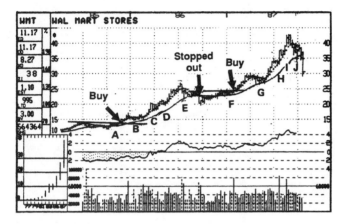

COURTESY OF MANSFIELD STOCK CHARTS

There is absolutely nothing wrong with occasionally getting whipsawed out of a stock in this manner and then rebuying it a few points higher once the danger signals have vanished. Look at those few points you gave away as the cost of insurance. Just as you pay premiums to protect your house against fire and theft, so, too, it is worth protecting your stock position against Stage 4 destruction. In this case, after making about seven points on the first transaction, you then should have moved back in as the stock powered above 25 and moved to new heights. This time your new initial stop should have been set at point F and raised progressively in the following months up to point I, right below 35. Then in October 1987 when that sell-stop was hit, you could have exited with a second fine profit, while so many others were scratching their heads and wondering what to do while the market plummeted.

The case of Wal-Mart would have taken you through whipsaws and some frustration, but you would have walked away with two fine profits. What will really make you tear your hair out is to completely lose a big profit and actually end up with a loss. This experience is as painful as it is unnecessary. At the beginning of this chapter I showed you several examples of such easy-come, easy-go cases. Intelogic Trace (Chart 6–26) is another stock that fits in that category. But now that you know how to properly use sell-stops, you'll never again be caught in that position. Many inves-

CHART 6–26

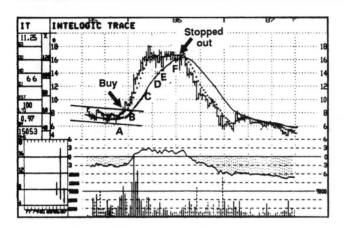

COURTESY OF MANSFIELD STOCK CHARTS

tors bought Intelogic Trace when it flashed a buy signal by moving above 8¼. Unfortunately, more than a few who rode the stock on its heady ascent just didn't know when to get off. They lost all of their profits and actually ended up with a loss!

From now on, the only roller-coaster rides that you take will be at the amusement park. If you bought IT when it broke out above resistance, you initially should have protected the stock with a sell-stop set at point A. In the following months, you should have raised it as shown on the chart. Once the MA flattened out and the stock broke below its sell-stop, you should have been glad that your sell-stop was activated, because you locked in a great gain before trouble set in. You didn't get the exact high, and it's unlikely that you ever will; but you did score a terrific profit in a matter of months. And, more importantly, you sidestepped the vicious Stage 4 decline that would have turned your big gain into a loss! To avoid just one of these ulcer-producing reversals—and believe me, there'll be plenty—is more than worth the price of the occasional whipsaw.

THE TRADER'S WAY

Several of the questions most frequently asked of me have to do with trading. How do you define a trader? Should you trade? Why bother trading? Is it better to invest or trade? Those of you who are veterans of the market battle know if you are more inclined to trade or invest. But newcomers often are perplexed about which road to take. Surprisingly, even some seasoned market players are confused in their approach. They may consider themselves investors but actually have a trader's psyche and therefore do poorly.

So before getting into the proper way for traders to time their sales, I want to wax philosophical for a moment. I don't really believe there is one absolute truth about whether it is better to trade or invest. I know many very successful traders, and there are certainly scores of winning investors. What I do know is that it is easier for most market players to win big by following the investing path to profits (especially new market participants). It involves less time commitment, less skill, and is certainly easier on your emotions. So why should anyone even consider trading? Simple. Traders need the challenge and the action! Whereas most investors are more conservative by nature and like to keep their lives relaxed and calm, traders are more inclined to live on the edge. They enjoy the thrill of battle and the competitive tensions that come with making decisions on the firing line.

Don't waste your time trying to determine if trading or investing is the best way to make money. There is no one best way; either approach can lead to success if skillfully applied. Instead, give some thought to understanding the kind of person you are and which approach you'd be comfortable with. Use a little introspection to find out what cloth you're cut from, and then become the best damned investor or trader that you can be! It leads to disaster if you decide to invest, but then get so angry because your stock dropped six or seven points that you end up dumping it just before the next upleg. So have an honest talk with yourself. If you obviously belong in one area or the other, then get there. Interestingly, there really are a number of market players who are in the middle and can adopt either approach. If you fall into this category, I suggest a mixed approach. Favor the investor's way, but do some trading if the market indicators (which I'll teach you in Chapter 8) signal the strong likelihood of a stiff selloff. Also consider taking some fast profits if your stock skyrockets in a hurry and becomes *very* overextended; if it moves far above its 30-week MA. In such a case it makes sense to lock in the huge gain on ⅓ to ½ of your position and ride the rest with a trailing investing sell-stop.

So much for philosophy. Now let's dig our teeth into some specifics. Just as there are clear-cut rules for investors, so there are for traders. These rules are a little less rigid because you've got to be ready to turn on a dime, but there are still definite guidelines to follow.

The first trading technique to perfect centers on the trailing sell-stop. Traders must be much more aggressive than investors in their use of this tool. Investors ideally want to stay with a position as long as the stock is in Stage 2. They accept the reality that there will be some pretty stiff setbacks along the way. In addition, months may go by when the stock moves sideways and consolidates before moving higher. Traders, on the other hand, realize that time is money. They not only want to sidestep all significant declines, they even want out if the stock is entering a neutral zone for several months. This makes sense because they can shift into a new stock that is ready to move into the exciting part of its cycle while the old situation simply zigs and zags. Therefore, a trader *shouldn't* wait for the 30-week MA to be violated on a selloff before selling. (In fact, if he can time the sale nicely when XYZ is well above the MA, the trader will often repurchase on dips back close to the MA.)

Just as we did with the investing case, let's study some specifics to better understand this concept. Stock XYZ in chart 6–27 broke out at 20⅜ after trading for several months in an 18¼ to 20¼ range. Once again, the stock should be purchased at 20⅜. But in this case, the initial stop should be handled differently. As a trader, you're looking for a faster but smaller upside move[5], so you should be willing to take a smaller initial loss if wrong. If the stock is going to be an A+ trade, it shouldn't drop significantly below the breakout point. So you should set the stop under the closest prior reaction low. If there isn't any, then you can play the following numbers game. While investors should *never* use automatic percentages, years of experience have demonstrated to me that those breakouts that are going to be big winners in a hurry almost never pull back

---

[5]On an annualized basis the move can actually be larger. After all, a 20 percent gain in one month is a 240 percent annualized move, while an investor who racks up a 100 percent profit in a year has obviously chalked up only a 100 percent annualized gain.

CHART 6–27

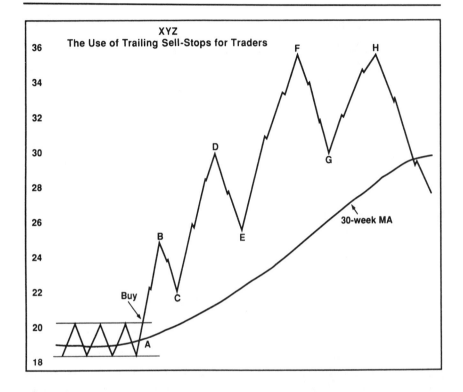

more than 4 to 6 percent below the breakout point. So if you can't find a nearby meaningful sell-stop point, you can place it 4 to 6 percent below the breakout level. However, make sure it's beneath a round number. For instance, if the breakout is at 20⅜, 4 percent is a little more than ¾ of a point, which is 19⅝. Five percent yields 19⅜. Since 19½ is psychologically like a round number, the position should be protected with a 19⅜ sell-stop (point A). (Under $20 consider each ½ point a round number, but above $20 place the sell-stop under an actual round number such as 21, 22, etc.)

Thereafter, XYZ moved up to its first rally peak at 25 (point B) before declining to 22 (point C). (Traders shouldn't pay attention to corrections of less than 7 percent. Only deal with the more meaningful moves.) Once your stock held at C and rallied back close to the prior top (point B), you should have raised the sell-

CHART 6–28

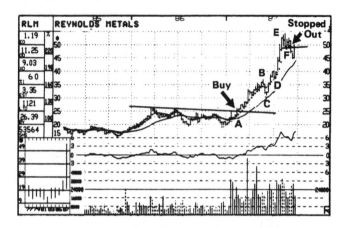

COURTESY OF MANSFIELD STOCK CHARTS

stop to just under point C (21⅞). Remember: if the prior low was at 22⅛ or 22, the sell-stop should be set below the round number, at 21⅞.

In the weeks ahead, XYZ rallied up to point D (near 30) before dropping back to point E (25½). Again, when XYZ rallied back up close to point D, the stop should have been raised up to 25⅜ (right under point E). In the same manner, the stop later should have been tightened to 29⅞ (point G). Eventually, after a double top formed (at peaks F and H), you were stopped out of the entire position at 29⅞ for an excellent gain in a hurry. One thing to always keep in mind is that a trader should *never* stay with a position if it breaks below the 30-week MA by even a fraction.

Chart 6–28 of Reynolds Metals (RLM) shows how trading sell-stops should be used in the real world. The stock should have been bought for a trade at 25⅛. It broke out of a continuation pattern after an impressive buildup in volume. Initially, the trading sell-stop should have been placed at 23⅞ (point A), under the round number of 24.[6] RLM then shot ahead in a hurry to 37⅜ (point B)

---

[6]To arrive at that level, multiply 25⅛ by 4 percent, which equals one point. That would bring the stop point to 24⅛, which doesn't make sense since it's right above the psychologically important round number. But 5 percent yields 1¼ points, which places the stop at 23⅞, right below the round number.

CHART 6-29

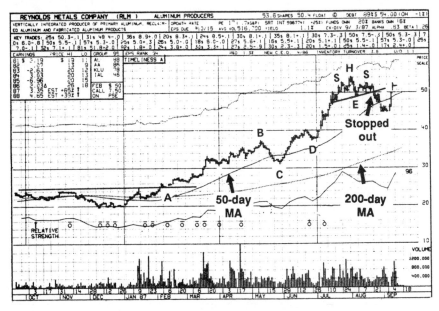

CHART COURTESY: DAILY GRAPHS AND LONG TERM VALUES

before undergoing a significant correction that dropped the stock to 31. After Reynolds rallied back close to its prior peak at 37, the stop then should have been raised to 30⅞ (point C). Later, after a rally to 40 was followed by a 7 percent correction, you should have prepared for your next move. As RLM moved back to its high, and then certainly as it surpassed it, the stop should have been raised to 36⅞ (point D). Thereafter, Reynolds embarked on another straight-up advance that reached 54¼ (point E) before the next meaningful correction unfolded. RLM bottomed, not so coincidentally, on the round number at 49. It then moved back to its prior peak. In addition, RLM formed a five-week neutral pattern that saw the stock drift sideways. After a substantial advance, this is always a worrisome trading sign. The trading sell-stop should therefore have been pressed even further to 48⅞ (point F).

While it isn't as obvious on a weekly chart (6-28) as on a daily chart (6-29), a small head-and-shoulders top pattern also formed. Therefore, once RLM broke below significant support at 49 it was time to take the nearly 100 percent profit that you earned in six months (200 percent annualized). It didn't matter that Reynolds dropped below 45 and then moved back above 50. The dynamic upside momentum was now a thing of the past, and a trader, unlike an investor, only wants to hold a position when all rockets are firing with full thrust!

TRENDING TOWARD PROFITS

The trading sell-stop technique that I just outlined is simple to use and will produce good profits on a consistent basis. But if you want to move to an even higher level of sophistication and score larger gains, you should learn to use trendlines and incorporate them into your trading plan.

In many cases, no valid trendline will form and you should simply use the trading sell-stop concept. But when an aggressive

CHART 6–30

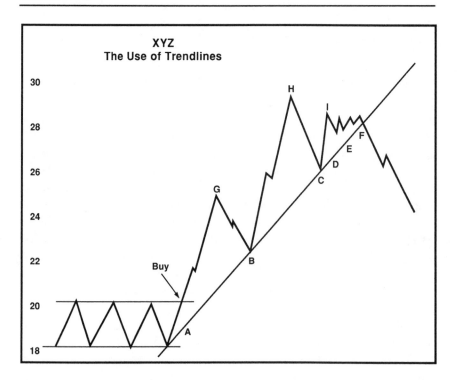

trendline does take shape, use it, because it's a way of locking in even more of the profit. At least a portion of the position should be sold when such a trendline is violated. Then the remainder can be handled via the sell-stop route, which will usually be at a somewhat lower level.

When integrating trendlines into your trading game plan, start out in the same manner as you did in the prior example. Set the initial stop at 19⅜ (point A) when you buy on the breakout at 20⅜. Then raise the sell-stop to B as the stock rallies back toward peak G. A clear-cut trendline is one that connects *at least three points*. If a trendline materializes, it should be brought into your analysis of where to place your stop. After XYZ rallied off of point C, the sell-stop should be placed under C. Here's where the trendline can start to help you. Now that it's been in force for several months and has been touched at least three times, you should raise the stop further to a point under the trendline. First you'll raise it to D, then a few weeks later to E and F. Since the trendline is a rising one, you can continue raising the stop on this half of the position even if the stock moves sideways, as it did following point I. One half of your position is now protected with a stop at point C, and one half is set very tightly at rising points D, E, and finally F. Eventually the sell-stop at F is set off as the stock drifts sideways. Even if it doesn't indicate a sharp drop, it's likely to lead to a neutral trading range. This is bad news for traders, so it's good to lock in the profit on half the position. Then when real weakness sets in, the second stop at point C is hit and another fine gain is secured.

Charts 6–31 and 6–32 of Computer Sciences (CSC) and Tultex (TTX) illustrate the advantages of using trendlines. CSC should have been bought for a trade when it moved above its downtrend line and above resistance at 38. The initial stop should have been placed under the round number of 36.[7] Then after a move above 40, followed by a reaction to 37⅜, the sell-stop should have been raised to 36⅞. Until this point, nothing has deviated from the trailing sell-stop method that we've outlined for traders. Now, however,

---

[7]Five percent of 38⅛ equals almost two points, which brings the stop to 36¼. Place it beneath the psychologically important 36 level.

CHART 6–31

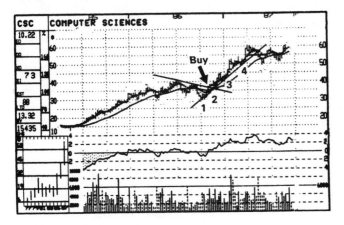

COURTESY OF MANSFIELD STOCK CHARTS

CHART 6–32

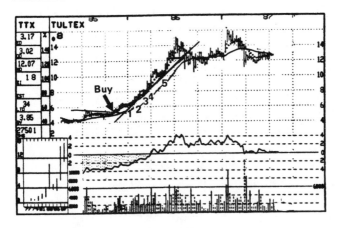

COURTESY OF MANSFIELD STOCK CHARTS

things start to change. You can draw an upsloping trendline that connects more than three points (numbers 1, 2, 3 and 4) on chart 6–31. That line should have been penciled in and extended into the future. Not so coincidentally, in the weeks ahead Computer Sciences hugged that line and kept trending higher. We now know for sure that we have a meaningful trendline on our hands. Therefore, the stop should be continually raised for at least half the position under the rising trendline. Be sure to keep it under the psychological round number. If you want to be *very* aggressive, you can use only one stop under the rising trendline. If you'd rather be a bit more conservative, it makes sense to press the stop (for half the position) very tightly under the continually rising trendline. The stop for the other half of the position should be placed under the last correction low. Interestingly, after CSC had a seven-month run on the upside, from the purchase price of 38⅛ up to 61, the two sell-stops approached each other. In late April and early May of 1987, the trendline was up to 57½, so one half of the position should have been protected with a 56⅞ sell-stop. The stop for the other half should have been set at 54⅞ since there was good support right above 55. In May, both were set off and a fine profit was locked in.

Note that the stock didn't get smashed. It dropped to 49¼ and rallied back above 55. The important reality to be aware of is that the trader's purpose was well-served. In the six months that he held the stock, it continually trended higher as it racked up a very tidy gain. But four months after the sell-stop was set off, CSC was only a bit higher than where it was sold. Since, as traders, we only want to be in the stock when it's thrusting higher, the trendline correctly showed us when the ride was over and it was time to exit.

Chart 6–32 of Tultex (TTX) is another good example of trading with the help of a meaningful trendline. TTX should have been bought at 5½ when it broke out above its downtrend line in late 1985. Starting in early 1986 (point 1 on Chart 6–32), an important uptrend line formed that hit two more points (2 and 3) over the next three months. It then touched the line two more times (points 4 and 5) over the next four months. So in addition to your use of a trailing sell-stop, this very meaningful trendline should have been factored into your trading game plan as the move unfolded. When it broke below the trendline at 13, the first half of the position should have been stopped out for a better than 130 percent gain in eight months. Then when the prior correction low at 12½ was violated, the remainder of the position should have been closed out. Again, the stock did not turn into a Stage 4 disaster. It's very meaningful that in the eight months *before* the trendline gave way it was up, up, and away. But eight months *after* the break, Tultex was 1½ points lower than where you got out! Listen to the message of the trendline, because it tells you when the upside momentum is ebbing and the air is starting to leak out of the bullish balloon.

MEASURING THE MOVE

Before leaving this section on trading, there is one more little-known trading technique that will improve your trading skills.

Over the years, technicians have come up with all sorts of fancy theories and games that are supposed to predict where a stock is headed. Believe me, I've dabbled with them all, from the simplest to the most complex. I'm not going to burden you with them because it's not worth the effort. But there is one simple concept that you should be aware of that does have a high degree of accuracy. When you add it to your arsenal of trading tools, you'll really be ready for the firing line. This trading measurement is called the *swing rule*. It doesn't appear often, but when it does, it can give you real insight into where an advance is likely to end. It's often so accurate that it's almost like reading next week's newspaper today! All you have to do is take the peak price before an important decline sets in and subtract the next low price from it. In Chart 6–33, you'll see that since XYZ peaked at 26 and the low formed at 16, you get a difference of 10 points—26 (point A) minus 16 (point B) equals 10 points.

The next step is to add the 10 points onto the peak price of A once XYZ betters the old peak of 26. So 26 plus 10 points equals 36. This level becomes a *potential* near-term target area. Obviously this is just an approximation. The move may end at 35 or 38, but as you near that area, it pays to be alert for signs that a near-term top is forming.

Aydin (AYD—Chart 6–34) reached a peak of 27⅝ in 1986 (point A) before breaking to the downside. When the destruction was over, the stock had been smashed to a low of 17½ (point B). AYD then broke out above resistance at 25 in early 1987. This move above the neckline also completed a head-and-shoulder bottom. The stock was soon marching to a very nice tune as it moved above its 1986 peak of 27⅝. The swing rule yielded a difference of 10⅛ points (27⅝ minus 17½ equals 10⅛). We could now make an in-

CHART 6–33

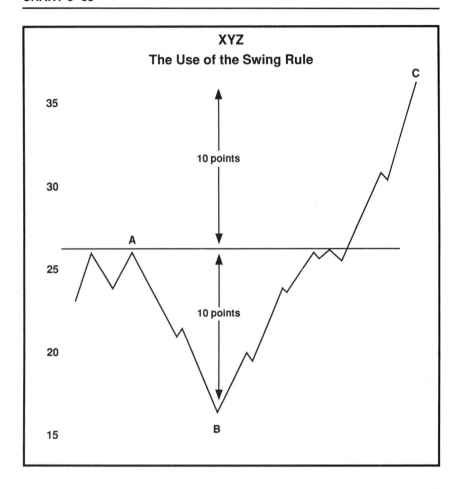

XYZ
The Use of the Swing Rule

telligent guess as to how high AYD might go before it would run out of gas. Add the 10⅛ points onto the peak of 27⅝ and you get a target of 37¾. As the weeks passed, Aydin moved closer and closer to that level before topping out and breaking below the uptrend line at 33⅞. And what price do you think the top at point C turned out to be? No, it wasn't our projected 37¾, but 37½! Not bad! So the best way to use this swing rule is to do partial selling of your trading position as close to the projected level as possible, and then sell the remainder when the stop is set off. In this case, it would be at 33⅞, when the price broke the trendline.

CHART 6–34

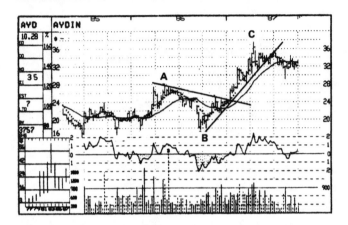

COURTESY OF MANSFIELD STOCK CHARTS

CHART 6–35

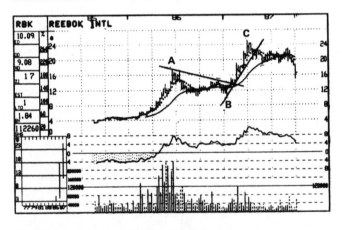

COURTESY OF MANSFIELD STOCK CHARTS

To show that AYD was no isolated occurrence, let's study the action of Reebok (Chart 6–35). The mid–1986 high was 17⅝ (point A). It then dropped down to point B, which turned out to be 10¼. Subtracting 10¼ from 17⅝ gives us 7⅜ points. Add the 7⅜ points to the prior peak of 17⅝ and we get a trading target of 25. The move actually ended at 25¼ (point C)!

CHART 6–36

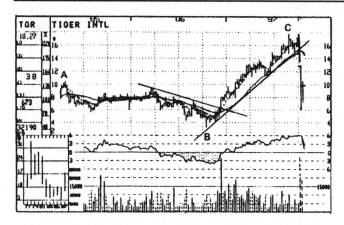

COURTESY OF MANSFIELD STOCK CHARTS

Finally, check out the action that unfolded in Tiger International (Chart 6–36). It flashed a buy signal in late 1986 when it moved above 6. But before that it dropped from its 1985 peak of 10½ (point A) down to 3⅝ (point B). That's a differential of 6⅞ points. To get an upside trading projection, add the 6⅞ onto the previous peak of 10½. Applying the swing rule yields an upside projection of 17⅜. Incredibly, the actual high for the move turned out to be 17¾ (point C), before TGR quickly fell below 6.

While every swing-rule projection won't turn out to be as perfect as these, the overwhelming majority will be surprisingly on target. So when trading a stock that gives you the opportunity to use this fabulous measuring device, take advantage of it! Sell at least a part of your position near the projection, then let your stop take you out of the remainder. By combining the proper use of sell-stops with trendlines and the swing rule, you are ready to do some disciplined and profitable trading.

LEARNING HOW TO WIN BY LEARNING HOW TO LOSE

No matter how good my system is, you will not win 100% of the time. That's a promise. How you deal with this fact of life will go a long way toward determining how big a winner you become. In fact, after all my years in the market, there is absolutely no doubt in my mind that one of the real keys to winning is learning how to lose. Think about it for a moment. Is it really so terrible to take a loss on one or two positions? To most people it is, and that's why they end up making poor decisions. But to market professionals, it's a fact of life, a cost of doing business. Specialists and other pros don't lose sleep if a given position ends up in the loss column. They concern themselves with two far more important factors: (1) the net result of *all* their positions (as long as it is strongly positive they are happy), and (2) where they will call it quits if a given stock moves against them.

This is the mature, rational—though rarely practiced—way to approach the market. When you play tennis, do you honestly expect never to hit a ball into the net? If you're a realist, you accept that some of your shots will misfire, and you don't get upset as long as you have a far larger percentage of match-winning shots. Training yourself to think this way is crucial. I'm sure you've seen, as I have, the person who blows sky-high over a poorly hit tennis ball or a missed putt on the golf course. Emotions are destructive if you don't deal with them properly. I've seen market players do reasonably well, especially in a bull market, only to have a single bad position undermine their entire strategy. Instead of realizing that the first small loss is the best loss, they get angry and stubborn as their stock plummets. When it's fallen to a level that appears cheap, they average down, throwing good money at a bad Stage 4 position. Even worse, as losses start to mount, the next destructive step is to start taking profits in those stocks that are still winners. In the short run this makes the investor feel better as he makes several entries in the plus column. But in the following months the portfolio will reflect the effects of this short-term fix. Very simply, this ill-conceived strategy loads up your portfolio with Stage 4 losers while you discard Stage 2 winners.

What drives us to this destructive behavior? In one word: ego! Too many traders and investors feel that if they pick a big winner they are a genius, but if they lose they are stupid. Neither is necessarily the case. If you win through poor tactics, you lucked out in spite of yourself. And if you took a loss but followed a solid disciplined approach, you acted wisely. Have a long talk with yourself and make sure your ego is under wraps when you make market decisions. Don't play the market so you can brag at cocktail parties about your winners. Invest your time and capital in the market because you enjoy the challenge of making a nice return.

The destructiveness of ego can be seen day after day. Sit around any brokerage office and listen to the conversations. You'll hear people saying that they are going to sell that dog just as soon as it gets back to where they are even. Why even? Why not when it rallies back to overhead resistance, even if that involves taking a small loss? For ego-driven investors, even means "I wasn't dumb." Their self-esteem is tied to their wins and losses. When they lose, this personality type just has to blame someone else—any handy scapegoat. And who's more handy than the broker into whose lap all blame is dumped. We've all come across some less than brilliant brokers, but brokers can't make you buy or sell a stock. And they can't make you stick with them even if they're truly incompetent. Ultimately, it's always your choice, so it's important that you learn to take responsibility for your actions. If those actions are positive, reinforce them; it they are negative, work to understand and alter them. Always be certain that you are in the driver's seat, not your ego. An extreme example of how potent the mixture of ego and trading failure can be occurred in Miami during the historic October 1987 crash. An investor who suffered severe losses shot and killed his broker before killing himself.

Promise yourself that you won't allow any one loss to be blown out of proportion. First, treat your portfolio like a mutual fund; look at the overall return of the whole. Second, make a pledge that you'll never hold any stock long or short without a protective stop. This will take the emotion out of the situation and guarantee that no single position will cripple your portfolio.

Now let's study some real-life situations that I had to handle in *The Professional Tape Reader*. While it's more fun reviewing the action of our many big winners, it's important to learn how to cope with situations that backfire.

I recommended American Capital Management (Chart 6–37) in January 1987 when it broke out above final resistance at 24 and the relative strength moved into positive territory. All systems appeared to be go, but instead of moving higher, ACA went into a stall. For the trader, this is *always* an important warning. If a stock doesn't come out of the gate strong on the breakout, a trader should

CHART 6–37

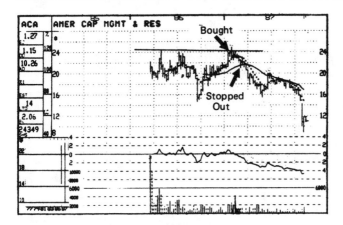

COURTESY OF MANSFIELD STOCK CHARTS

immediately lighten his position while protecting the remainder with a very tight stop set about 5 percent beneath the breakout (under a round number). In the case of ACA, that would translate into a sell-stop at 22⅞. So for traders the loss was really minimal. Even investors can use a little common sense and lighten up when a stock fails to move above the breakout level. In the meantime, the investor's sell-stop was set right beneath the moving average at 22. Therefore, the position was closed out for a 9 percent loss once the stock started to weaken. If this discipline hadn't been followed, a small loss would have turned into a 65 percent disaster as ACA hit a low of 8¼ several months later.

Chart 6–38 shows another potential winner that turned sour–Rollins Environmental (REN). Once again, there was no serious problem as our method handled the curve ball very nicely. Rollins gave a continuation buy when it moved above final resistance at 23½. After moving to 26, it quickly pulled back *below* the breakout at 23½, which was a good reason for traders to get out with a fractional loss. Stocks that turn into great trades rarely drop back below the original breakout point. For investors, the stop should have been placed at 21⅞, since the prior lows were right above 22. This is where I placed it in *PTR*. In addition, the 30-week MA was at 22, so when REN broke below 22 it was time to say goodbye to

CHART 6–38

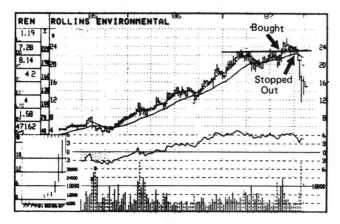

the position with a 7 percent loss. A few weeks later, that exit point almost looked like a profit as the stock plummeted to 11½ for what could have been a 50 percent-plus loss!

The lesson is obvious. Protect all of your positions with stops and don't ever make an exception because a certain stock is a special situation.

THE PHILOSOPHY OF SELLING, OR DON'T GIVE BACK PROFITS NEEDLESSLY

It's not enough to understand the mechanics of selling. You must also understand the winning philosophy that accompanies the methodology. Most market participants view profits and losses in a way that I can only categorize as strange. Their view also makes for odd and destructive decisions. Ask eight out of ten investors who bought stock XYZ at 40 how much they've lost now that the stock is down to 20, and they'll answer nothing! The conventional wisdom says that as long as I don't sell the stock, I haven't taken any loss; or it's just a paper loss. That's ridiculous! Your stock is only worth the price of the last print on the tape. It's an asset that can be sold any time the market is open. If you decide to cash in your chips on any given position, you can take that money and do as you wish with it. But because of this nonsensical view that a stock in which they are losing 50 percent is not a loss, they hold and hold, waiting for it to come back to even so they won't have to feel stupid. Not only are they suffering needless additional shrinkage of capital, they are missing out on the chance to shift the funds into new Stage 2 situations. The converse is also ridiculous. If they bought a stock at 40 and it's run up to 80, they feel they don't have a profit because they haven't sold yet. Instead, they talk about playing with 'their' money. They should recognize that they have real profits that will be lost if not properly protected.

Once you redefine your thinking in this manner, you automatically start to act differently. Think about it. If you buy 1,000 shares of XYZ at 40 and it advances to 80, your $40,000 is now worth $80,000. You can take that money and move into another stock. If you want to use it as a down payment on a house, that, too, is your choice. And if you don't tend to business and allow your stock to fall from 80 back to 40 because you didn't use a sell-stop, you lost $40,000 of your hard-won assets.

I strongly suggest that each weekend you tabulate the value of your portfolio. Don't worry if it swings a few percent from week to week. That's the way of the market. But if you see your assets drop by 20 to 25 percent, something is wrong. If you're using sell-stops, perhaps you are taking too much risk by buying stocks that are too far above their stop-loss points. If that isn't the case, then it's possible that you are taking far too many small losses in a row because the negative market climate is whipsawing you in position after position. In such a situation, just move to the sidelines until the probabilities of success become favorable. In Chapter 8, I'll teach you how to keep in touch with a few easy-to-calculate indicators that prevent this. But in the meantime, by continually tabulating your results, you'll take significant changes in your assets more seriously and never allow profits to slip away.

Look at Chart 6–39 of TS Industries, which got bashed in the October 1987 crash, and you'll see what I mean. Many investors who had accumulated large profits lost it all, plus some. If you had stayed on top of the stock, there was absolutely no excuse for that to happen. I recommended TNDS in *PTR* in early 1986 when it was below 10. It rose in perfect Stage 2 fashion for the next one and a half years, never once violating its rising 30-week MA. It didn't even

CHART 6–39

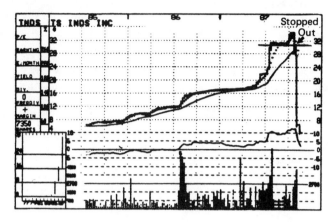

COURTESY OF MANSFIELD STOCK CHARTS

violate any minor support levels in that entire period. Then, in late September 1987, the stock hit a high of 34½ after having established a solid base of support right above 31. Since the MA was losing upside momentum and leveling out, I raised the sell-stop to 30⅞. A few weeks later that stop was touched and the stock was closed out for better than a 200 percent gain. But what is even more startling is what happened to all of those investors who had no game plan, and to those market players who thought they could continue to give TS Industries plenty of room to gyrate. In the few weeks after I closed out the position, the stock dropped a sickening 92 percent, hitting a low of 2¾! In three weeks, the entire gain of the prior two-year advance was wiped out! This is the sort of market nightmare that you'll never have to lose sleep over as long as you faithfully practice the discipline that you now know.

QUIZ

1. The only time it is acceptable to average down in a   **T**   **F**
   Stage 4 situation is when the volume pattern is positive.
2. When dealing with an over-the-counter stock, you are   **T**   **F**
   permitted to use sell-stop limit orders but *not* straight
   sell-stop orders.

3. For investors, the key to successful selling is learning   **T F**
   to properly use trailing sell-stops.

4. The only time either a trader or investor should ever   **T F**
   hold a Stage 2 stock without a protective sell-stop is
   when *both* the group and overall market trend are bullish.

5. You bought stock XYZ when it moved above the downtrend
   line at 78½. The prior high at point A is 82. The correction low
   at point B is 72¾. If XYZ moves above point A, where would
   you project the trading top to occur?
   A. 87¾   B. 82   C. 89¼   D.91¼

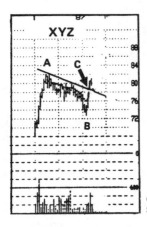

COURTESY OF MANSFIELD
STOCK CHARTS

6. Stock XYZ turned favorable on a trading basis when   **T F**
   it moved above its downtrend line at 36. A good uptrend line then formed in the following months that
   connected *at least* three points.

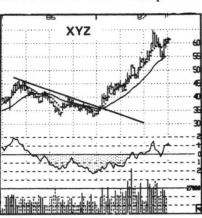

COURTESY OF MANSFIELD
STOCK CHARTS

7. The sell-stops that are shown on the Unocal chart   **T F**
   (letters A through E) are valid trading sell-stops.

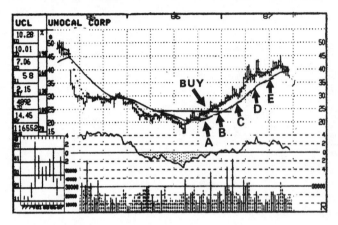

COURTESY OF MANSFIELD STOCK CHARTS

ANSWERS

1. False. It is never acceptable to average down in a Stage 4 situation.
2. False. You are *not* permitted to use any form of stop order over-the-counter. You must therefore work with your broker on these orders.
3. True.
4. False. Both traders and investors should never hold any position without a protective sell-stop.
5. D. 91¼. The stock is Sequa Corporation Class B, and the up-move ended in late August 1987 at 91½.
6. True. The chart is Aluminum Corporation of America, and the following trendline should have been drawn, touched at four points.

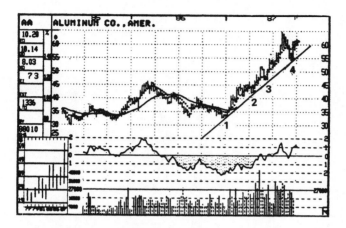

COURTESY OF MANSFIELD STOCK CHARTS

7. False. Trading stops should be placed much tighter beneath the correction low, not all the way beneath the 30-week MA. However, the points A, B, C, D and E are valid investing stops.

CHAPTER 7

Selling Short: The Less Traveled Road to Profits

Although the market for stocks is upwardly biased when viewed over long periods, a good one-third of the time it's headed down. This also applies to individual stocks. Most investors view this downward phase as a time to be out of the market, or out of particular stocks. They content themselves during this time with the paltry return offered by banks and money market funds, awaiting the end of the so-called bad market.

Individual investors aren't the only ones who spend long periods sitting on their hands. Their brokers are no better—just more dangerous. They fill their days and earn their commissions during down markets by recommending buys on fallen stocks—stocks that usually still have a good distance yet to decline.

This chapter is one of the most important in the entire book. It's about short selling. Read it carefully and with an open mind. If you're unfamiliar with the concept of short selling, go back to the definitions on short selling and breakdowns in Chapter 1.

It never ceases to amaze me how many market players refuse to sell short! Many won't give it a moment's thought. They would no more short a stock than put the deed to their houses on double zero in a Vegas casino: they view it as being that risky. Therefore, it's understandable why they react so negatively when the subject is broached. But those fears are unfounded, and they are actually losing out on a chance to make a great amount of money in a hurry. It's a statistical fact that stocks decline faster than they rise. So if you learn how to capitalize on these smashes, you'll be way ahead of the game.

CHART 7–1

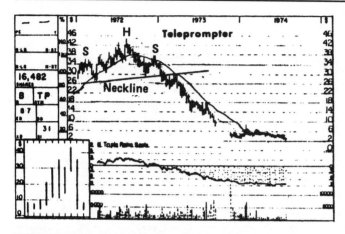

COURTESY OF MANSFIELD STOCK CHARTS

Stocks fall apart much faster than they rise because fear causes a panic reaction while greed takes a while to simmer.[1] These two vulnerable charts (7–1 and 7–2) were recommended as short sales in *The Professional Tape Reader.* They clearly show the profitable chemistry that occurs when you mix a negative technical pattern with a bear market!

Many people are optimists and it's against their nature to try to profit from negative situations. But if you only play the long side of the market, it's like driving a car that has only a forward gear. Even though you need that gear a much greater percentage of the time, it's dangerous not to have reverse for those few occasions when you need to back up out of a jam. The same applies to the stock market. Over time, bull markets predominate over bearish ones. For example, between 1960 and 1987 only eight of the years were bearish, but to have misplayed those years would have taken away a large portion of your gains. Not to have capitalized on the bear markets by selling short would have handicapped your portfolio still further. The simple and logical way to approach the mar-

---

[1]The crash of October 1987 reinforced this truth. The market averages gave back in a few days the gains of the entire previous year!

CHART 7–2

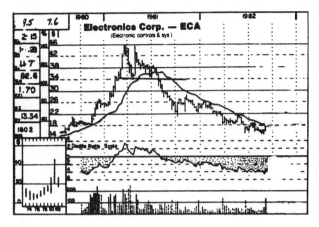

COURTESY OF MANSFIELD STOCK CHARTS

ket is to learn that just as the best stocks should be bought in a bull market, the most vulnerable ones should be sold short in a bear market.

WHY IS SHORT SELLING SO FEARED?

If you follow my rules, I believe you'll see that short selling presents no greater risk then does buying. If this is the case, then why do so many people refuse to sell short, and why are they absolutely phobic about this very important and profitable technique? Here are a couple of the most common answers that I've heard over the years.

Many investors feel it's un-American to sell short. They believe we have to root for our companies to do well. They seem to think it is similar to cheering for your local baseball or football team, and they don't want to be disloyal. Since most Americans have a natural tendency toward optimism, short selling is often viewed as a negative pastime.

My reaction to the above is simple. There is absolutely nothing wrong with recognizing the reality of both the marketplace and economy. Cycles are a fact of life, and there is nothing patriotic about holding a stock while it enters a Stage 4 decline. In the same way that it's rational to sell and avoid a large loss when a stock starts to crash, it's also reasonable to profit from that decline.

Also, short selling actually serves a very valid economic function. Short selling increases the stock's liquidity on the downside, so when an issue gets smashed, its decline is eventually cushioned. After all, a person who has sold XYZ short has to repurchase that stock at some point. Every short sale represents future demand for the stock. When it declines and short sellers buy back the stock, this demand actually slows the drop.

Finally, none of the professionals with whom I speak ever view short selling as unpatriotic. More importantly, they sure don't refrain from doing it themselves. I may be overly cynical, but I really don't think most professionals are unhappy that the public has bought the un-American bit, thus leaving the shorting arena to them.

A second bogey-man that keeps so many from selling short is that classic excuse, *you can lose everything you have!* The thinking (or nonthinking) goes something like this: If you buy XYZ at 40, the worst that can happen is that the company goes bankrupt and the stock ends up dropping to zero. But if you sell short, there is no upside limit. It can advance toward infinity. Since infinity brings to mind the size of the universe and other imponderables, this theoretical danger is enough to make most investors stop right in their tracks. They dismiss the idea of short selling and go back to what they perceive as being safe, such as buying Stage 4 patterns in a bear market.

While there is a remote theoretical possibility of a stock jumping higher and higher, thus wiping you out while you are short, there is *zero* possibility of that happening when you follow my methods. You've now read and digested enough of my approach to know the answer even before I tell you what it is: a protective buy-stop. This device will guarantee that you never suffer the horrible fate of infinite loss and eternal pain and suffering. It's no different from what I taught you on the buy side. In the same manner that a properly placed protective sell-stop will make it impossible for you to ever carry any stock from 40 down to zero, so, too, will an intelligently placed protective buy-stop assure that you'll never hold XYZ short as it advances from 40 to 200! Once you learn how to implement this important tool, you'll quickly see that it's nonsense to listen to your friends and relatives who warn you against the evils of shorting. You won't lose the house, car, and even the kids, as so many amateurs fear. On a worst case basis, you'll suffer a 10 to 15 percent loss on a position that moves against you. This is no different than what happens on the long side when one of your purchases doesn't work out and your sell-stop is set off.

Once you learn to view the market properly, you'll see that it is a simple numbers game. There is absolutely no difference between buying Stage 2 stock XYZ when it breaks out at 40 and protecting that position with a 35⅞ sell-stop, and selling short Stage 4 stock ZYX at 40 and protecting it with a 44⅛ buy-stop. In both cases you have a 10 percent loss if the position goes against you. Forget about the unlimited risk nonsense. With my method, you will never carry a long to zero or a short to infinity.

COMMON MISTAKES WHEN SHORTING

Before showing you the correct way to sell short with big potential and minimum risk, here are some of the most common mistakes that investors make on the short side.

1. *Using overvaluation as your criteria for shorting.* Don't ever fall into the trap of thinking that a high P/E means you should sell short. I've talked about the subjectivity of overvaluation before. It's such a fuzzy concept when considering short-sale candidates that you should swear off of it entirely. I could fill up page after page of this book with examples of stocks that looked to be too high based on their P/E ratios but went much higher in the months ahead. Chart 7–3 of Data General looked fundamentally attractive to sell short in early 1984 when that junior bear market started. It was selling at an astronomical 35 times earnings, and the market looked ready to get hit. But during the next eight months, while the Dow Jones Industrial Average shed over 200 points, DGN rose from 30 to close to 60! This stock was in a solid Stage 2 uptrend, and you already know not to even consider shorting a stock in that stage.

Interestingly enough, there are many stocks that move into Stage 4 and turn out to be really big winners on the short side even

CHART 7–3

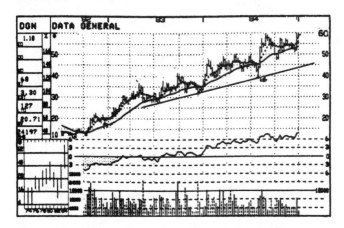

COURTESY OF MANSFIELD STOCK CHARTS

though they have low P/Es when the sell signal is given. Wayne-Gossard (Chart 7–4) was selling close to 10 times earnings in late 1972 when it flashed a sell signal by breaking below 11. One year later it was at an even lower P/E as the stock crashed to 4½. The lesson is clear: fundamental overvaluation is not the way to uncover a choice short sale even though it is the most common method among the rank and file of market players.

   2.   *Selling short because the stock has advanced too far.* Another very destructive approach used by many traders and investors is selling short when they feel a stock has run up too far. If you like Russian roulette, this is your kind of game. But it's just a matter of time until the gun goes off and you get hit with a huge loss. People who play this game are selling short while the stock is charging ahead in Stage 2, and then they can't understand why they get clobbered. But now that you understand stage analysis, you can see why they get their heads handed to them by trying to guess a Stage 2 top. Chart 7–5 of Angelica is a perfect example of what can happen when you play this guessing game. In April 1981—at the onset of a bear market—Angelica had more than doubled and was at its high at 14. Eight months later, it was up to 25 despite a 200-point drop in the Dow.

CHART 7–4

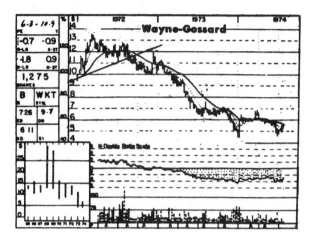

COURTESY OF MANSFIELD STOCK CHARTS

CHART 7–5

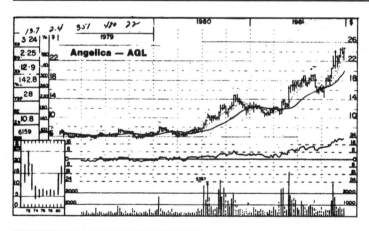

COURTESY OF MANSFIELD STOCK CHARTS

3. *Falling for the sucker short.* The stock market has the equivalent of a too-good-to-be-true offer. We've all seen cases where you know that the deal is just too good to be offered for such a pittance. A closer investigation usually reveals that your instincts were correct and there really are no free lunches. In the market this takes the form of a sucker short. This is a stock that has risen so far in excess of its apparent sensible value that it seems destined to fall. Every market cycle has a number of sucker shorts and they end up doing a nose dive—but usually long after you've been squeezed out of your short position for a great loss. Such stocks combine both factors that I've cautioned you to avoid: a high P/E, and a sharp advance. In addition, the stock usually gets a lot of media attention because of its eye-popping runup. Finally, and most dangerous of all, it has a very large short interest[2] relative to the average daily trading volume. Whereas many stocks have a short interest equal to three to four times the average daily trading (which is on the high side), these too-obvious shorts often have a short position five times or more the average daily volume.

Before examining two case histories that show just how dangerous these sucker shorts can be, you should know where to get the short interest figures. Once a month (around the 21st), the New York and American Stock Exchanges compile the latest totals on the stocks with the largest short interests. These numbers are reported in *The Wall Street Journal* (Chart 7-6, column A) along with the average daily volume (column B). If you divide column A by column B, you get the ratio. For instance, Home Shopping Network's short interest is 4,283,306. The average daily volume is 137,595. The ratio is then a whopping 31 (4,283,306 divided by 137,595)!

Both Bowmar in 1972–73 and Home Shopping in 1986–87 illustrate exactly what I'm talking about. Back in the early 1970s, Bowmar (Chart 7-7) rose from 2 to 10, then 15, then up to 20. It was wild, and every time a few more points were tacked on, more and more fundamental reports came forth showing that the stock lacked substance and was destined to crash. The fundamentalists were right, because even if the pocket calculator that Bowmar produced ended up on every desk in the country, the stock was still getting pricey. What these analysts and the many market players who sold the stock short didn't understand was that as long as BOM was in Stage 2, high could become much higher. The second factor they failed to take into account was that so many people

---

[2]*Short interest* is the number of shares of a particular stock that are currently sold short.

CHART 7-6

SHORT INTEREST HIGHLIGHTS

	9/15/87	8/14/87	% Chg	Avg Dly Volume
Astrex Inc	93,300	93,300	0.0	2,090
†Astrotech Int Corp	320,035	338,879	−5.6	78,923
At&e Corp	1,140,092	1,188,402	−4.1	20,833
†Atari Corp	1,351,500	1,215,900	11.2	183,876
Atlas Cons Mng B	57,194	56,194	1.8	46,719
†Bally Manu Wts	153,134	161,605	−5.2	12,552
†Bat Ind Adr Ord	876,938	151,130	480.3	198,928
†Blocker Energy	393,000	439,222	−10.5	347,100
Bolar Phar. Co.	639,759	1,075,225	−40.5	111,485
Bowne & Co Inc	4,570	41,635	−89.0	54,371
Brown Forman Clb	58,892	62,908	−6.4	41,876
†Bsn Corp	389,763	407,653	−4.4	22,909
Canand Wine Cla	50,900	47,300	7.6	17,223
†Cardis Corp	321,100	260,000	23.5	9,776
Carnival Cruise	72,196	67,094	7.6	209,166
Central Fund Can	4,000	83,461	−95.2	34,647
Chambers Dev Cla	67,500	71,657	−5.8	19,766
Charter Med Cl A	10,428	39,200	−73.4	43,604
Citizens First Ban	90,267	120,778	−25.3	15,361
Cml Corporation	61,300	70,300	−12.8	10,433
†Color Sys Tech	188,600	180,500	4.5	13,942
†Conquest Exp Co	222,900	179,256	24.3	35,933
Cons Oil Gas Inc	79,907	89,061	−10.3	16,771
†Customedix Corp	152,542	108,375	40.8	35,438
†Damson Oil Corp	642,217	676,107	−5.0	124,495
†De Laurentiis Ent	217,777	129,100	68.7	17,995
Delmed Inc	65,347	65,347	0.0	32,666
Diagnos Ret Sys B	60,700	15,600	289.1	19,090
Dillard Dept Store	150,350	145,963	3.0	42,938
†Dome Petrol Ltd	121,942	123,873	−1.6	174,019
Echo Bay Mines	523,820	498,617	5.1	396,342
Elsinore Corp	66,398	55,403	19.8	29,557
†Entertain Mkt	1,186,296	1,134,385	4.6	33,466
†Foothill Group Inc	316,800	316,396	0.1	17,576
Frischs Rest	323,293	323,795	−0.2	4,038
Fruit Of The Loom	63,071	63,823	−1.2	98,004
Gen El Cr Geyws	65,500	79,600	−17.7	15,023
†Geotherm Res	252,657	253,057	−0.2	7,414
Giant Food Inc A	50,839	61,169	−16.9	56,623
Goldfield Corp	86,072	90,374	−4.8	19,590
Granges Explor	19	26,040	−99.9	9,047
Great Lake Chem	34,207	6,045	465.9	25,885
Greenman Bros	174,339	175,330	−0.6	14,914
Gulf Canada Res	5,818	41,543	−86.0	120,057
Hard Rock Cafe	46,600	15,800	194.9	6,052
†Hasbro	388,609	437,345	−11.1	125,909
Heritage Ent Wt	25,831	0	....	6,676
†Home Shop Net	4,283,306	4,212,510	1.7	137,595

were shorting the stock. It attracted almost a quarter of a million shares on the short side; that was about 10 times the average daily volume. By itself, such an abnormally large short position can propel the stock higher as the shorts scramble over each other to repurchase the stock whenever it begins to rally. That's exactly what happened as Bowmar advanced to 30, 35, and 40. Week after week, more and more short sellers got wiped out as the stock

CHART 7–7

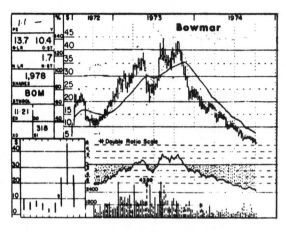

COURTESY OF MANSFIELD STOCK CHARTS

climbed to a peak of 45 and even defied the first 10 months of the 1973 bear market. Of course now that you understand stage analysis you should see that there is no way you would ever have been short throughout 1972 and 1973, simply because the long-term MA was rocketing higher.[3]

Never forget this point: *Don't ever short a stock that is above its rising 30-week MA.* If you understand all that I've taught you about buying, then you know how to sell short—you just don't realize it yet. Everything is simply reversed. Just as you should never buy a stock that is trading below its 30-week MA, you should never sell short any stock that is still above its rising 30-week MA no matter how enticing it may seem.

As an interesting sidelight, after topping out in late 1973 near 45, Bowmar later broke below its MA, and the MA turned down. By now most of the shorts were ruined and disgusted. They didn't want to hear about the stock. Following the market's perverse way, Bowmar then crashed over the next two years, dropping below $1 per share!

---

[3]The only time the MA stopped rising and the stock broke below it, there was a temporary sharp selloff. You really shouldn't have shorted it even for that time span because of the large short interest. If you did, however, you would have covered for a breakeven trade when BOM moved back above the MA.

CHART 7-8

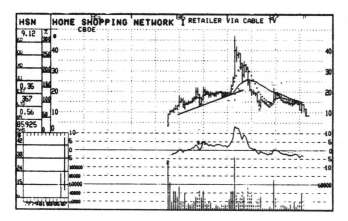

COURTESY OF MANSFIELD STOCK CHARTS

Home Shopping Network (Chart 7-8) is another example of a sucker short, but of more recent vintage. Chart 7-8 doesn't do full justice to the incredible fireworks that occurred in 1986 and early 1987 in that stock, because it split twice, which equals a six for one stock split. But one glance at the graph should give you an idea of how the shorts' stomachs were churning. The initial public offering (IPO) was at 18, and the stock closed the first day at an unbelievable 47¾. Now the game was underway. Investors who got in at 18 had over a 150 percent profit the first day the stock started trading! In the next few sessions, it shot ahead to 50, 55, 60, then 65, and that was only the beginning. Now prospective short sellers really started coming out of the woodwork. To them, the stock had to come down. So the short interest built up to over 10 times the average daily volume as more and more speculators bet on a crash. In the meantime, brokerage reports declared that the stock was overvalued, but it was in Stage 2 and the short position was too high. So what happened? To the confoundment of the short suckers, HSN rose vertically from 100 to a presplit peak of 282 (which equals 47 on Chart 7-8 when adjusted for the splits)! Then, as is usually the case, after all of the too-early short sellers got wiped out, the stock finally topped out and broke below its moving average, tumbling all the way back down.

OTHER SHORT-SELLING ERRORS

The three types of shorting errors I've just pointed out certainly aren't the only ones you must be aware of when looking to make money on the down side. It's also important that you don't sell short a stock that is too thin. By too thin, I mean an issue that has relatively little trading volume each day. If the average weekly volume is under 15,000 shares, look elsewhere. Remember, if it trades only a few hundred shares a day when you try to cover the stock (repurchase your shares), your buying will cause the price to rise. In addition, when a stock trades thinly, it doesn't take much buying to panic the other shorts, causing a short squeeze (shorts trying to repurchase their shares, thus driving the price higher).

Another grave error is to sell short a stock that is part of a very strong group. All the principles that I've taught you on the buy side still apply, but in reverse. You want to sell short a vulnerable stock that is in a weak group, especially when the overall market is negative.

Chart 7–9 of Aluminum Company of America looked weak when the stock broke below the MA at 36 in early 1973 (point A). Later that year, when it again broke below the MA at a much higher level (47-point B), it looked even more vulnerable. In both cases, you should have passed on it and looked elsewhere for your bear-market action, because Chart 7–10 of the aluminum group was showing far too much strength as the relative strength continued to trend higher.

On the other hand, it's not at all surprising that PSA (Chart 7–11) crashed and turned out to be a great short sale, as the airline group (Chart 7–12) was in trouble right along with the individual stock.

The final error to be on guard against is that of selling short without placing a protective buy-stop. *Never do this!* If your short sale is on the New York or American Exchange, then physically place the protective buy-stop[4] order on a good-'til-canceled basis. But if it's over-the-counter, make sure your broker has it on his market monitor and will immediately cover it for you if it hits your buy-stop level.

---

[4]On the American Stock Exchange it's a buy-stop limit order.

CHART 7–9

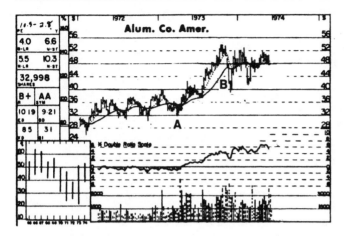

COURTESY OF MANSFIELD STOCK CHARTS

CHART 7–10

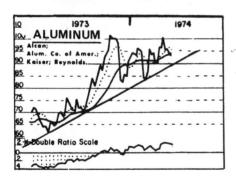

COURTESY OF MANSFIELD STOCK CHARTS

SUMMARY OF SHORT-SELLING DON'TS

- Don't sell short because the P/E is too high.
- Don't sell short because the stock has run up too much.
- Don't sell short a sucker stock that everyone else agrees must crash.
- Don't sell short a stock that trades thinly.
- Don't sell short a Stage 2 stock.

CHART 7–11

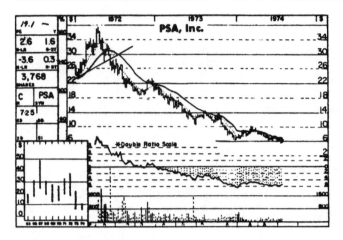

COURTESY OF MANSFIELD STOCK CHARTS

CHART 7–12

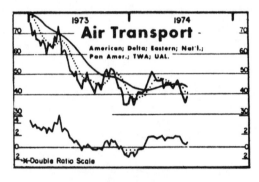

COURTESY OF MANSFIELD STOCK CHARTS

- Don't sell short a stock in a strong group.
- Don't sell short without protecting yourself with a buy-stop order.

HOW TO DO IT RIGHT

Now that we know what not to do, let's start learning how to sell short successfully in a disciplined and unemotional manner. The starting point is to look for a stock that has had a substantial advance over the past year. However, don't stop there, as so many amateurs do. It is important that you make sure your short-sale candidate is in Stage 3 with a flat MA, or, even better, an MA that is starting to decline. Also look for a stock that has trended sideways for several weeks. Moving sideways is a sign that a distributional top formation is unfolding that will help power your stock on the downside. Finally, look for a clear-cut level at or preferably below the MA that will signal the start of a Stage 4 downtrend if it's violated.

Chart 7–13 illustrates this point. As long as XYZ was trending higher and the MA was rising, you shouldn't have even considered shorting the stock. But after the MA leveled out and a top was completed (point A), the probabilities of a major decline became high.

WHEN TO SELL SHORT

The next question to resolve is: When is the best time to initiate your short sale? Is it when the initial breakdown occurs (point A),

CHART 7–13

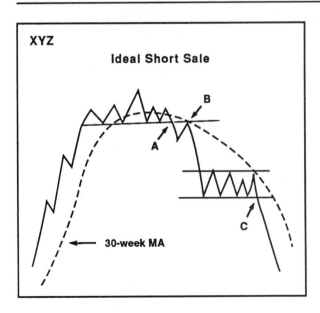

or when the pullback rally takes the stock back toward the break-down area (point B)? Again, everything that we learned on the buy side is valid when we're shorting. We just have to reverse the steps. I said earlier that when dealing with upside breakouts the risk is lower if you buy on pullbacks, but there is always the chance that you'll miss out entirely and never buy the stock if it doesn't pull back. I therefore stressed that the best tactic for investors is to buy half the position on a breakout, and the other half on a pullback toward the breakout point. Traders, on the other hand, should go for it and buy their entire position on the breakout. The rules for short selling are the same. Traders should sell short their entire proposed position on the breakdown. This is especially important for traders to realize. While pullbacks toward the breakdown level do occur in better than half the cases, they nevertheless occur far less frequently than pullbacks toward breakout points. The reason is simple. Stocks decline because of fear, and when panic gets out of hand, it's simply a matter of bombs away! Nevertheless, con-servative investors who want to keep their risk to a minimum should sell short only one half of the proposed position on the initial breakdown, and then short the other half on a pullback.

Chart 7–14 of General Medical—a short sale recommendation in *The Professional Tape Reader* back in 1973—illustrates what I'm talking about. As long as the stock remained in Stage 2, we refused to join the crowd and call it overvalued even though its P/E was a ridiculous 47. But once the MA stopped rising and a top formed, it was time to put it on our short-selling shopping list. Then after it broke down at point A, the fun began as it plummeted lower and lower.

TAKING SOME PROFITABLE STEPS

Just as there is a disciplined sequence that you should use when considering buying, so, too, there is one for short selling.

1. The Market. The very important starting point is the overall market trend. While I'm not going to tell you that you can never sell a stock short when the major market trend is bullish, this should be the exception, certainly not the rule. Just as I showed you back

CHART 7–14

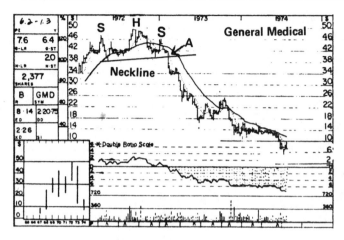

COURTESY OF MANSFIELD STOCK CHARTS

in Chapter 5 how an outstandingly bullish chart pattern such as National Semiconductor could have been bought in the 1973 bear market, so, too, an outstandingly bearish chart pattern can be sold short even when the overall market trend is favorable. Buying National Semiconductor in a bear market should have been done as a hedge against the many short sales you had outstanding. By the same token, if you find an outstandingly negative chart pattern that one stock should be a hedge against your many longs. In general, however, it's best to keep it simple. When the market's major trend is bullish, you want to look for buys. And, conversely, when the investment climate is clearly negative, you want to look for short sales. The starting point will be market averages that are clearly negative (as they were in 1962, 1966, 1973–74, 1977, and 1981–82). Then you want to do aggressive short selling. Once the major trend turns clearly bearish, as it did in early 1973 (see Chart 7–15), it becomes easy to rack up big profits on the short side. So once we are sure that all of the market averages are below the 30 week MAs and are in Stage 4, and the majority of our other long-term gauges (which I will teach you in Chapter 8) are also negative, it's time to start hunting for some good short-sale candidates.

CHART 7-15

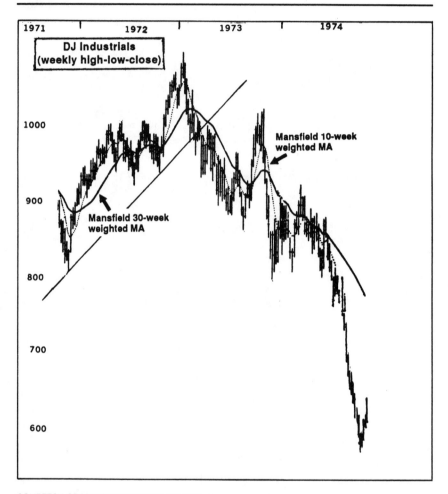

2. The Group.   The next step is to isolate those market sectors that are showing significant potential vulnerability. To do this, we look at the group charts for negative formations.[5] We want to make

---

[5]The Mansfield Chart Service has a section that covers all of the S&P group sectors. Always study it in conjunction with the individual charts.

CHART 7–16

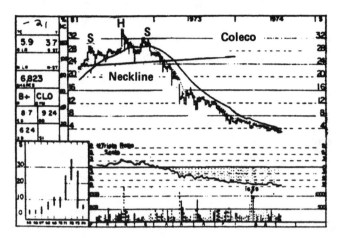

COURTESY OF MANSFIELD STOCK CHARTS

CHART 7–17

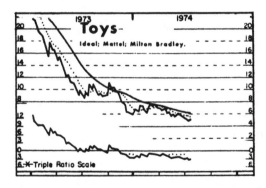

COURTESY OF MANSFIELD STOCK CHARTS

sure the group has broken below its 30-week MA. Another key is that the relative-strength line is trending lower. Finally, it's important that several charts from that sector are acting technically weak.

As Charts 7–16 and 7–17 show, the really major scores on the downside come from the one-two punch of a bearish market group and individual stock chart from that sector. It is no coincidence that Coleco, which was a *PTR* short-sale recommendation in early

1973, turned into a huge winner on the down side. This stock had everything going for it; the overall market trend was bearish, the group was negative, and Coleco's chart pattern was horrid once it broke down and completed its head-and-shoulder top formation. (Later in this chapter I'll cover this very important and profitable formation in great detail.)

3. The Individual Chart Pattern.   Now let's refine the process further. There are several factors that go into making up an ideal short-sale candidate. We don't want just an OK short that is going to go down; we want A+ shorts. Here are the filters that will help you separate the champs from the chumps. Make sure the stock has had a significant runup before the top has formed. If the top unfolds after a mediocre Stage 2 advance, it's very likely to have a minor drop that will just take it back into its prior base area, which won't be a thrilling ride. But if your short-sale candidate has taken off like a rocket before the Stage 3 top forms, the probabilities are very strong that a big downhill slide is in store. The second factor requiring strict attention is whether or not there is a significant area of support close to the breakdown point.

Here are two charts that both formed Stage 3 tops and then broke down into Stage 4. Chart 7–18 of Northwest Airlines had

CHART 7–18

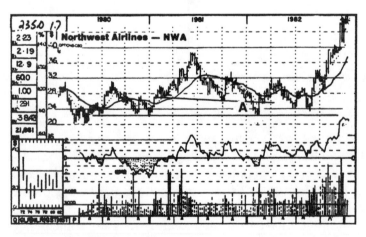

COURTESY OF MANSFIELD STOCK CHARTS

only a so-so decline because there was solid support near 22, which wasn't far below the breakdown at 26⅞ (point A). Not surprisingly, the decline halted as NWA neared 22. On the other hand, Chart 7–19 of Hiram Walker had no further nearby support once it broke 20 (point A) and, like Humpty Dumpty, it suffered a great fall.

4. Relative Strength.   Never sell a stock short that has very positive relative strength (RS), especially if the RS line is trending higher. If such a stock breaks down and you own it, of course you'll sell it; but you do not want to sell that stock short. While it's OK if the relative strength is above the zero line on the Mansfield chart, it must have clearly topped out and started trending lower. It is even more negative if a breakdown on the price chart is accompanied by a drop into negative territory by the RS line. These stocks are the short sales that usually turn out to be the A+ winners.

Chart 7–20 of U.S. Steel in 1974 is a perfect example of a stock with strong relative strength that should not have been shorted even when it violated support at 42 (point A). When it broke down, the RS line was still very healthy; therefore, the stock did not turn out to be a profitable short sale. At the same time, Chart 7–21 of Allen was an excellent stock to sell short late in 1972. Its relative strength weakened badly and pierced the zero line as the stock

CHART 7–19

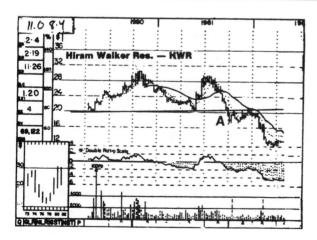

CHART 7–20

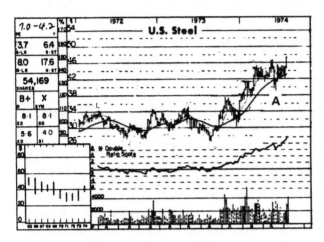

COURTESY OF MANSFIELD STOCK CHARTS

CHART 7–21

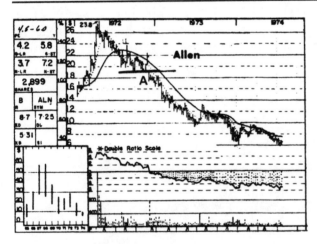

COURTESY OF MANSFIELD STOCK CHARTS

dropped below support at 19 (point A). One glance at the chart shows what happened once Stage 4 appeared in all its glory.

5. Volume. Now, pay careful attention! Volume is crucial when we're dealing with upside breakouts on the buy side. You should never buy a breakout that does not have confirming volume. If you do buy one and volume doesn't confirm, then you should sell it on the first minor advance. *The short side is 100% different.* While it's nice if volume does pick up significantly and confirm the downside breakout, volume is not a necessary ingredient for a winning short sale. It takes power to make a stock rise, but a stock can truly fall of its own weight. There are many cases, such as Jonathan Logan (JOL) back in 1973, where volume did not confirm the downside breakout and the stocks turn out to be spectacular winners. JOL (Chart 7–22) completed a major top when it broke below its trend-line at 55 (point A). Note how low volume was at that point (B). This didn't stop the stock from tumbling close to 90 percent! It's even more negative if volume increases on the breakdown and then contracts on the pullback toward the breakdown area. You don't need to make volume a major priority when you're looking for potential winners on the short side, while you most definitely do under the rules for buying.

6. Support.   The last factor to check out is how much nearby support is beneath the stock. The ideal short sale is one that has had a steep Stage 2 advance with only small congestion areas along the way. This situation will slip rapidly when the retrorockets are fired. On the other hand, a stock that has risen slowly and has a

CHART 7–22

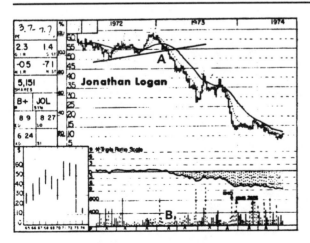

COURTESY OF MANSFIELD STOCK CHARTS

large trading zone not too far below the breakdown level will be far more resistant to decline.

Charts 7–23 of Pacific Scientific and 7–24 of Banc One illustrate this point. Pacific had a straight-up Stage 2 advance with no significant congestion areas of support along the way. Not surpris-

CHART 7–23

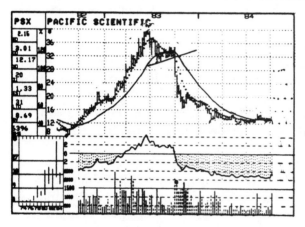

COURTESY OF MANSFIELD STOCK CHARTS

CHART 7–24

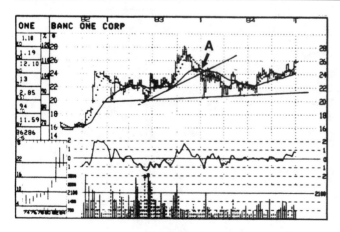

COURTESY OF MANSFIELD STOCK CHARTS

ingly, there was symmetry on the downside as it fell even faster than it rose.

Chart 7–24 of Banc One Corporation presents us with a very different pattern and result. First, the advance was slower and far less exciting. In addition, it traded for quite some time in the 20 to 24 zone before breaking out and moving above 28. When Banc One broke both its 30-week MA and trendline (point A), the decline was *very* slow. It also failed to break below the major support at 20 despite several attempts. So always favor a chart that has minimal support below it when narrowing down your shorting candidates.

PLACING THE ORDER

Once you determine the one or two stocks that you want to sell short, here's how your order should be placed. If stock XYZ breaks down at 24⅞, put in an order to sell short the desired amount of shares with a 24⅞ stop and a limit of 24⅜. Here is another difference from the buy side. On the buy side, in actively traded issues, we said to only make the spread between the stop and limit price ¼ of a point. When you are shorting, however, you should make it at least ½ a point and, in inactive cases, a bit more. Here's why. There's an archaic rule on both the New York and American Stock Exchanges called the *uptick rule*. It states that you can only sell a stock short after it trades at a higher price. In my opinion, this is a ridiculous lack of logic which grew out of the 1929 crash. To prevent so-called bear raids, the exchanges—in their infinite wisdom—decided they would not let stocks be sold down too sharply by short sellers. This shows a tremendous prejudice for bull markets on the part of the exchanges. Can you really imagine them telling you that you can only buy a stock if it downticks? That's nonsense, and someday I believe the uptick rule will go the way of weekend trading! Due to the uptick rule, you want to give yourself a bit more leeway to get your short sale off.

As on the buy side, your order should be entered on a good-'til-canceled basis. With over-the-counter stocks, you must depend on your broker since you cannot physically place stop orders. The advantage is that there is no nonsensical uptick rule over-the-counter. Therefore, if you see XYZ breaking below 25 bid, and

24⅞ is the point at which you should sell it short, as soon as the bid goes to 24⅞, your broker can immediately sell it short for you. That really is quite a big plus in a crashing market!

NEVER TOO LATE?

Thus far we've discussed short selling near the breakdown point. But is shorting feasible when a stock has already had a substantial decline? The answer is an emphatic yes. While it would be more ideal to go short near the top because the profit potential is larger, remember that the really big losers have a habit of becoming even bigger busts before they hit rock bottom. Shorting well into a Stage 4 decline is a good trader's tactic because the selloffs that immediately follow are usually fast and furious. But this tactic is only to be used if a consolidation pattern forms beneath the declining MA and then a new breakdown occurs.

This type of trading is comparable to continuation buying in Stage 2. Just as continuation buys are more for traders, this formation is more for an aggressive market player and trader. But such a short does have its merits since the decline can be very rapid when it makes the renewed breakdown. Shorting a stock like Winnebago (Chart 7–25)—which had already dropped from close to 50 to 22—after it consolidated and then broke down again at 21⅞ (point A) made a lot of sense, as it produced an additional super gain in a hurry. Good candidates for this type of shorting are stocks that are part of a group which has fallen completely out of favor. It's even better if you find one—such as Winnebago back in 1973—that had a fancy institutional following. When the institutions' love turns to loathing, it's a safe bet there will be a long downward trail of panic selling.

Despite an already steep price fall, the downside percentage potential can still be considerable. Twenty-two to 3 (as in the case of Winnebago) is a tremendous percentage drop irrespective of the large prior decline. Just make sure that you don't short such a stock without the proper pattern first forming. Be sure a consolidation has taken place, and a new breakdown occurs. And you must choose a proper entry point so there will be plenty of resistance and a sound place to enter a protective buy-stop overhead.

CHART 7–25

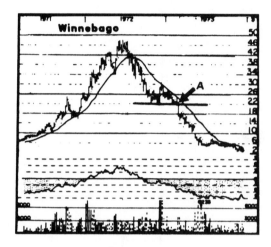

COURTESY OF MANSFIELD STOCK CHARTS

ESPECIALLY PROFITABLE FORMATIONS

Back in Chapter 4, I showed you the importance of spotting head-and-shoulder bottom formations, since they lead to incredibly profitable upside advances. The converse is also true. Head-and-shoulder top formations (especially when they come after a dynamic advance) are among the most profitable short-selling signals. While they don't occur with great frequency, they do form more often than head-and-shoulder bottom patterns, and they do appear often enough to be a source of great gain. In fact, when you start to see a bevy of these formations occurring, it's a signal that a major market top is moving into place.

The first ingredient of a valid head-and-shoulder top pattern is a stock which has been very strong and already had a substantial advance. The beauty of this formation is its ability to spot trend reversals. If there's no big prior upmove to reverse, forget it; it's not going to be exciting. Volume should be well above average on the advance, as the latecomers rush in close to the end of the move. Then along comes a correction, as profit-taking sets in (B-C on Chart 7–26). Once the selloff runs its course (point C), the stock

CHART 7–26

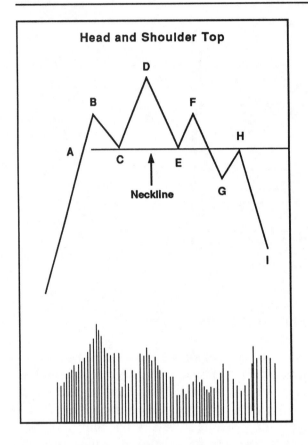

then shoots ahead to another new high (point D). No problem yet, except that on this second rally, volume usually stops expanding and is often less than on the preceding rise. This is the first sign of potential trouble. The dwindling volume reflects lessened buying interest at this lofty level.

A second correction (D-E) then quickly sets in. This is another sign that something is starting to go wrong. After breaking to a new high (point D), the stock appears to be embarking on a new upleg as the buyers' greed glands start to work overtime. Instead, the stock only moves ahead a few points and then quickly sells off once again. The clincher that tells you weakness is setting in is how far back this second decline (D-E) carries. As I've shown you before, when dealing with support areas, the former peak (B) should act as support when the stock starts to decline. The fact that the decline instead carries the stock all the way to the prior low (C) is a distinct negative.

Now you have a potential left shoulder (A-B-C) and head (C-D-E) as well as a trendline (C-E) connecting the two correction lows. This trendline is the potential neckline of the head-and-shoulder top formation and must be watched very carefully. If it breaks, watch out! Now it all hinges on the next rally. Will the upward momentum reassert itself, or is the stock getting too tired, and sellers increasingly anxious? Whatever you do, don't jump the gun. Don't anticipate that most of the pieces of the puzzle are in place for a short sale. In about one-third of the cases, these potential top formations will not move to completion and will instead end up breaking out on the upside.

If, as in the case of Chart 7–26, the next rally (E-F) fails to exceed the previous rally peak (D), or—even worse—ends its advance at the same point as the left shoulder peak (B), then look out. If it drops back toward the neckline once again, you have a clearly recognizable right shoulder. Volume will usually be lighter on the right shoulder. While it isn't crucial that volume is heaviest on the left shoulder or the head, *don't trust the formation if the heaviest volume appears on the right shoulder.* If that much buying power is still present, there is a high probability that the formation will prove a short seller's trap. So look elsewhere.

Finally, the next decline (F-G) takes the stock below the neckline. At this point, the potential head-and-shoulder top becomes a reality. This is the most bearish pattern that can form, so if you ever find yourself holding a stock that has just completed one, don't hope and pray—sell it immediately! And if conditions are right (overall market trend and group are negative), go for it and sell the stock short!

There are a few other subtleties that you should be aware of. The first can easily be summed up in a rhyme that I've used for years: the bigger the top, the bigger the drop. The longer this bearish formation takes to form, the more powerful the eventual downmove will be. While all head-and-shoulder top patterns are negative, one that forms in three weeks isn't as powerful as one that unfolds over a nine-month span. This makes sense because the more time the stock spends forming the pattern, the more buyers who are trapped in that top area. And it's those late-for-the-party buyers who will supply the downside fireworks when they begin to panic many points lower!

A second factor to remember is that the wider the swing from the neckline to the peak, the more vulnerable the pattern is. The reason for this is that the more volatile the stock is when the top forms, the greater the risk buyers are willing to take in that high-risk zone. They really had to believe the fundamental story or rumor to buy in the face of such wild swings. That great confidence turns to great disappointment and panic when the bearish reality sets in.

Now let's look at some actual case histories of head-and-shoulder top patterns as theory merges with reality. First go back and look at Charts 7–1, 7–14, and 7–16. Teleprompter, General Medical, and Coleco were all *PTR* short-sale recommendations that formed head-and-shoulder tops before moving into Stage 4.

Metromedia (Chart 7–27) is another classic example of the power of this bearish pattern. Volume was very low on the right-shoulder rally, and the group was also weakening. Metromedia did tease a bit, breaking below the neckline a few times before declin-ing. At no point, however, did it give you a reason to get out, as the MA continued to decline and the stock did not move signifi-

CHART 7–27

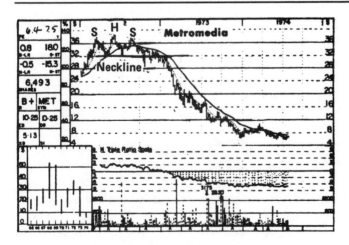

COURTESY OF MANSFIELD STOCK CHARTS

CHART 7–28

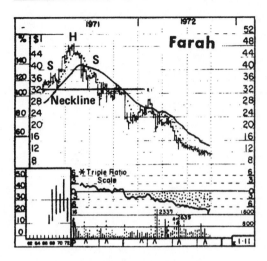

COURTESY OF MANSFIELD STOCK CHARTS

cantly above it at any time. Later in this chapter, I'll show you where your protective buy-stop should be placed and how to lower it to lock in more and more of your profits as the stock plummets. Once Metromedia developed downside momentum, it became a dream short. It crumbled from its break of the neckline at 31⅞ down close to 5!

Farah (Chart 7–28) was another excellent short back in 1972 after it, too, completed a head-and-shoulder top. Breaking below its neckline at 33, it had dropped close to 10 in one year as Stage 4 ran its downward course.

Diamond-Bathurst (Chart 7–29) really demonstrates just how powerful this pattern can be. In 1986, in the midst of one of history's great bull markets, DBH formed a head-and-shoulder top over a nine-month period. When it broke below its neckline at 24, it dropped an incredible 55 percent in the next three months! Always be on the lookout for these formations, as they are both potent and profitable. Finally, if you see them forming on page after page of your chart book (as was the case in the late 1972–early 1973 period), it's an important indicator for the overall market. Very simply, it's a clear-cut sign to change your thinking from long to short.

CHART 7–29

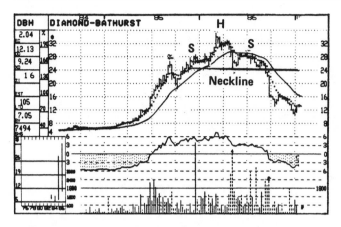

COURTESY OF MANSFIELD STOCK CHARTS

PROJECTING A TARGET

In a few pages, I'll show you how to use buy-stops to lock in your gains on short sales. But there is one more profitable technique I want to share with you first. Back in Chapter 6, I showed you how to use the swing rule to make uncannily accurate projections on the buy side. That same principle applies on the downside too.

Using Chart 7–30 as a model, take the low price that a stock hits (point A) while it is in a top area and subtract it from the highest level that the stock reaches thereafter (point B) before it breaks below the prior low (A). Since the stock peaked at 60 (point B) and the prior low (point A) was at 40, you get a difference of 20 points (60 minus 40). The next step is to subtract that 20 points from the old low (point A). 40 minus 20 points equals 20. This level then becomes a potential trading target. Just as on the long side, this measurement is usually quite accurate, and it pays to be alert for signs of a trading bottom forming near there.

Hughes Tool dropped to a low of 30 (point A in Chart 7–31) in late 1981. It then rallied back up to 45 (point B). That measurement equals 15 points (45 minus 30 equals 15). Therefore, once Hughes Tool violated support at 30, the swing rule projected a downside target of 15. A few months later, HT hit 14⅜ (point C), which turned out to be the low of the year for 1982.

CHART 7-30

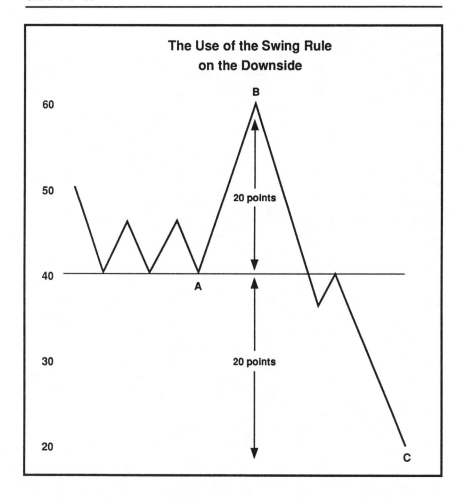

The Use of the Swing Rule
on the Downside

Maremont (Chart 7-32) underwent a really wild sequence, as it first dropped close to 31 (point A) before rallying sharply to a peak reading of 59½ (point B). This was a very unusual wide swing that predicted a devastating fall *if* Maremont broke below point A. After all, 59½ minus 31 equals 28½ points. Subtracting that 28½ points from the point A bottom at 31 yields what appears to be a ridiculous reading of a drop to 2½. Once Maremont did break below point A, it bottomed at 6, not far above the swing-rule target level.

The same technique can be applied to moves in the overall market averages. Projecting a bottom for the 1981-82 bear market

CHART 7–31

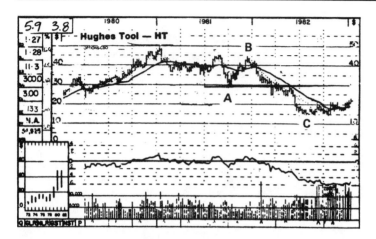

COURTESY OF MANSFIELD STOCK CHARTS

CHART 7–32

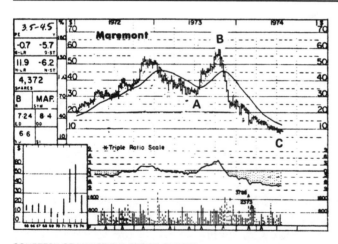

COURTESY OF MANSFIELD STOCK CHARTS

was as easy as A, B, C (see Chart 7–33). At point A, the Dow Jones Industrial Average dropped to a low of 894. In the spring of 1981, the Dow had an intraday high (point B) of 1,031. That yields a difference of 137 points. Later in the year, when the DJI violated its low at point A, a downside projection of 757 was flashed. As

CHART 7–33

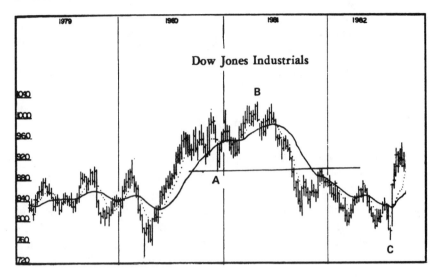

COURTESY OF MANSFIELD STOCK CHARTS

hard as it is to believe, when the Dow ultimately bottomed and ended that bear market, the low in August of 1982 was 770!

Therefore, when you're trading a stock on the short side, the downside swing rule gives you an excellent tool. Once the stock drops down close to its target area, take your profit on half the position and play the remainder using a protective buy-stop.

PROTECTING YOUR SHORT WITH A BUY-STOP

By now you should have a pretty good idea of what I'm going to say next. There are no big surprises. It's merely a matter of adapting the buy-stop concept that I taught you in Chapter 3 to the short side. If you reverse everything that we went over in Chapter 6 about sell-stops, you should already know what to do. I'll run through one ideal example and a few case histories to make sure you have it down pat. To me, this is one of the real keys to profitable short selling. First, it will give you peace of mind when shorting. Don't underestimate the importance of mental calm; your emotions can end up overwhelming your chart-reading ability time and time again if you get nervous about market action. Second, this discipline will make sure any loss is relatively small if the short-sale position moves against you. Finally, once your stock starts crashing, it will guarantee that your profits increase as you move further and further into Stage 4.

Before going further, promise yourself that you will absolutely *never* go short without first placing a protective buy-stop on a good-'til-cancelled basis with your broker. Just as on the long side, calculate where the buy-stop should be placed before you dial your broker. A very important part of the process for picking a good short-sale candidate is being able to protect it with a buy-stop that is not too far from the ideal short-selling price. This negates the old short-selling bug-a-boo that the stock can run to infinity. If your short sale fulfills all the other criteria, but the protective buy-stop must be placed 30 to 40 percent from the point of short sale, look for another stock. In the same manner, if you come across two potential short sales that look equally vulnerable and fulfill all of the other criteria, but one can be protected with a 10 percent buy-stop while the second one has its buy-stop 20 percent from the shorting level, then go with the lower-risk candidate.

After you sell your stock short and place the protective buy-stop, it's very important to know how to methodically lower the stop in the following weeks to lock in more and more of the gain. Let's go through the process carefully.

Prior rally peaks and the 30-week MA will be the two key factors you will focus on when setting your protective buy-stops. When you set the initial buy-stop, pay less attention to the MA and more to the prior peak. For example, in Chart 7–34 you'll note that after a very sharp Stage 2 advance, stock XYZ formed a Stage 3 top as it trended sideways in the 60 to 70 zone. It eventually violated support at 60 (point C) and broke below the 30-week MA, which had flattened out. This was a Stage 4 sell signal, and the point to sell the stock short was at 59⅞. The initial buy-stop should have been placed right above the prior rally high (point B) of 65. Therefore, the good-'til-cancelled buy-stop would be placed at 65⅛. If, however, the prior peak had been 64⅝ or 64¾, you would still place the buy-stop at 65⅛. It's the same concept (but in reverse) that I told you about when placing sell-stops. Like buyers, sellers are affected by round-number psychology. A heavy batch of sell

CHART 7–34

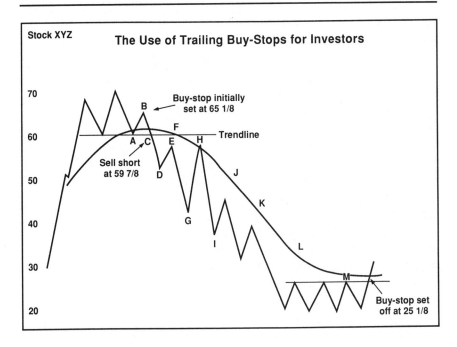

Stock XYZ — The Use of Trailing Buy-Stops for Investors

Buy-stop initially set at 65 1/8
Trendline
Sell short at 59 7/8
Buy-stop set off at 25 1/8

orders are likely to accumulate at 65 instead of 64⅞ or 64¾. There-fore, *always* place the buy-stop above the round number whenever it's close to it.

The next step is to relax and let the market action unfold. In the unlikely event that your short sale moves against you, your protective buy-stop will keep your loss to a minimum and you will be able to make it up on a future trade. More likely, however, the stock will start tumbling and the profits will build up. Here's how to keep those profits from evaporating. As long as your short sale is below its declining 30-week MA, give it plenty of room to swing. Trail the buy-stop behind the declining price in the following man-ner. After the first selloff that bottoms at point D, and then the first significant oversold rally of at least 8 percent, get set to lower the protective buy-stop. You don't actually alter the buy-stop until after the rally reaches its peak (point E) and then moves back toward its prior low (point D). If a move above that rally peak at E also takes the stock above the 30-week MA, then an investor lowers the buy-stop to a point right above that level. But if, as in this example, the peak falls short of the MA, an investor should still place the buy-stop above the MA (point F). Later in the cycle, when the MA levels out, become more aggressive and press the buy-stop to a tighter position right above the rally peak.

Next the stock drops sharply to point G, which is normal Stage 4 behavior. After rallying sharply back toward the declining MA (point H), the rally fails and the stock starts heading south once again. Don't worry if the stock nudges slightly above the declining MA. It's only a cause for concern if it moves significantly above it. After the rally terminates and the stock drops back toward the prior low (point G), then the buy-stop should be lowered right above the round number of the prior rally peak at point H. In the following months the protective buy-stop should be lowered sequentially to points J, K, L, and M before the position is eventually stopped out at 25⅛ for a substantial profit. Note that the tactics change slightly once you've reached a Stage 1 base area and the MA is no longer declining. The protective buy-stop is lowered to point M above the significant area of resistance even though this buy-stop point is below the 30-week MA.

Now let's look at some actual case histories so you can get some practice at placing buy-stops.

Blair (Chart 7–35) completed a small head-and-shoulder top formation in mid–1972, then broke below its neckline at point A, where the stock should have been sold short at 19⅞. The initial protective buy-stop should have been placed right above the rally peak at point B. Then, as Stage 4 started dropping the stock lower and lower, the protective buy-stop should have been lowered to points C, D, E, and so forth, all the way down to point K (near 7½). When Blair moved above 7½ and your protective buy-stop was hit, an excellent profit was locked in even though that did not turn out to be the absolute low point. That's fine, because our method locked in better than a 60 percent gain in a disciplined, unemotional manner, and took us out of the short-sale position very close to the low.

The same winning tactic is illustrated very nicely by Dow Chemical (Chart 7–36), which suffered severely during the 1977 bear market. Dow completed a Stage 3 top formation and moved into Stage 4 once it broke below both support and its 30-week MA

CHART 7–35

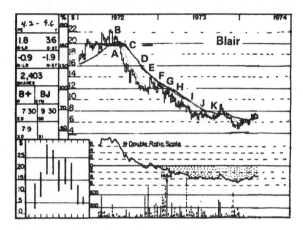

COURTESY OF MANSFIELD STOCK CHARTS

CHART 7–36

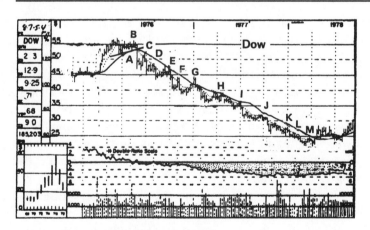

COURTESY OF MANSFIELD STOCK CHARTS

at point A, near 53. Initially, the position should have been protected with a close protective buy-stop set at point B—right above
the prior rally peak. In the following months, the buy-stop should
have been lowered to points C, D, E, and so on, until it was finally
lowered to point M at 25⅛, where the position was closed out for

a fabulous profit. Note that if you didn't have this discipline working for you, you would have started giving back a good portion of your excellent gain as the stock worked its way back toward the mid–30s in the following months. Instead of being in that frustrating would have-could have-should have position, our system of buy-stops got us out within 3 points of the bottom and allowed us to remain relaxed and in control of the situation throughout the entire decline.

Even though the market will definitely throw some frustrating curves at you along the way, this is the disciplined, unemotional, and profitable way to go. Always protect all your positions, both shorts and longs, with stops. Remain entirely mechanical no matter what headlines or TV news flashes you see.

USING BUY-STOPS THE TRADER'S WAY

The rules for traders' buy-stops are just the reverse of the long-side sell-stops. As on the long side, traders must be more aggressive than investors in their use of stops. While an investor wants to give a short sale plenty of room for gyrations—as long as it doesn't ruin the overall negative pattern—a trader only wants to stay with the position as long as it closely follows the game plan. As soon as the position begins to deviate, it's time to get out and look for a new short position. The trader must look at gyrations as either potential reversals or possibly the beginnings of sideways trading zones that will tie up his capital for long periods. Just as on the long side, a trader shouldn't wait for the 30-week MA to be violated on a rally before covering a short sale.

Chart 7–37 shows you just how the trading game should be played on the short side. First of all, stock XYZ moves in a side-ways Stage 3 pattern between support near 60 and resistance near 70. Eventually it breaks below significant support at 60, flashing a sell signal at 59⅞ (point A). That's where the stock should be shorted. In this case, the initial buy-stop should not be handled in the same manner as for the investor. Just as on the long side, it's imperative that traders keep their losses to a minimum, so the protective buy-stop should be set in the following manner. If there is a prior peak very close to the breakdown level, use that as the

CHART 7–37

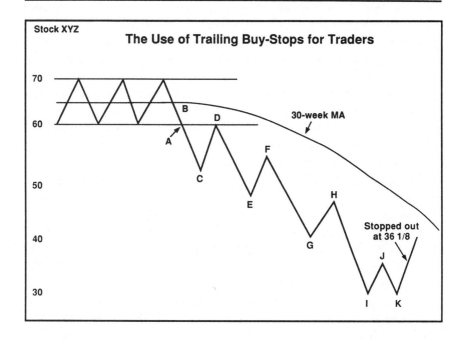

point to set your buy-stop. If, however, there is no close stop, and you have to set your initial buy-stop 10 to 15 percent above the short-sale price, place the buy-stop 4 to 6 percent (point B) above the breakdown level (point A). Make sure it's above a round number. For instance, if the breakdown is at 59⅞, 5 percent would be 62⅞. Therefore, place it above the round number of 63 at 63⅛.

In the following weeks, XYZ dropped to point C before undergoing the expected pullback rally toward the initial breakdown. Once the rally failed at point D, and the stock dropped back to the prior low at C and broke below that point, the trading buy-stop should have been lowered to point D. Thereafter, the stock dropped quickly to point E before staging a new rally that failed at point F. Then, when a new decline dropped XYZ back to point E and broke below it, the buy-stop should have been lowered to point F; and, in the same manner, to point H and then J. Eventually, a double bottom formed and the stop at J of 36⅛ was set off, locking in a fine trading profit. Never forget: place the buy-stops right above the round numbers when you are close to them. (For instance, if the rally at J had terminated at 35¾, the buy-stop should have been set at 36⅛.) One last important point: as on the long side, don't pay attention to oversold rallies that don't advance at least 7 percent or more. (Investors should use an 8 to 10 percent threshold.) The wiggles and jiggles that take place in the 3 to 4 percent range are just that—wiggles rather than meaningful moves that should determine strategy. And one final tip, which by now should certainly not surprise you: Traders should *never* stay with a short position that moves above its 30-week MA, even momentarily.

Chart 7–38 of Seaboard World shows how traders should use buy-stops in the real world. Seaboard completed a major head-and-shoulder top formation when it broke below the neckline at 10⅞. The initial trading buy-stop should have been placed about 6 percent above the 10¾ entry price (6 percent of 10¾ yields a price of 11⅜). Therefore, the buy-stop should have been placed above the round number (under 20 each ½ point counts as a round number) of 11½, at 11⅝ (point B). In the succeeding months, the stop should have been dropped to points C, D, E, F, and finally G, at 5¼. After dropping to a low near 4, Seaboard nudged above the MA, and above point G. Traders would be stopped out at 5¼ for an excellent profit. As a trader, you should not have been at all concerned that

CHART 7–38

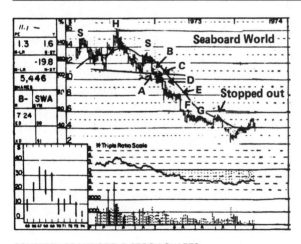

COURTESY OF MANSFIELD STOCK CHARTS

the stock subsequently broke to yet another new low before bouncing back up. A big profit was scored in a hurry in a disciplined manner. As Bernard Baruch commented about how he had become so wealthy, "I always made the mistake of getting out too early."

TRENDLINES ON THE DOWNSIDE

The last technique that traders must add to their arsenal of profitable methods is the use of trendlines when selling short. The same concept that I showed you in Chapter 6 of using trading trendlines on the long side is valid when selling short—however, in reverse.

If no valid trendline forms (one that hits at least three points), then simply use the trading buy-stop technique. When a clear-cut trendline does form, it certainly pays to utilize it. At least a portion of the short position should be covered when such a trendline is violated. The remainder can be protected with a buy-stop, which will usually be at a somewhat higher price than the trendline.

Chart 7–39 illustrates how to add trendlines to your bear-market game plan. Initially, the buy-stop should be set at 53⅛ (point A). Take 6 percent of 49⅞, which equals 52⅞, and place the buy-stop above the round number—53⅛. As the stock starts doing its Stage 4 thing, the buy-stop should be lowered, first to point C, then to point D. After that the strategy changes. Rally peaks B, C, and D form a valid downsloping trendline. You should recognize this and incorporate it into your strategy. In the following weeks, as XYZ goes into free-fall, you should lower your buy-stop to points E, F, G, and so forth, on half the position, using the trendline as a guide. Since it is angling downward, you can continue lowering the buy-stop on this half position even if the stock moves sideways, as it did following point K. Half the position is now protected with a buy-stop above H, and half is set very tightly at point J. Eventually, the sideways action nudges the stock above the trendline and the buy-stop at J is set off for an excellent profit. Even if the penetration of the trendline doesn't indicate a sharp upside reversal, it is likely to lead to a neutral trading range. This is a great time for traders to do at least partial profit-taking. When real strength appears and the second buy-stop (point H) is hit, another excellent gain is locked in and the position becomes history.

CHART 7–39

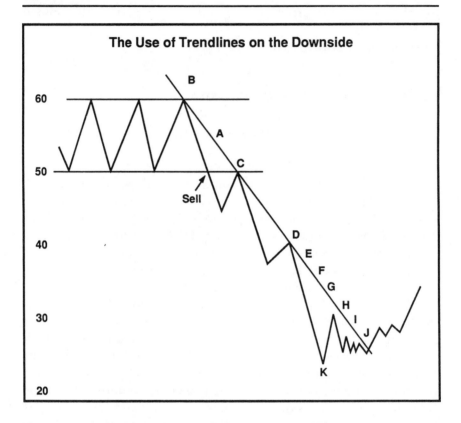

The Use of Trendlines on the Downside

Chart 7–40 of Peabody Galion points out the advantages of using trendlines. Peabody should have been sold short when it broke below its upsloping trendline (A-B). The initial buy-stop should have been placed above the round number of 41 (point D).[6] After the sharp selloff toward the 26 area and the rally back to 34 (point E), another wave of selling set in. At first the buy-stop should have been lowered to E. But by then a clear-cut trendline formed that was touched more than three times, and the buy-stop should have then been lowered to points F, G, and H in the following weeks.

---

[6]Five percent of 38⅞, which was the breakdown point, equals almost 2 points, which brings it to 40⅞. So place the buy-stop above the psychologically important 41 level.

CHART 7–40

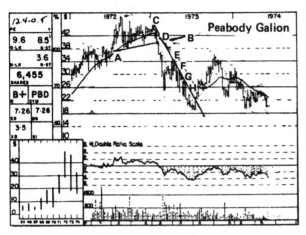

COURTESY OF MANSFIELD STOCK CHARTS

Finally, after an exciting downward ride Peabody moved above its downsloping trendline at point H, rallying above 22. An excellent profit was thus established on half the position. When Peabody demonstrated enough strength to go above its MA near 26, it was time to clear out of the remainder of the position with another fine trading profit. Interestingly, although that first selloff low did not turn out to be the absolute low for the 1973–74 bear market, PBD was still very close to that level a year later. Once again the traders' purpose was well served, as the trendline kept them in for the sharp downside smash and then helped them exit before the choppy sideways action. Always be alert to these important trendlines; they can make short selling both fun and highly profitable.

ANOTHER WAY OF REDUCING RISK

The use of put options is yet another way to play the downside with relatively little risk. By buying a put you have the right to deliver that stock at a specified price until a given date. Thus if you buy a put on XYZ at 50 for a price of $250, and XYZ then falls to 30 before the expiration date of the option, you're in great shape. You can buy the shares in the open market at 30 and deliver them to the original seller of the put at 50. The 20-point difference minus the cost of the put is your profit (in this case, $1,750 excluding commissions). Buying a put on a stock you think is going to collapse gives you the same rooting interest as going short. The advantage is that the most you can lose is the price of the put—in this case, $250.

On the negative side, the premium you pay for the put does cut into your profit potential, and if the move doesn't develop before your option expires, you're out the cost of the option. For the average market player, short selling is the preferable tactic. For seasoned speculators, put buying can be a fine way of limiting risk while also increasing your leverage. (In Chapter 9, we'll go into options in greater detail.)

In conclusion, you should understand that Stage 4 situations actually offer you another opportunity to make money, and there is no more risk to selling short than to buying—as long as you follow my few important guidelines and *always* use protective buy-stops!

QUIZ

1. Due to the inherent high risk of short selling, only aggressive speculators should use this tactic.   **T   F**
2. It is *never* a good idea to sell short a stock that is above its rising 30-week MA.   **T   F**
3. You should never sell a stock short without protecting the position with a buy-stop order.   **T   F**
4. After a sharp Stage 2 advance, a head-and-shoulder top formation is the most bearish pattern that can form.   **T   F**
5. You should sell short only on pullbacks toward the breakdown level.   **T   F**

6. The accompanying chart is a good short sale at point   **T   F**
   A even though the P/E ratio is on the low side at 10.

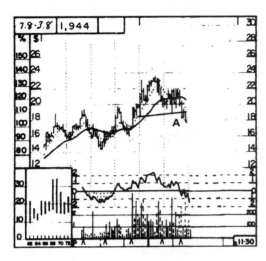

COURTESY OF MANSFIELD STOCK CHARTS

7. Despite the 35 percent drop from its high near 40,   **T   F**
   this stock is still a good short sale on the new breakdown at point A.

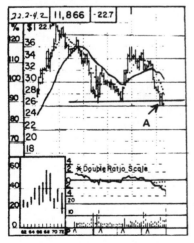

COURTESY OF MANSFIELD STOCK CHARTS

8. After crashing from its high near 38 down to a low of 20¼ in 1973, this stock rallied sharply to 30¾. When renewed selling pressure set in and the stock broke to a new low below 20¼, the downside target according to the swing rule was:

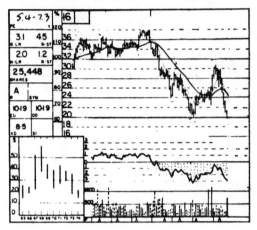

COURTESY OF MANSFIELD STOCK CHARTS

   A. 14⅛
   B. 9¾
   C. 2½
   D. 12

9. Which one of these three stocks is the best short sale at its respective point D?

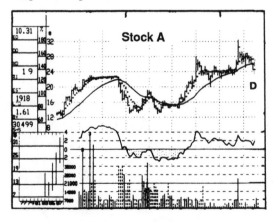

COURTESY OF MANSFIELD STOCK CHARTS

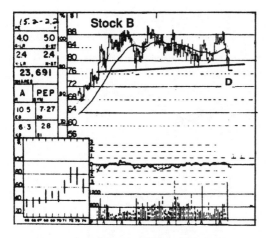

COURTESY OF MANSFIELD STOCK CHARTS

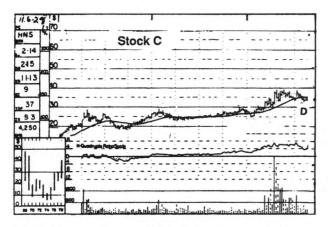

COURTESY OF MANSFIELD STOCK CHARTS

10. Stock XYZ should be shorted if it breaks below major support at 30. How should the order read that you give your broker when you want to sell 1,000 shares short?
  A. Sell short 1,000 XYZ at 29⅞.
  B. Sell short 1,000 XYZ 29⅞ stop.
  C. Sell short 1,000 XYZ 29⅞ stop–29⅝ limit.
  D. Sell short 1,000 XYZ 29⅞ stop–29⅜ limit.

11. Which one of these three stocks is the best short sale at its respective point D?

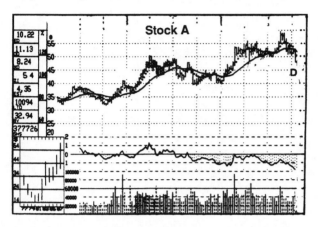

COURTESY OF MANSFIELD STOCK CHARTS

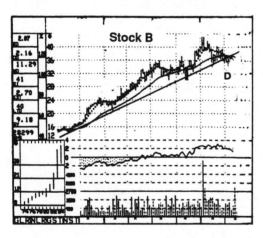

COURTESY OF MANSFIELD STOCK CHARTS

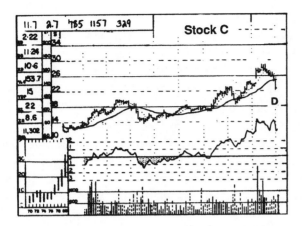

COURTESY OF MANSFIELD STOCK CHARTS

ANSWERS

1. False. As long as proper tactics are used, short selling is no more dangerous than buying, and everyone should do it in a bear market.

2. True.

3. True.

4. True.

5. False. About 50 percent of the best short-sale candidates never pull back to the original breakdown levels. You should therefore sell short at least half of your intended position on the breakdown, even though it is safer to short on pullback rallies.

6. True. The chart is Manhattan Industries in 1972. After breaking down at point A, it underwent a major Stage 4 decline that didn't reverse until Manhattan broke below $2 per share. So much for low P/E ratios!

7. True. The chart is of Genesco in 1972. Despite the sharp prior selloff, this was an excellent continuation-type short sale such as Winnebago (Chart 7–25). If you sold it short near 26 (point A), it dropped 90 percent before bottoming below 3!

8. B. The chart is of TRW in 1973. According to the swing rule, the stock had a projected downside target of $9\frac{3}{4}$ ($30\frac{3}{4}$ minus $20\frac{1}{4}$ equals $10\frac{1}{2}$; then $20\frac{1}{4}$ minus $10\frac{1}{2}$ equals $9\frac{3}{4}$). As things turned out, the actual bottom turned out to be $10\frac{1}{8}$ before a new Stage 2 advance got underway.

9. B. Stock B is Pepsico, which was an ideal short in 1973. The relative-strength line dropped into negative territory on the breakdown after several months of draggy action. In addition, the MA was heading lower. Finally, the top was over a year in the making, and "the bigger the top, the bigger the drop." In this case, Pepsico crashed all the way down to $29\frac{1}{4}$ before reversing back to the upside.

   Stock A is TWA in 1987. There were two reasons *not* to short the stock at point D. First, the 30-week MA was still rising. Second, the relative strength was still quite strong. Even though it did decline much later in the year, three months after point D it was up to 35, which would have given you a whopping loss.

   Stock C is Hanes in 1978. Again, the relative strength was far too strong to sell it short. Three months later it had almost doubled as it moved above 60!

10. D. If you want to sell a stock short if it breaks below 30, use a stop at $29\frac{7}{8}$ with a limit *at least* half a point lower, since you have to wait for an uptick (if it's on the New York or American Exchange). Therefore, D is the correct answer.

    A is incorrect. If you say to sell at $29\frac{7}{8}$, that means sell at $29\frac{7}{8}$ *or better*. Therefore, if the stock is trading at $30\frac{1}{8}$, you'll still sell it short on the next uptick even if it never breaks below 30.

    B is incorrect. By placing a straight stop order, if XYZ breaks 30 and doesn't uptick until $27\frac{1}{2}$, that's where you'll sell it short, since there is no limit to your short sale. That's why a limit on the order is essential.

    C is the second best answer, but the limit of $\frac{1}{4}$ of a point is too tight for a short sale that needs an uptick.

11. A. Stock A is Sears Roebuck in 1987. It was far and away the best short sale, as the relative strength was sick and the MA was heading lower. It's not surprising that once point D was hit at $49\frac{7}{8}$ in the next few weeks, the stock crashed to 26.

Stock B is US Tobacco in 1984. The relative strength was far too strong to sell it short. So it's not surprising that four months later, you'd have been sitting with a loss, as UBO was up to 40.

Stock C is Thiokol in 1980. It should not have been sold short, as the MA was still rising and the relative strength was very strong. THI never dropped lower than point D during the remainder of 1980 and, instead, moved up to 38½ later in the year.

CHAPTER 8

USING THE BEST LONG-TERM INDICATORS TO SPOT BULL AND BEAR MARKETS

Wouldn't it be great to have bought aggressively in January 1975, March 1978, and August 1982? Each of those junctures occurred right before major bull markets were about to get underway. And it would have been even nicer to have moved to a very defensive position in January 1973, late 1976, July 1981, and early October 1987, before major bear markets took their toll. *The Professional Tape Reader* did—and you can too!

In July of 1982, many economists were writing about a severe recession that would last for another year or more. With the Dow Jones Industrial Average (DJI) below 800, a widely followed market guru was predicting a crash to at least 500—and the public was listening and believing. After having been bearish for the prior twelve months, I wrote in the July 22, 1982, issue of *PTR,* "We are in the embryonic stages of a new bull market. And for the first time since we turned bearish at the June 1981 top, we now want you to use all dips for buying." Three weeks later, the market touched its intraday low at 770 and the rest was history. One of the greatest bull markets in this century was launched.

At the other extreme, the public was absolutely euphoric in August of 1987. One leading financial magazine even wrote an article with the overly optimistic title, "Dow 3000: Not If, But When." The super bulls were tripping all over themselves to come up with higher and higher market projections; Dow 3,500 was considered a sure thing, and 4,000 was seen as reasonable because our prices were so much cheaper than those of the Japanese market. In this wildly bullish environment, I sounded like a real party pooper when I wrote in the September 17, 1987, issue of *PTR,* just days after the all-time high of 2,746 that "there are some ominous clouds forming on the horizon." In the following weeks, my technical indicators became more and more negative and I had subscribers build up substantial cash reserves. Then on October 15th, I wrote that "this is most definitely *not* a time to abandon a defensive posture." That following Monday, October 19th, saw the worst one day crash in history as the Dow dropped an incredible 508 points!

How did I do it? Simply by doing my technical homework and listening to the message of my long-term indicators. After you study this chapter, you too will be able to confidently spot major top and bottom areas with precision. I keep tabs on well over 100 technical indicators and report on the 50 best gauges in every issue of *PTR.* These 50 indicators comprise my *Weight of the Evidence,* which is how I judge the technical health of the market's three trends—long, intermediate, and short-term. My method differs from that of many other analysts who track a few gauges in which they have faith. The reason I favor my broad-based approach is because over the years I've learned that any technical tool, no matter how good its record, will throw you a curve at some point. If you lean too heavily on just a few indicators, your system will sooner or later take you out into left field. But if you learn to listen to the collective message of the majority of these fine gauges, your probabilities of ending up on the wrong wavelength are quite small.

While it's always important to keep in touch with the major trend, it's absolutely vital when the market moves into a high-risk zone (such as late 1972 and early October 1987), or a low-risk area (such as early 1975 and the summer of 1982). These are the times when false signals and whipsaws are most likely to pop up on your individual stock charts. By identifying when you are entering a high-risk area, you can build up large cash reserves and become extremely selective in your purchases. In addition, you can test the waters with a short sale or two. On the other hand, when our trusted indicators point out that the market is entering a low-risk zone, at the end of a bear market, it makes sense to start locking in profits on short sales, building up cash reserves, and getting ready to start doing selective buying.

At other times, when everything is strongly bullish (such as August 1982–June 1983), or clearly negative (such as January 1973–October 1974), you should move aggressively with the trend. It's therefore very important that you are always aware of the technical health, or lack thereof, of the market's major trend. I spent a lot of time reflecting before writing this chapter because I wanted to find the perfect middle-ground approach for you. Obviously, I'd like you to keep in touch with all 50 of my excellent technical gauges so you are very sharp when dealing with all the curve balls the market can throw at you. At the same time, I know you don't have the time and staff that I do to keep up so many indicators. So I carefully researched all of my technical tools and came up with those few that you need to follow to stay finely tuned to the major trend. These gauges are easy to keep up, and if you had listened to their majority opinion, you would have identified every bull and bear market over the past several decades.

STAGE ANALYSIS FOR
THE MARKET AVERAGES

The starting point is obvious. By now you should certainly feel very comfortable with stage analysis, so let's apply it to the market averages. This is one of the easiest gauges to keep up and yet is the most important one. You have no choice with this one. If you keep up just one long-term indicator, this is it. Track it in a weekly chart service or plot it yourself.

If you decide to keep up this indicator yourself, refer to page 313 in Chapter 9 which deals with calculating a moving average (MA). Every Friday, plot the closing price and write it on a data sheet. Then calculate and keep up a 30-week MA of that data.

Next, interpret the action. Just as with stage analysis for individual stocks, once a potential Stage 3 top forms on the DJIA, you must proceed with caution. Then when the Dow breaks below its 30-week MA and breaks down into Stage 4, it's time to become very defensive. Suspend buying even if you see a few stocks breaking out on their charts. Be sure to sell any stocks that are showing poor relative strength. Pull up your protective sell-stops as tightly

CHART 8–1

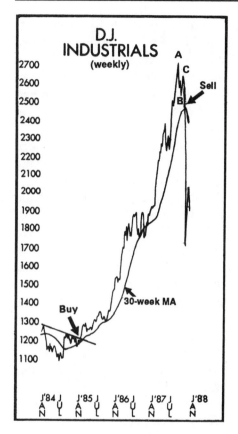

SOURCE: *The Professional Tape Reader*

as possible on your few remaining long positions. Finally, start
hunting for ideal short-sale patterns.

While this key long-term indicator certainly isn't infallible and
will give an occasional whipsaw signal, it is incredibly reliable. No
bear market in the past several decades has unfolded without this
gauge flashing a negative signal. Study Chart 8–1 and you'll see
one of the main reasons I turned bearish before the October 1987
crash. After moving above its 30-week MA in August 1984, and
then moving into Stage 2 in early 1985, the DJI had a real moonshot
on the upside. For the next two and a half years it was up, up, and

away as the average more than doubled while remaining above its rising 30-week MA.[1]

But in late 1987, some dangerous things began to happen. First, the average moved to a new high in late August (point A) before selling off sharply (to point B). This was followed by another rally in early October (point C) that failed to reach the August peak. This A, B, C sequence had an obvious toppy potential to it. When the DJI later broke below the prior low at point B, at least an intermediate-term top was signaled.

While these negative zig zags were taking place, an even more serious problem was taking shape. The 30-week MA was losing upside momentum and starting to level out. This gave the chart a worrisome Stage 3 appearance. The last strike was thrown at the market when it finally broke below the 30-week MA near 2,450. This was a strong Stage 4 sell signal, and a sign that the party was over. A new bear market was beginning. Within the next few sessions the market started to accelerate on the downside, suffering its greatest one-day percentage drop in history! While many others exclaim that the crash came out of the blue, you now know differently.

It was exactly the same in 1929. Many words have been written about that long-ago debacle, but few are true. I've seen some authors assert that the only way to have avoided the 1929 disaster was to have exited the market as early as 1928, when stocks started becoming really overvalued. Others have said that crash also was totally unpredictable. Nonsense. History and cycles truly do repeat themselves and, as the phrase goes, those who fail to learn from history are doomed to repeat it.

You didn't have to say goodbye to stocks in either 1928 or 1986 when they became fundamentally overvalued. If you had, you would have missed out on two fabulous rallies. In both cases, simply spotting the Stage 3 potential tops and then reacting to the

---

[1]The only time the Dow temporarily edged below the MA in late 1986, there was no negative signal given since the MA was still rising. In addition, the DJI never broke below support.

CHART 8-2

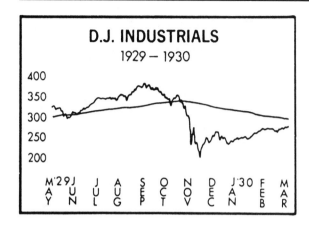

SOURCE: Dow Theory Letters

Stage 4 breakdowns of the 30-week MA would have put you far ahead of the Wall Street crowd (see Chart 8–2 of 1929 crash) while letting you stay safely in the game until the final inning.

Now study Chart 8–3, which shows the Stage 3 tops and eventual breakdowns into Stage 4 of the DJI for several bear markets. In every case, the story was the same. Once a Stage 3 top formed and the MA stopped rising, it was time to be careful. The final negative signal was a significant break below the 30-week MA. Thereafter, once the MA started heading south, you should have remained in your bear-market storm shelter until the MA showed signs of leveling out. Remember, it's not enough for the industrials to temporarily pop above the MA (as in late 1969) if the average continues pointing lower.

On the other hand, this important long-term indicator is not a Johnny-one-note type of gauge. Unlike many others that I've researched over the years, stage analysis is equally adept at spotting the start of bull and bear markets. After a major decline, once a Stage 1 base starts to form, it's time to get set for the next bull market signal (see Chart 8–4). Once the level 30-week MA is penetrated on the upside, it's time to look aggressively for buys on your stock charts.

CHART 8-3

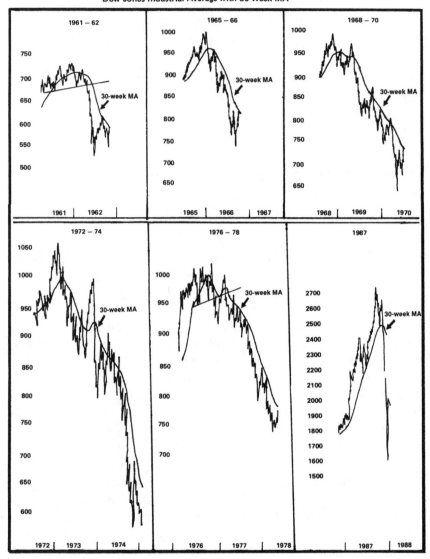

BEAR MARKET TOPS
Dow Jones Industrial Average with 30 Week MA

COURTESY OF MANSFIELD STOCK CHARTS

CHART 8–4

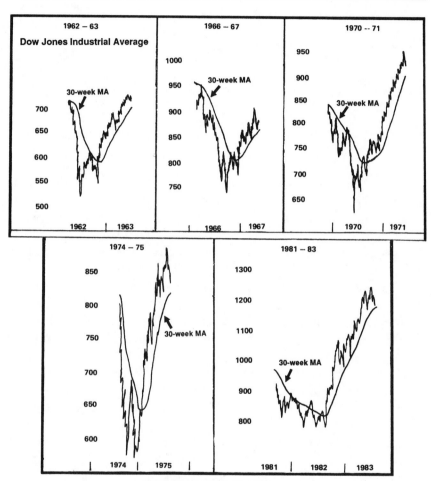

Bull Market Bottoms

THE ADVANCE-DECLINE LINE

The next important market indicator to track closely is the New York Stock Exchange (NYSE) advance-decline line. An A-D line takes the difference between the number of issues advancing on a given day (a positive number), and the number declining (a negative

CHART 8–5

Diaries			
NYSE	**FRI**	**THUR**	**11/13 WEEK**
Issues traded	2,004	2,015	2,175
Advances	692	1,296	820
Declines	912	386	1,135
Unchanged	400	333	220

SOURCE: Reprinted from *The Wall Street Journal,* November 16, 1987, p. 65, © Dow Jones & Company, Inc. 1987. All Rights Reserved.

figure). Here's how a day-to-day reading of the A-D line can help keep you on the right side of the market's primary trend. You can begin your calculations at any time by arbitrarily picking a large base number such as +50,000.[2] You then calculate the difference between advances and declines on a daily basis. For example, if 692 issues are up and 912 issues are down (see Chart 8–5 from *The Wall Street Journal's* Market Diary; disregard the unchanged issues), you come up with a net figure of −220. Subtract this number from your base figure of 50,000 and you get +49,780. If the next day's action produces more advances than declines, you add that number to the previous day's running total.

As long as both the advance-decline line and the DJI are moving higher in gear with each other, there's nothing to worry about; it's very unlikely that the market will experience even a significant correction. However, when this indicator starts to lose upside momentum as the DJI continues to charge higher, that's a *negative divergence* signalling market trouble ahead.[3] If the divergence takes place over a short period of time (several weeks), the decline is likely to turn out to be a correction within an ongoing bull market. If, however, the negative divergence continues to take shape over a long period of time (several months), that's a problem. On top of all this,

---

[2]The starting number you pick doesn't matter since the scale for the A-D line is arbitrary. It is a cumulative line that you will add to if there are more advances than declines each day, and subtract from if there are more declines than advances.

[3]After a rally to a new high in the DJI, and the advance-decline line or another market average refuses to confirm by also moving to a new high, that non-confirmation is a negative divergence. It is a reason to become defensive.

if the DJI and the A-D lines break down from important top formations, a new bear market is ready to descend on Wall Street. This clear-cut signal has worked time and again throughout market history. You are much more likely to see the A-D line reach its peak before the DJI because, as confidence wanes, money moves out of the secondary stocks and into the higher-quality blue chips. Historically, the NYSE advance-decline line reaches its ultimate peak five to ten months before the blue chips top out. Once the A-D line stops rising, start becoming more and more suspicious about how much longer the bull will be able to stay alive.

When it comes to a major bottom forming, the probabilities strongly favor that the DJI will reach its ultimate low and then refuse to drop further, while the A-D line continues to move lower and lower. Rather than being a negative sign, as many market players believe, this is actually a long-term positive indication. It is the opposite of the negative divergence that forms in a Stage 3 top and thus is called a *positive divergence*. Such a divergence shows that some sectors are starting to shape up even as others continue getting clubbed. Whether you're dealing with a top or a bottom, remember that the longer that a divergence lasts, the more significant the eventual reversal will be.

In *The Professional Tape Reader,* I keep up advance-decline lines for the New York Stock Exchange, American Stock Exchange, the over-the-counter market, and the Dow Jones Industrial Average. While all provide insight into the market's subsurface technical condition, the only one that is crucial for you to keep up is the NYSE advance-decline line. It's not only listed every day in the Market Diary of the *Wall Street Journal,* but in just about every local newspaper's financial section.

When you chart this gauge, make sure you graph it on the same chart as the Dow Jones Industrial Average. Both should be plotted on a daily basis. It will literally take you a matter of seconds to keep up this gauge, but it will vastly help you increase your profit potential. All you have to do is split your charting paper in half and come up with a reasonable scale for the DJI and chart that on top. On the lower half of the graph chart the cumulative figure each day for the NYSE advance-decline line. Decide that each line on your paper is worth a given amount of net units of advances over declines (say 200 units per line). On the next day, if the DJI closes down 20 points, find that point on the Dow graph, plot it, and draw the line. When dealing with that day's A-D data, if the prior day's reading was + 50,000 and today there are 200 more declines than advances, the cumulative figure of + 49,800 must be charted. Since each line equals 200 units, you drop down one line on the graph to chart today's reading. If, instead, there were 1,200 advances and 400 declines, then the net change for that day would be a reading of + 800 units. Thus you would move up four lines (since each line equals 200 units) to plot the A-D on your chart.

Market history is filled with examples of the NYSE advance-decline line reaching its peak prior to that of the DJI and refusing to go one bit higher no matter how much further the industrials surged ahead. This syndrome demonstrates a market advance which is becoming dangerously selective. As confidence lessens, more and more money flows out of the broad market and focuses on only the highest-quality companies. This is always an important early warning signal that the bull market's day of judgment is close by, and that you must watch your charts and indicators extra closely for further signs of the end.

Chart 8–6 illustrates this pattern perfectly. While the NYSE A-D line reached its peak in May of 1961 (point A), the DJI didn't stop climbing until late that year (point B). There was almost a seven-month lead time between the two peaks. Several non-confirmations cropped up along the way as the industrials moved to new highs in August, September, November, and December of 1961, while the A-D line refused to do likewise. This was ample warning that serious trouble was brewing. When the industrials broke below major support, as well as the 30-week MA, in early 1962, it clearly was time for the bear to start growling.

This same bearish syndrome appeared in 1965. First the A-D line topped out in May 1965, even though the DJI continued rising for nine more months. New DJI highs were registered in October 1965, and in January and February 1966, but all were unconfirmed by a new high in this important indicator. The advance-decline line's prior peak, as well as the series of unconfirmed new DJI highs, were strikes one and two. Strike three, and the signal that the 1966 bear market was getting underway, was the break below both key support and the 30-week MA in March of 1966.

CHART 8–6

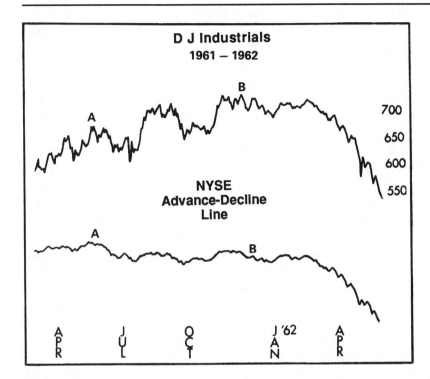

SOURCE: Dow Theory Letters

Perhaps the biggest and one of the best divergence warnings from the A-D line appeared in the March 1972–January 1973 period. This gauge reached its peak ten months before the January 1973 DJI top. In that long period of time, there were four new DJI highs that this indicator refused to confirm. This was a very powerful warning. It was hardly surprising that the DJI broke support as well as the 30-week MA in late January 1973, commencing the most devastating bear market in over 40 years.

Finally, this same tell-tale pattern appeared in 1987 before the worst one-day crash in the history of the market. While so many others were busy rationalizing that the crash was a product of our large budget and trade deficits, followers of this very reliable gauge knew differently. The two deficits were a silly excuse; they were both present as the market zoomed higher during the first eight months of 1987, as well as when it crashed.

The reality is that the market fell apart for the same reason it always gets walloped—it became too weak technically to advance any further. Whenever this happens, the path of least resistance is always down. Look at Chart 8–7 and you'll see that this excellent gauge was invaluable once again in 1987. The NYSE advance-decline line reached its peak in March 1987 (point A). At that point, the DJI was struggling to reach 2,400. In the next five months, the bearish advance-decline syndrome appeared in all its glory. The A-D Line huffed and puffed but could not blow past its March peak. Yet, during the same period, the DJI moved above 2,700. Four unconfirmed highs were registered by the DJI in April, June, July, and finally August 1987. By the time the Dow's intraday high at 2,746 was hit, the only argument that was taking place among most market players was how soon Dow 3,000 would be topped. This was significant foreshadowing, and a few weeks later when the DJI broke below its major support near 2,490 and then its 30-week MA, the die was cast. A bear market was in the cards. The only surprise was that what usually takes several months to accomplish occurred in just a few short weeks, as the computerized sell programs compressed the action.

It's important to be aware that a bullish divergence forms in a far different manner. After the 1929–32 crash both the NYSE advance-decline line and the DJI moved in synch on the downside. Then in July 1932 both gauges registered new lows before starting sharp rallies. Almost eight months later, in late February, 1933, an interesting phenomenon took place. The DJI hit bottom and then started to rally. The advance-decline line, however, told a different story. The A-D line continued declining throughout the entire month of March while the industrials rallied. This is typical action as a major bottom forms. Since confidence is naturally in short supply after a protracted decline, buyers are extremely cautious when they first put their toes back into the buying pond. Buyers initially gravitate toward the quality issues while shunning the more speculative ones. Therefore, it's not surprising that this favorable sequence of a new low in the A-D figures unconfirmed by a corresponding low in the DJI can be found at several major bottoms over the years.

CHART 8-7

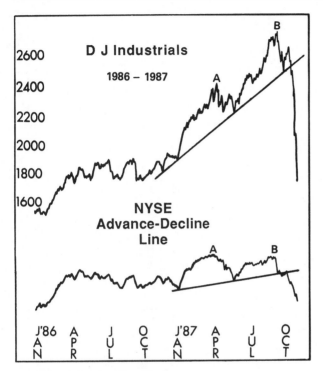

SOURCE: *The Professional Tape Reader*

Another textbook case of this phenomenon occurred in late 1957 (Chart 8–8). After being smashed in the second half of that year, the DJI hit bottom in October (point A). Over the next two months, all declines saw the industrials hold above the October low as a Stage 1 base started to form. But the A-D line remained under pressure during that period, and it broke to new lows (point B). This divergent action soon was followed by the great 1958–59 bull market.

This bullish pattern reappeared after the 1962 crash (see Chart 8–9). Those technicians who knew their market history were in a position to buy while the Street was in a panic over the Cuban missile crisis. The Dow reached its crash low in late June of that year (point A), months before the headline events. During the following eight weeks, both gauges enjoyed a nice technical rally.

CHART 8-8

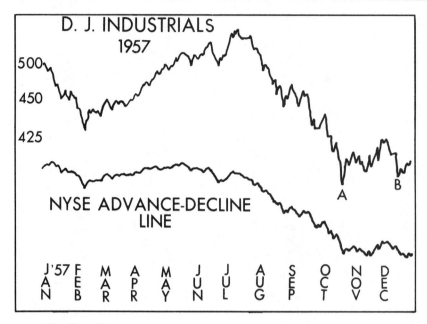

SOURCE: Dow Theory Letters

Then came the historic September–October selloff with Cuba, missiles, and Russian warships shaking up far more than just Wall Street (point B). Interestingly, amid all the fear and the A-D line hitting a new low, the DJI held on the one-yard line and refused to break below its June 1962 bottom. With anxiety at epic levels, this was a very powerful divergence signal. Once Khrushchev turned his ships around, the market started a fabulous three-and-a-half year bull market.

This very profitable pattern again appeared on the financial scene in mid–1970. After the wicked 1969–70 bear market, the DJI bottomed in May 1970, while the A-D line continued to crash until it finally hit its low in July. This was a great timing signal that the 1970–73 bull market was ready to go into orbit. Finally, this positive pattern showed up on the charts in the June–July 1984 period, after the January–July junior bear market. Within days, the incredibly powerful July 1984–August 1987 bull market was underway.

CHART 8–9

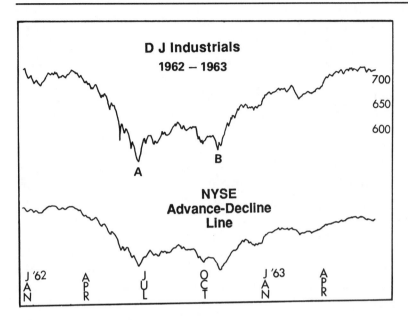

D J Industrials
1962 – 1963

NYSE
Advance-Decline
Line

SOURCE: Dow Theory Letters

MEASURING THE MARKET'S MOMENTUM

There are several other ways to use the NYSE advance-decline figures. Weekly figures give you another perspective for long-term analysis. Daily figures can also be charted on a point-and-figure basis rather than in the bar-chart manner that I've just taught you. Finally, short-term oscillators can be constructed for trading purposes. Each facet provides an added insight into what the market is up to. I use all of these in *The Professional Tape Reader* because I feel these important statistics are basic to technical analysis. But you can get a pretty good advance-decline overview if you just follow the daily figures on the divergence basis I just taught you, in conjunction with one other long-term method. This indicator has the advantage of being (1) very accurate, (2) easy to interpret, and (3) quick to calculate. I call this gauge my *momentum index (MI)*. It is actually a 200-day moving average of the NYSE advance-decline figures.

By measuring momentum in the market you are actually applying Newton's law of physics, except that when dealing with stocks it should be rephrased to say that *a trend in motion can be expected to continue until it reverses*. In other words, forget about minor zigs and zags and keep your eye on the major trend. This is where the momentum index (Chart 8–10) can help you.

The first step is to collect the NYSE advance-decline data for the latest 200 market sessions. If you are industrious, you can go to your local library and get the numbers from back issues of *Barron's*. If you don't have the time, simply start jotting down the figure as of today and in forty weeks you'll have a complete set of data. The next step is to add up all the pluses and minuses for the 200-day period. After you get this total, divide it by 200. This answer is today's momentum index.

After collecting the data for 200 days and calculating today's index number, this gauge is very simple to maintain if you use the following shortcut. There is no need to add up the entire 200 days of data again. As with calculating any MA, simply add the new day's data into your calculator (when adding, you enter whatever sign you see) and *subtract* the 201st day's data. When you subtract,

CHART 8–10

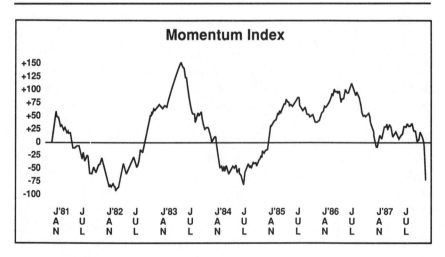

SOURCE: *The Professional Tape Reader*

you must remember that you have to reverse your sign.[4] Don't forget to physically cross out the 201st day on your data sheet; otherwise tomorrow you may not realize that it's already been taken out, and you'll mistakenly use the same day again. The final mechanical step is to take the difference of these two day's data (the new day and the 201st day) and divide it by 200. When you get that answer, add it to yesterday's MI reading and you have today's new momentum index.

Here's a real-life example of how to quickly execute this calculation. On November 11, 1987, the MI reading was minus 63. With this information in hand, let's see how you should have calculated the answer the next day. On November 12th, there were 941 more advances than declines on the New York Exchange. Thus I put a plus 941 in my calculator. Next I checked the data sheet and saw that the reading from the 201st day (January 29, 1987) was minus 82. Remembering to reverse signs, I entered a plus 82 into my calculator and crossed out that 201st day on my data sheet. The total of the plus 82 and plus 941 equals a plus 1,023. Divide the 1,023 by 200 and you get a reading of plus 5.1. The final step is to add the plus 5.1 to yesterday's momentum index reading of minus 63, yielding a new MI reading for November 12th of minus 57.9.

Over the years I've developed a few useful rules for interpreting this helpful indicator.

1. The most important signal is a crossing in either direction of the zero line. If the momentum index has been in negative territory and then crosses above the zero line, that's a favorable longer-term signal. On the other hand, a drop from positive to negative territory is a bearish indication.

2. The longer the time period that this gauge has been either above or below zero, the more meaningful the signal is when it moves across the zero line.

3. The most significant moves are those which take place when this indicator has been deep in positive or negative territory for

---

[4]If the data from the 201st day was a plus 400, you must enter it in your calculator as a minus 400. Conversely, if the 201st day that you're dropping was a minus 600, then you put it in the calculator as a plus 600.

quite a while and then crosses the zero line. This stands in contrast to those occasions when the MI hovers near the zero line and then pops across it.

4. The most meaningful bearish signals occur when the MI has been in positive territory for quite a while and, at the extreme, moved *far* above the zero line before giving a bearish signal.

5. In a bull market this gauge will almost always reach its peak *before* the Dow Jones Industrial Average does. Even though it may hang on to a marginally positive reading for the remainder of the bull market, an early warning signal is given even while it's still in positive territory by a sharp drop from its peak reading. One look at chart 8–10 will show you that the pre-crash action in 1987 was a textbook case of this syndrome in action. The MI actually reached its peak in mid–1986, even though the Dow had another year of bullish action ahead of it. While there was no reason to sell just because the MI was starting to lag, it was clear that it was becoming dangerously late in the day for the bull market. Note that even though the first eight months of 1987 were a bullish fantasy, this gauge was quite mediocre throughout that period. The fact that the Dow could move up so many hundreds of points and not have an impact on this indicator was certainly an important warning. In October, *before* the October 19th Black Monday crash, this indicator dropped into negative territory. This was yet another warning that contrary to Wall Street majority opinion, the coming decline was not a correction in an ongoing bull market but a full-fledged bear smash.

This long-term indicator has identified the onset of several other bear markets in very timely fashion. Excellent sell signals were flashed in January 1962, early 1969, early 1972, spring 1981, and January 1984.

This indicator is more helpful at spotting tops than bottoms. Sell signals generally come relatively early at tops, giving advance warning; but they are somewhat late at bottoms, acting more as a confirming signal. As long as you are aware of that, however, the MI can still be a great aid to you on the bullish side, too, by helping you distinguish flash-in-the-pan rallies from the real thing. Confirming buy signals were flashed in February 1961, the spring of 1963, April 1967, January 1971, early 1975, August 1982, and January 1985.

Over the years this fine long-term gauge has foreshadowed many important market moves. When combined with the few other long-term indicators that you're learning in this chapter, you have an excellent arsenal of technical tools to cut through the fog created by Wall Street and the media.

SIMPLE BUT EFFECTIVE

The next long-term indicator is very useful in gauging the market's true subsurface technical condition, but *don't* ever use it in a vacuum. It shouldn't be judged alone, but only as part of our team of indicators. Whereas the DJI in relation to its 30-week MA gives very specific signals, this gauge does not. It does tell us when the market's technical health is quietly starting to fail, even though everything may still look great on the surface. On the other hand, it will also often show subtle strengthening, even though the averages are still getting bombed. Its message will almost always be very early, giving you plenty of time to plan for a change in market direction. Then, when the majority of our other long-term indicators start to agree with this early signal, you'll know it's time to make an important move.

I want to stress the importance of keeping in touch with the new high-new low figures. There are actually a few different sets of figures and each is helpful in its own way. The most commonly followed high-low numbers are the daily ones published each morning in *The Wall Street Journal* and most local newspapers. These figures, however, are based on all stocks, including preferreds. While they are helpful, I prefer the common-stock-only data. They are harder to obtain but are available in some papers such as *Investor's Daily*. These figures are excellent for traders to track on a daily basis, as they often foreshadow very meaningful short-to-intermediate-term moves. I track them in *PTR* along with all of the other indicators that we've been going over. Since I want you to get the maximum return on your limited-time investment, I suggest you track the weekly figures rather than the daily ones. The weekly new highs and new lows will point out much more meaningful moves and also filter out a lot of trading static that investors don't need to be concerned with. Also, you'll save a lot of time in keeping up the indicator.

Now that we've settled on the weekly data, we're still presented with another choice. Just as with the daily figures, there are the conventional figures which appear in most newspapers (and are based on all stocks, including preferreds) and those that reflect common stocks only. While both are useful, and I keep an eye on both sets of statistics, I again prefer the common-stock-only weekly figures.[5]

To see the subtle differences in the two sets of data, let's examine the numbers for the trading week ending October 23, 1987. This was the crash week that included Black Monday, October 19th. The conventional NYSE figures showed 12 new weekly highs versus 1,516 new weekly lows. To calculate this indicator subtract new lows (which are negative) from new highs (which are positive). The net reading for this week was a minus 1,504. This was one of the largest negative readings in market history.

The corresponding weekly figures for the common stocks only were 8 new highs versus 1,058 new lows. The net figure was a minus 1,051. You can see that when you exclude preferred stocks, warrants, and the like, there is a significant difference in the sizes of the two numbers, although not usually in the overall direction. So although the common-stock-only figures are preferable, if you have to use the conventional data, it is still valid. The greatest variance between the two sets of data occur when interest rates stage a significant move, which has a profound impact on preferred stocks.

As you have already seen, the calculation is easy. When it comes to charting, all you have to do is set up a scale for the DJI on the upper half of your graph paper and one for this gauge on the lower half. Each weekend, plot the closing Friday DJI level versus this figure.

Now let's move on to interpretation. While there are several ways to use this data, I find two to be easiest and most profitable.

First, when this gauge is consistently in positive territory, it is a favorable long-term indication. When it is in negative territory week after week, you're dealing with an unhealthy market.

---

[5]One problem: they are difficult to find in most newspapers. One source is *M/G Financial Weekly,* P.O. Box 32333, Richmond, VA 23293.

Second, when an important divergence takes shape, a reversal in the trend is starting to form. A perfect example stands out on Chart 8–11, in 1982 (point E). Even though this gauge remained in negative territory—showing that the major trend was still bearish—something very bullish and exciting was taking place. While the DJI continued to move lower and lower throughout the first eight months of 1982, this key indicator started trending higher during that period. This showed that fewer and fewer stocks were actually following the widely-watched average in its downward direction; it was a sign of subsurface technical strengthening. This was a perfect case of a positive divergence and was one of several key non-confirmations that helped me turn bullish in July of that year, before the historic bull market started in August. In the same manner, in late 1974 the market continued to move sharply lower while this gauge started sloping gently higher. This was a beautiful foreshadowing of the powerful 1975–76 bull market.

On the other hand, while the DJI was moving higher in the late 1972–early 1973 period, the differential was trending lower (point A). This action clearly tipped off the coming 1973–74 bear market. The same pattern again was in evidence in late 1976 (point C), early 1981 (point D), and late 1983. All three negative signals occurred right before significant bear markets.

Now look at the 1987 super rally (point G). While the market zoomed ahead, this indicator refused to move higher and actually trended somewhat lower. This showed that something was rotten beneath the surface. When the gauge further weakened in October, in tandem with several of our other indicators, you knew that big trouble was on the way. The October '87 crash certainly fulfilled that prophecy. It should therefore be obvious that this easy-to-construct long-term indicator is one that you must always keep an eye on!

NO ISOLATIONISM HERE

With today's instant communications, and all of the United States trading partners having more than a passing interest in the strength of our dollar, the foreign stock markets are more tuned in to each

CHART 8–11

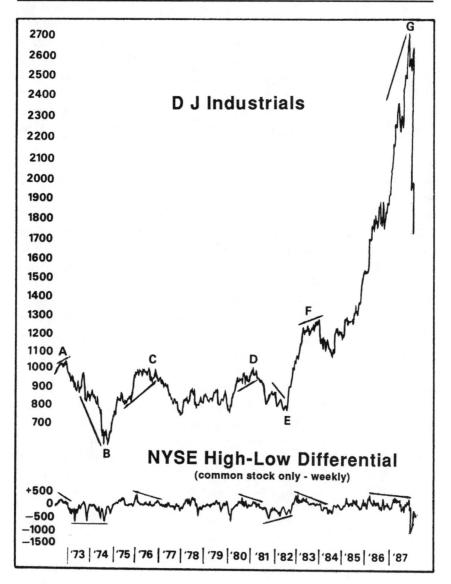

SOURCE: *The Professional Tape Reader*

CHART 8–12

Global Stock Markets

		In Local Currencies			In U.S. Dollars[1]	
Index	% Change	11/12	52-wk Range	% Change	11/12	52-wk Range
The World	−2.0	312.1	410.2- 295.9	−2.2	390.9	495.9- 334.1
E.A.F.E.[2]	−2.0	438.2	574.5- 412.5	−2.3	703.6	876.1- 550.0
Australia	−2.2	234.7	433.2- 222.2	−1.1	143.0	285.3- 135.0
Austria	−4.6	202.0	270.2- 197.8	−5.2	441.8	532.2- 421.6
Belgium	+1.1	270.0	395.0- 261.5	+0.6	380.2	514.1- 339.6
Canada	−0.9	330.7	460.4- 316.3	+0.0	271.4	374.5- 252.2
Denmark	−1.1	339.2	417.5- 334.9	−1.5	390.0	463.5- 345.2
France	−2.5	301.7	467.6- 278.3	−3.1	292.1	427.4- 271.9
Germany	−2.9	164.8	264.0- 147.3	−3.3	357.2	505.4- 326.7
Hong Kong	+7.2	1517.5	2803.4-1415.0	+7.3	1080.0	1994.1-1006.6
Italy	−1.4	387.4	598.9- 370.4	−1.7	194.7	290.0- 187.8
Japan	−4.5	1047.8	1360.1- 835.0	−4.8	2782.1	3439.2-1831.5
Mexico	+6.1	36186.4	78086.-7592.2	+4.5	269.2	618.2- 115.2
Netherlands	+4.6	229.2	332.5- 199.8	+4.4	436.7	567.3- 389.8
Norway	−3.9	426.8	728.5- 370.4	−4.7	474.0	784.3- 417.6
Sing/Malays	−1.9	454.3	848.3- 442.8	−1.8	682.3	1236.4- 666.7
Spain	−3.5	198.1	284.6- 163.0	−4.6	121.6	163.7- 84.2
Sweden	−4.8	689.8	1058.3- 655.2	−5.4	585.3	857.3- 560.7
Switzerland	−0.5	150.3	220.7- 138.6	−1.1	464.4	619.6- 440.5
U.K.	+3.6	509.8	736.2- 469.5	+3.1	374.8	500.7- 280.8
U.S.A.	−2.2	232.8	313.9- 210.5	−2.2	232.8	313.9- 210.5

Base: Jan. 1, 1970=100
[1]Adjusted for foreign exchange fluctuations relative to the U.S. $.
[2]Europe, Australia, Far East Index.
Source: Morgan Stanley Capital International Perspective, Geneva.

Source: Barron's

other than ever before. Properly interpreted, this increasing inter-dependence can be a very useful long-term indicator for our market.

It is very easy to keep track of what is going on around the globe by utilizing the statistics that *Barron's* reports each weekend in their International Trader section (see Chart 8–12).[6] They report

[6]In addition, they have an excellent Market Laboratory section in the back of the paper that makes the publication very worthwhile for any serious technician.

on 18 world stock markets in addition to our own. Prices for all markets are given in terms of local currencies and U.S. dollars. Since the dollar has gyrated in yo-yo fashion in recent years, I find it more meaningful to use the local currency prices. All you have to do is chart these markets on a weekly basis and watch for significant chart formations.

My studies have convinced me that the most profitable market moves in the United States occur when the overwhelming majority of world markets are in agreement. This is true on both the upside and downside. Way back in early 1973, *PTR* stated, "The London Industrials staged the sharpest single day's drop in its entire history . . . a broad top has been completed and a bear trend clearly established . . . but rather than fret about the losses Britons are in for, keep in mind the serious warning this leading indicator is for our own market." Both their market and ours soon crashed.

It wasn't just London (Chart 8–13) that got in trouble. *All* of the foreign markets did. Australia, France, London, Japan, and West Germany were especially negative, breaking down from major Stage 3 top patterns. France (Chart 8–14) gave an especially timely sell signal as it broke below major support and completed its top in late 1972, several weeks ahead of the DJI's peak in January 1973.

The same story line unfolded in 1981 right before the April 1981–August 1982 bear market blindsided Wall Street. Austria (Chart 8–15)

CHART 8–13

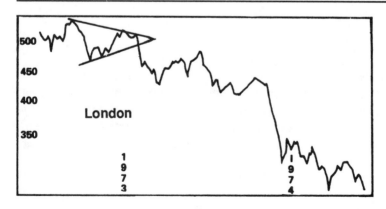

SOURCE: *The Professional Tape Reader*

CHART 8–14

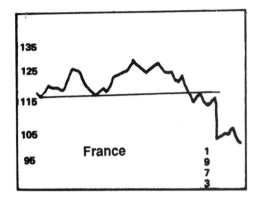

SOURCE: *The Professional Tape Reader*

CHART 8–15

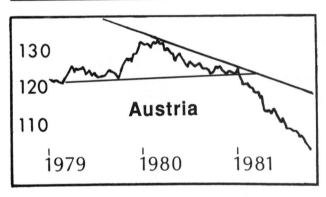

SOURCE: *The Professional Tape Reader*

flashed a bear-market signal in early 1981, several months before the U.S. market topped out. In addition, France (Chart 8–16) once again was right there with its bear-market signal as our market was reaching its peak. Both of these early warnings made it clear that it was time for you to get your investing house in order, as the probabilities were high that bearish trouble would soon reach our shores. Just in case there was any doubt, Australia, Canada, Hong Kong, and Singapore all chimed in with their own bearish message. The end result

CHART 8–16

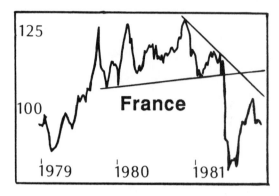

SOURCE: *The Professional Tape Reader*

was a very rough 16 months as the 1981–82 bear market ran its course.

The good news is that this long-term indicator works equally well on the bullish side. Amid all of the gloom and doom that was rampant on Wall Street back in the first half of 1982, this gauge was definitely an early ray of sunshine. The United Kingdom (Chart 8–17) started trending higher in late 1981, and both the Netherlands and West Germany formed solid Stage 1 bases while our own bear market ground relentlessly lower. Then all three confirmed that bullish tidings were ahead for our market starting in the second half of 1982, as they all staged major upside breakouts.

It's obvious this is a financial pulse that you want to monitor closely. However, it does demand considerable time, so here's good news: A simple way to follow this indicator is to chart *only* the world market average on a weekly basis. *Barron's* supplies this number in its table of Global Stock Markets (Chart 8–12). It will give you a very close approximation of what is going on with all of the foreign stock markets. Just chart it each weekend. In addition, calculate and chart a 30-week MA for the data.

As you can see on Chart 8–18, this key long-term gauge flashed an important buy signal when it moved above its 30-week MA in the summer of 1982 (point A). It remained in a favorable position until the late-1983 period when a Stage 3 top formed. Thereafter, in early 1984 this average weakened even further, breaking below

CHART 8–17

SOURCE: *The Professional Tape Reader*

CHART 8–18

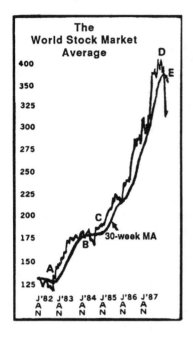

The
World Stock Market
Average

SOURCE: *The Professional Tape Reader*

the MA (point B). This negative action correctly dovetailed with the January–July 1984 junior bear market. This gauge showed exceptional strength later in 1984 (point C) as it broke out on the upside ahead of the U.S. market. This proved to be an excellent signal of the exciting 1985–August 1987 bull move that was gathering steam in the United States. Then after close to three years of incredible strength, the world average started tracing out a clearcut Stage 3 top (point D). This was another reason to become defensive after the August peak in the United States. Finally, once key support and the 30-week MA were violated in October (point E), you had another clear sign that to continue dreaming about Dow 3,000 would be suicidal!

AS GM GOES . . .

During the late 1950s, cabinet member Charles Wilson commented that "what's good for GM is good for America." General Motors is no longer the dominant corporation it was then, but it still casts a very long shadow. The market is not a democracy. The bullish and bearish votes that each stock casts toward the major trend most definitely do not count equally. The most heavily traded and owned institutional favorites matter far more than the over-the-counter secondary stocks. Of all these shakers and movers, there is one that you must always keep your eyes glued to—General Motors. Never listen to the message of this key stock in a vacuum, but when it flashes a major signal that is in synch with the majority of the gauges in this chapter, *do not ignore it!*

An added bonus is that this indicator takes so little time to follow. Just be sure to note General Motors' action when you flip through your charts. There is a popular method that many use to measure this key stock's health (or lack thereof). It's called the four-month rule. Simply stated, if GM doesn't make a new high (or low) within four months, it is a signal that GM's prevailing trend is reversing. Over 70 percent of the signals of the four-month rule have been profitable in the past 50-plus years. Even more impressive is the fact that not one of its failures was off by much more than 10 percent. And to its credit, many of the signals on the plus side scored fabulous gains.

I follow the four-month rule in *PTR,* and it's worthwhile for you to do so also. But what I've found to be far more helpful in timing the market is to apply stage analysis to the General Motors chart. If the two methods disagree, *always* go with the message being flashed by our charting technique. When it completes a Stage 3 top and breaks down into Stage 4, it's time to worry even if a new GM high was hit last month. The reverse is true when General Motors breaks out of a Stage 1 base. One other factor to bring into the picture is the concept of divergence analysis, with which you should now feel more comfortable. When GM refuses to make a new high (or low) in tandem with the DJI and the other leading averages, it's an early warning that you'd better be alert.

Chart 8–19 shows an excellent example of GM helping to spot an important bottom. During the 1973–74 bear market, new lows came along on schedule to verify that the worst bear slide in a generation was intact. But in mid–1974, life changed for GM. First it broke above its downtrend line, next it completed a double bottom, and finally it jumped above its 30-week MA. This very favorable signal coincided with the start of the dynamic 1975–76 bull market.

CHART 8–19

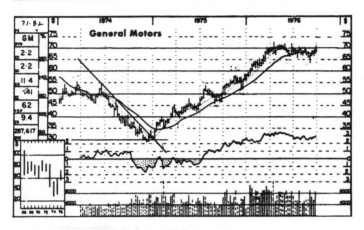

COURTESY OF MANSFIELD STOCK CHARTS

The market was no more tricky during the 1981–82 bear trend (Chart 8–20). While the averages moved relentlessly lower, GM started to form a Stage 1 base as early as the first quarter of 1982. In May of that year, the stock moved into Stage 2, which was a very early warning that the bear was close to expiring. Interestingly, I turned bullish in July when the majority of my indicators finally got in favorable gear with GM; but it wasn't until August that the market averages hit their bear-market low and the bull was born. Don't believe what so many market players do—that you have to bargain-hunt because bear markets reverse so quickly. This is absolutely not true! There is plenty of technical foreshadowing that takes place before an upturn materializes. When you do your technical homework, you'll spot it.

Unlike some gauges, such as my momentum index, the GM signals at tops are as timely as those flashed at major lows. In early 1966, GM flashed danger as it refused to better its 1965 high, even though the DJI catapulted to a new peak reading. This divergence was an important warning. Another negative signal was the poor relative strength and toppy Stage 3 action that formed in early 1966. Finally, there could no longer be doubt that trouble was on its way once it broke below support and the MA. Soon thereafter, the 1966 bear market was in the record books as prices broke sharply.

CHART 8–20

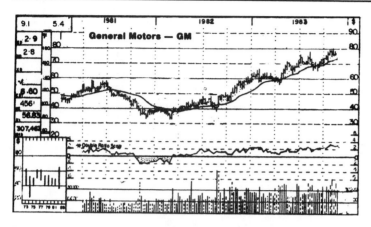

COURTESY OF MANSFIELD STOCK CHARTS

This indicator didn't tip off the 1969–70 bear market—that would be too subtle. It yelled it! While the DJI moved back within inches of its 1966 high in December 1968, GM failed miserably. It didn't come close to its 1966 high, and in early 1969 it broke below its MA. Trouble was on the way.

GM did an equally good job of warning of danger before the 1973–74 bear market. Not only did GM not move to a new high in January 1973, as did the DJI, it couldn't even come close to its 1971 peak. That divergence was scary. And when it smashed below support and the 30-week MA in early 1973 (see Chart 8–21), you should have known it was time to turn away from the good news and start selling.

Finally, let's examine more recent action. Did this indicator offer any selling clues before the historic October 1987 crash? You bet it did! As with every other gauge in this chapter, GM said sell before the 1987 crash. Look at the 1987 price action in Chart 8–22. Even though General Motors hit a new high that August, trouble was signaled only a few weeks later. This is why I always place much greater emphasis on flexible systems like stage analysis than a rigid system like the four-month rule. Those investors and analysts who blindly follow the latter method believed there would be nothing to worry about at least until December. But when you look at the chart, you

CHART 8-21

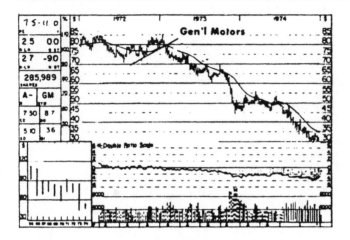

COURTESY OF MANSFIELD STOCK CHARTS

CHART 8-22

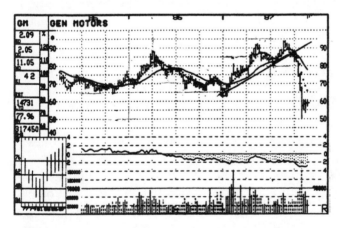

COURTESY OF MANSFIELD STOCK CHARTS

should see why danger was clearly signaled in the late September–early October period. GM suddenly reversed and first broke below its long-term uptrend line. Then it violated its 30-week MA. While all of this was taking place, the DJI was rallying from near 2,500 up to the mid-2,600s. This was a reason to be concerned. If the other few gauges that you've just learned were in fine shape, you could have worried a bit less. But *every* one of these indicators was in poor shape. I therefore advised *PTR* subscribers to move to a very defensive position. Remember, it's tough for any market to go up in a sustained attack if GM can't join in; and equally hard for the bear to keep its grip if GM refuses to go down. Therefore, this simple indicator is one to watch closely. When it flashes a definitive signal that is in harmony with the majority of this chapter's excellent long-term gauges, you'll be ignoring its message at your own peril.

CHEAP OR DEAR

This next long-term gauge shows that I really am a pragmatist. Although I strongly believe in the technical approach, I always strive to be as objective as possible. When giving seminars, I often joke that if throwing darts at the stock listings would give me the right answer 80 percent of the time, it would become the 51st indicator in *PTR's* "Weight of the Evidence." Technical or fundamental, all I want is greater insight into tomorrow's likely market action. Unfortunately, the predictive value of most of the fundamental gauges that I've tested isn't reliable enough. A few are, however, and the best one is the price/dividend ratio. This very long-term tool expresses stock prices as multiples of dividends. In other words, what would it cost you—in terms of stock price—to buy a dollar's worth of dividends?

Before digging deeper into the theory, here's how to calculate the P/D ratio. Each weekend in *Barron's* Market Laboratory section, there is a table (see Chart 8–23) titled "Indexes' P/Es & Yields." The *Barron's* of November 23, 1987, had the following input: The yield on the Dow Jones industrial average as of the close on November 20th was 3.58 percent. Elsewhere in the Market Laboratory section we find out that the DJI closed at 1,914. The

CHART 8–23

Indexes' P/Es & Yields	Last Week	Prev. Week	Year Ago Week
DJ Ind.-P/E	15.2	15.3	15.9
Yield, %	3.58	3.54	3.64

SOURCE: Reprinted from *Barron's,* November 23, 1987, p. 154,

next step is to multiply the DJI close by the percentage yield (DJI Friday's close times percent DJI yield equals dividend payout of DJI). In this case, the figure is 68.52 (1914 times 3.58 percent—which must be changed to .0358 when put in decimal form—equals 68.52). That $68.52 is the amount of dividend currently being paid by the 30 Dow blue chips. We are now ready for the final step. Since the indicator is the price/dividend ratio, all that we now have to do is plug in the price of the DJI and then divide by the dividend (1,914 divided by 68.52). This gives us a P/D ratio reading of 27.9 (round the decimal off to one place).[7]

We're now ready to swing into action. This very-long-term gauge is excellent for spotting *major* top and bottom zones. Everyone talks in terms of the market being cheap or expensive, but that is subjective. This, however, is a way of objectively deciding. Declines in the P/D ratio toward the 14 to 17 area have appeared at times when common stocks were uncommon bargains. On the other hand, when stocks become dear in terms of their return, then it's time to be on guard against a major top forming. A move above 26 has historically been a dangerous reading, while a figure above 30 has been a sign that stocks are extremely overvalued.

Before going further, make sure you realize that although this is not a pinpoint indicator, it is incredibly helpful, but *only* when used in conjunction with the timing gauges in this chapter. Understand that a favorable or unfavorable signal will often appear well

---

[7]Now that you understand the theory behind the gauge, the quick way to calculate is simply to divide 100 by the percentage yield (i.e., 100 divided by 3.58 = 27.9).

CHART 8–24

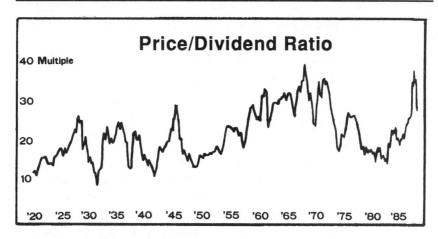

SOURCE: *The Professional Tape Reader*

before it is time to take action. A bearish figure means the market is entering a high-risk zone that will almost surely be followed by a crash. But that bear market may still be a year or more away. So if all of our other long-term indicators are still bullish, continue to play the long side with a close eye on the exit. The opposite is true when this gauge turns favorable. A perfect example occurred when the P/D ratio dropped to a very low and favorable level in 1932. This gauge correctly showed that an incredible bull market was in the wings, but you shouldn't have become aggressively bullish until our timing tools (such as the DJI in relation to its MA) turned positive.

On the favorable side, very bullish readings were registered in 1932, 1937, 1942, 1949, 1974, and 1980. Each and every one was followed by a very profitable bull market. But some readings, such as those registered in 1932, 1942, and 1980, were over a year early. So view this indicator as one that spots a bullish or bearish potential forming, but until the spark (which our timing gauges spot) occurs there is no explosion, even though gas is pouring into the room.

On the negative side, high-risk levels were reached in 1929, 1936, 1939, 1959, 1961, 1965, 1968, 1972, and 1987. The 1987 signal was especially helpful as the price/dividend ratio neared the 40 level—the most dangerous reading of the previous 20 years and one of the highest in history! It's not surprising that the October 1987 crash was so severe, since this gauge was showing plenty of excesses to be wrung out of the tape. Once again, this ratio turned clearly negative in early 1987, though the majority of our other long-term indicators didn't join the bearish party until after the August 1987 peak.

GOING AGAINST THE CROWD

All of the gauges that we've been reviewing have at least one thing in common—they are objectively measurable. They are all based on specific statistics (such as advances and declines, or new highs and new lows). There is one indicator, however, which is subjective and doesn't rely on any specific signals, yet is very helpful. It's known as the *theory of contrary opinion.*

This theory relates to the innate herd instinct that afflicts investors.[8] A basic tenet of this theory is that people feel most secure when they are in the mainstream. For this reason, investors form a consensus opinion. They reinforce each other's beliefs and block out evidence that would support other conclusions. In the market, this behavior leads to excessive optimism just before a crash, and general pessimism at the very bottom. People who use the theory of contrary opinion to good effect try to find out what the consensus opinion is, then act in just the opposite manner.

Before going any further, I want to caution you. Contrary opinion (CO) is a very valuable tool when used properly. Unfortunately, not one investor in a hundred really understands it, although everybody and his broker wants to be sophisticated and think they are using CO. Do not make the mistake of so many contrary-opinion buffs and try to force an answer from CO every week or even every few months. A true CO signal may not arise for a year or more. It is only valid when a prevailing theme starts to play through the media and is thoroughly accepted from Wall Street to Main Street. Don't think CO consists of merely calling

---

[8]One of the best practitioners of contrary opinion was Garfield Drew who for many years wrote *The Drew Odd Lot Studies.*

your broker, finding out he is bullish, and then deciding you are bearish. The trick is to wait for a very obvious one-sided opinion to form, whereby everybody suddenly believes he knows something, and then to become suspicious of that conventional wisdom. I thoroughly believe in the slogan that says, "When everybody knows something, it isn't worth knowing."

When a truly one-sided opinion really grabs the Street, it becomes so heavy you can almost cut it with a knife. One other word of caution: I disagree with those who believe that contrary opinion alone is enough. Not true. I view CO as a psychological potential, just as the price/dividend ratio represents a value potential. Neither one should ever make you buy or sell stocks if all the timing gauges disagree. When CO gets the agreement of the other technical tools, then get set, because a big market move is getting ready to unfold.

The next question is: How should you try to judge contrary opinion? Most analysts choose to use the bullish and bearish sentiment figures that are compiled by services such as Investors Intelligence.[9] While I track these figures and do find them useful, they fluctuate quite a bit. For really major signals, I much prefer to skim through the financial press. Magazine and newspaper headline writers don't mean to be an indicator, but are they! Since they are trying to sell papers, they want to hit the right nerve. If they sense that the public is jittery, fear is what they feature; while in bullish times, we see a steady torrent of optimistic headlines.

A headline or magazine cover is often all that is needed to trigger a prompt "that's got to be wrong" response on your part. Then, when our other indicators agree, you know the market is ready for a really important move. A perfect example of the cover-story syndrome was provided in late 1974. After the worst bear market since 1929, one of the leading financial magazines put a picture of a big black scary bear on its cover. For emphasis, they showed the bear knocking down the pillars of Wall Street. Since so many of my other long-term indicators were also turning positive at the time, this was a perfect time to disregard the fear syndrome gripping Wall Street and start buying.

---

[9]Investors Intelligence, 30 Church Street, New Rochelle, NY 10801.

Another classic contrary-opinion signal was flashed in the summer of 1978. A different major business magazine ran a cover story titled "The Death of Equities." Not surprisingly, the market staged a major advance that lasted almost three years. Harder to believe—but just as true—that same magazine ran a new story on the same topic five years later. This time they featured a charging bull on the cover with a headline that read "The Rebirth of Equities." Interestingly, this was late in the spring of 1983. Only a few weeks later, in June, speculative stocks registered a major high and then crashed. The blue chips struggled higher for a few more months before getting hit hard in the January–July 1984 junior bear market.

I don't mean to pick on any specific magazine or newspaper, because the media is merely representing the psychology of the moment. Just be aware that it shows up time after time in the press, and you have to learn to use it properly rather than letting it wrongly affect you.

Even better than *a* headline are *many* headlines, all reinforcing the same sentiment. Look at the montage (Chart 8–25) that appeared in *The Professional Tape Reader* in late 1974 and you'll see

CHART 8–25

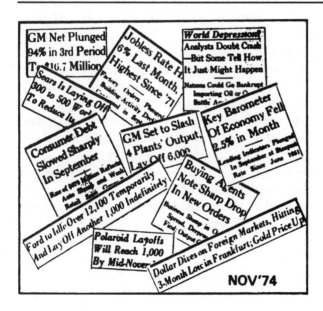

CHART 8–26

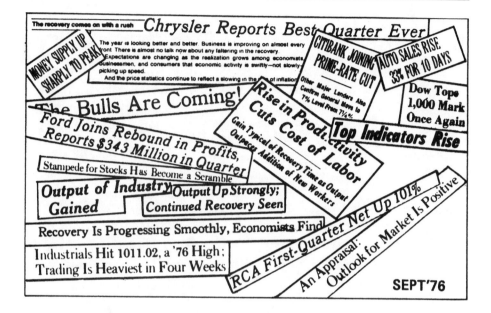

exactly what I mean. After the devastating 1973–74 bear smash, headlines spoke of huge layoffs, plunging earnings, and a possible world depression. We all know, or should know, that the market is supposed to top out on good news and hit bottom on bad news. All too many investors forget that truism and move *with* the news. Headlines reporting such scary news drive the consensus of opinion to believe the market is going to crash much further. That's when an important bottom is invariably formed. It's no coincidence that the market at the time of these headlines was within a few weeks of terminating its worst crash since the Great Depression.

Now shift your attention to Chart 8–26. When I ran this montage of overoptimism, the Street was really whipping itself into a bullish frenzy. One of the most prestigious newspapers in the country told us "The Bulls Are Coming!" In addition, the prime rate was dropping and earnings were rising. Wouldn't you know that the market was within days of reaching its 1976 peak of 1,026. Since so many of the long-term indicators were also turning negative, it was very predictable that the September 1976–February 1978 bear market was starting.

CHART 8–27

The pattern is always the same. Another fine example of contrary opinion was provided in the summer of 1982 (Chart 8–27). While so many analysts and investors were convinced that a severe recession and Dow 500 were just around the corner, I flashed a major buy signal because the overwhelming majority of my key indicators turned positive against this negative news backup.

Finally, let's examine what the psychological climate was in 1987 as that major top was forming. One of the scariest headlines from a CO point of view was the one I reprinted in late August that said "Dow 3,000: Not If, But When." (Chart 8–28) For a major financial magazine to feel so strongly that the upside was the only side was a significant signal. Added to my other technical gauges that were weakening, this caused me to adopt a very defensive position which helped *PTR* subscribers sidestep the historic 1987

CHART 8–28

crash. To make matters worse, once the market started sliding, it was met with calm rather than panic.

From now on, be very aware of headlines. When this indicator finally speaks, and when it gets agreement from our other gauges, be sure you listen to its message.

CHAPTER 9

ODDS, ENDS, AND PROFITS

You're almost there! If you never learn a winning market tactic other than those I've already taught you, you're going to do very well in the market—as long as you faithfully apply my techniques. Now we're going to put the finishing touches on your education. To refer back to our tennis analogy, you definitely know enough to be a winner, but now you're going to learn the advanced techniques that can make you a champion. Now that you have mastered stage analysis, be aware there are several other areas beside stocks where it can be applied very profitably!

FUN WITH FUNDS

The first area to move into is that of mutual funds. This is a game that is both easy to master and has relatively low risk. Most investors view mutual funds as very long-term investments that should be bought and locked away through thick and thin. This is foolish for several reasons. First, once you know how to time major moves, why in the world would you want to sit through a Stage 4 bear trend? Second, more and more funds have gone the no-load or low-load route.[1] Finally, there are now many funds that offer both an

---

[1] No-load funds charge no fee for buying or selling the fund. It is purchased and sold at the net asset value. A low-load fund charges a relatively small fee, usually in the 2 to 3 percent area.

aggressive stock fund as well as a money market fund. To induce you to keep your money in their coffers, they allow switching back and forth between funds, usually with just a phone call. This immediately sets up the potential for a very profitable trading and investing game. All we have to do is buy an aggressive fund when the market turns clearly bullish (such as in mid–1982 and late 1986), and sell and move into a money market fund when Stage 4 appears (as in January 1984 and early October 1987).

When I first started recommending mutual-fund switching many years ago, there were only a handful of funds that offered this opportunity. But the growth of the mutual fund industry has made it commonplace.

The weekly chart of Stein Roe Capital Opportunity (Chart 9–1) shows how easy it is to implement this strategy. In the summer of 1982, the 30-week moving average finally leveled out after trending lower for 14 months. Then, when the fund moved above its 30-week MA at $13.50, a low-risk buy signal was flashed. Since you can't physically place sell-stops on mutual funds, you must use mental stops (meaning that if it closes below your sell-stop point, you'll immediately call the fund and sell it). In this case the stop should have been set initially under the low at point A. Once this chart turned favorable it was simply a matter of holding on while the fund rocketed higher. One year later when Stein Roe broke below its MA, it was time to move out of the aggressive fund into a money market fund with a 100 percent profit in hand.

The advantage of using mutual funds to capitalize on the market's cycles is that you don't have to pore over page after page of individual stock charts. All you have to do is keep up a few charts of some of the better-acting funds along with their 30-week MAs.[2] This only takes a few minutes on the weekend and is well worth the effort.

If you aren't familiar with how to calculate a 30-week MA, relax. First, reread my description of the moving average in Chapter 1. Then come back to this example and you'll get it easily.

---

[2]Later in this chapter, I'll list some no-load mutual funds that allow telephone switching and which have had a good record over the past several years.

CHART 9–1

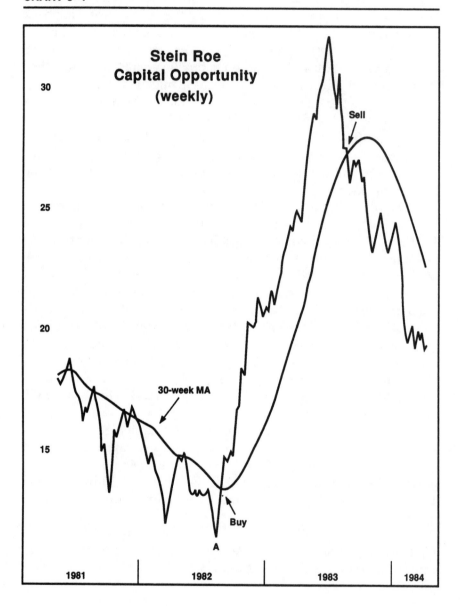

Stein Roe
Capital Opportunity
(weekly)

Fund XYZ (Chart 9–2) had the following weekly (Friday) prices over the past 30 weeks:

CHART 9–2

	How to Construct a 30-Week MA				
Week	Price	Week	Price	30-Week Total	30-Week MA
1	30.0	16	28.0		
2	29.5	17	27.9		
3	29.2	18	28.0		
4	29.5	19	28.1		
5	29.6	20	28.0		
6	29.4	21	27.9		
7	29.2	22	27.8		
8	29.0	23	27.7		
9	28.8	24	27.8		
10	28.9	25	27.9		
11	28.8	26	28.0		
12	28.6	27	27.7		
13	28.5	28	27.6		
14	28.4	29	27.5		
15	28.3	30	27.4	853.0	28.43
		31	27.2	850.2	28.34

To get the first plot for your 30-week MA, simply add up the 30 weeks on your calculator or computer and get the total (853). Put that answer in the total column. Then divide by 30 and you have your starting point for the MA (28.43). In the following weeks, there is no need to repeat the lengthy process of adding up the new 30 weeks. Simply add the 31st week (27.2) to last week's total, then subtract out the oldest week (the oldest week's total in this case is 30.0—remember to cross it out on your data sheet) from last week's total of 853. This gives you a new total of 850.2. Divide by 30 and you have the new 30-week MA of 28.34. With this method and a pocket calculator you can keep up several moving averages with just a few minutes work.[3]

The weekly chart of the Value Line Special Situation Fund (Chart 9–3) shows that after getting a buy signal in late 1986, you would have gotten an even more timely sell signal in early October 1987 before the historic crash. The decline that took place within the next few weeks was nothing short of astounding. By following

---

[3]When your fund has an ex-dividend in excess of 3% you should adjust your chart. Simply subtract the amount of the dividend from the current price and place on the new scale. As for the MA, subtract the dividend from the prior 30 week's data and re-calculate the MA.

CHART 9–3

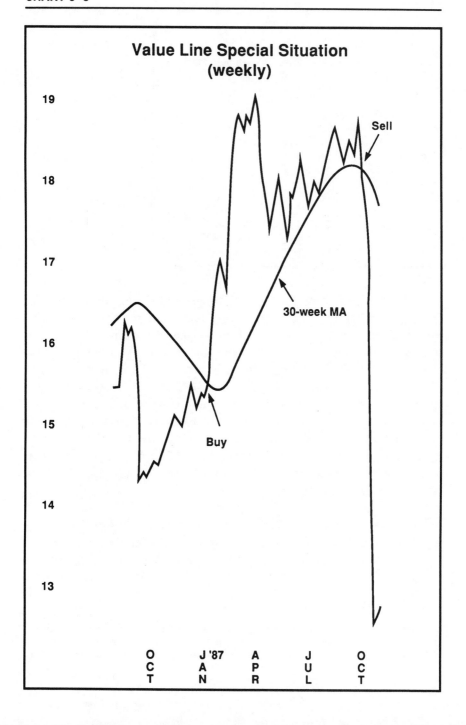

our system, you could have calmly watched that historic crash from the safe harbor of your money market fund.

Before proceeding, let's deal with the question that you're probably getting ready to ask. Since this exciting mutual-fund technique looks so easy and profitable, should you forget about stocks and use it exclusively? My answer is: for most of you, no! The potential is more dynamic in individual stocks than in funds, so it would be a mistake to totally ignore that area. But depending on your personality and the time you can allot to the market, you should work out the mix between mutual-fund switching and stock purchases. If you are very committed to the market and want to devote a couple of hours a week, you should obviously place a greater emphasis on stocks and less on funds. But even this type of investor should place some capital in the switch-fund game. I especially recommend that you use fund switching for your IRAs (Individual Retirement Accounts) and pension funds, while putting your more aggressive money into individual stocks. If, on the other hand, you have very little time available to devote to the market, then it certainly makes sense to lean much more heavily on funds than stocks.

The simple rules I've just shown you for buying and selling when the 30-week MA is violated works very well for investors. There will be very few signals, and they can catch all the major moves. Traders, however, must use a *daily* chart with a 30-*day* MA. The potential is even greater, but more work and attention are required. In addition, there are more frequent signals and whipsaws. That is why you should decide if you are more comfortable investing or trading.

SHORT-TERM FUND TRADING

Chart 9–4 of Scudder International Fund shows how accurate the trading approach can be. After catching a super advance from late 1986 (point A) until May of 1987, the fund sent a short-term sell signal as the daily price edged below the 30-day MA. While the sell signal turned out to be a whipsaw, a great profit was locked in and the fund should have been repurchased when it broke out again and moved to a new high in late June (point B). Again, this second

CHART 9–4

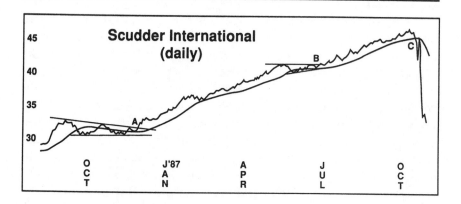

upside ride was exciting and profitable until a timely sell signal was
flashed in early October (point C), right before the October crash.

Be aware that when you are dealing with daily fund charts you
should pay equal attention to the chart formation and 30-day MA
to keep whipsaws to a minimum. While you should always trade
out of the fund if it breaks below the 30-day MA, buy the fund *only*
if it both crosses above the short-term MA and breaks out above
resistance, as Scudder did at points A and B.

The next question that arises is how to determine which no-
load mutual fund to purchase when several give simultaneous buy
signals. While they're all likely to be winners, if fund A advances
15 percent while fund B runs ahead 30 percent in the same time
span, it's obvious which one we want to be holding. It's easy to
determine the likely winner of the race when you learn to use a
few tricks. The secret doesn't lie in getting the fund's prospectus
and trying to figure out which stocks look best and which areas the
fund is invested in. First of all, this would be ridiculously time-
consuming. Secondly, mutual-fund managers change their portfolios so rapidly that the prospectus you're reading is most likely
out-of-date. A method that is far simpler and has a much greater
probability of success is to compare the relative strength of the
different buy candidates in the 60 to 90 day period before the buy
signal is given. First, check out the percentage advance in this
period from the low to where it is when the buy signal is flashed.
The fund with the greatest percentage gain while still in a Stage 1

base almost always leads the pack in Stage 2. A second helpful hint is given if one fund breaks out a few days before a second fund. The fund that broke out first is exhibiting better relative strength. Finally, check out the action of the moving average. If one fund breaks out above an MA that is still declining while the second fund jumps above a level MA, then the second fund is the preferable choice. If, as often happens, all three of these relative-strength measurements point to the same buy candidate, don't hesitate—buy it! On the other hand, if you get mixed signals and there's no clear-cut answer, then the likelihood is that all will perform in a similar manner.

Don't think this method is strictly for risk-avoiders and old fuddy-duddies. A well disciplined approach to no-load mutual-fund switching can yield surprisingly good results with a minimum of potential downside risk. To see what I mean, look at Chart 9–5, which shows the results that were achieved in *The Professional Tape Reader* over an eight-year period. While the methodology used was a little different (most of the trading signals were based on my proprietary Group Intensity trading index, which is reported in each issue of *PTR*), the results that you would have achieved using the simple method I just taught you would be quite close to those in the table. Note that $100,000 increased more than fivefold in this time span to over $530,000! This works out to be a compounded annual increase of 23 percent, which sure beats the heck out of 5½ percent at the bank, where so many people leave their IRA money.

As I promised, here is a list of some of the no-load funds that have impressed me with their action over the past several years. In no way is the list meant to be all-inclusive. When rating services such as Lipper Analytical come out with their new performance figures, it's easy to see which funds are acting best and merit your attention. For those who want to know which few funds to begin charting, this list is a good starting point:

Columbia Growth, P.O. Box 1350, Portland, OR 97207 (800-547-1037)

Constellation Growth, 11 Greenway Plaza, Suite 1919, Houston, TX 77046 (800-231-0803)

Fidelity Fund (one of several funds in the Fidelity Family of funds), 82 Devonshire Street, Boston, MA 02109 (800-544-7777)

CHART 9–5

$100,000 Invested in Stock Mutual Funds and Liquid Asset Funds

Date	Fund	Gain or Loss In Holding Prd	Total
4/2/79 – 6/4/79	Money Fund	+ 1,764.25	$ 101,764.25
6/4/79 – 9/10/79	100%Drey 3rd Cent	+ 15,468.90	117,233.15
9/10/79–11/12/79	Money Fund	+ 2,278.78	119,511.93
11/12/79– 2/19/80	100%Drey 3rd Cent	+ 34,192.60	153,704.53
2/19/80– 4/21/80	Money Fund	+ 3,816.82	157,521.35
4/21/80– 9/26/80	100%Drey 3rd Cent	+ 49,294.25	206,815.60
9/26/80– 1/14/81	Money Fund	+ 8,250.54	215,066.14
1/14/81 – 5/1/81	100%Drey 3rd Cent	+ 3,492.88	218,559.02
5/1/81 – 6/5/81	Money Fund	+ 3,342.76	221,901.78
6/5/81 – 7/2/81	100%Drey 3rd Cent	- 3,289.33	218,612.45
7/2/81 – 8/14/81	Money Fund	+ 4,455.25	223,067.70
8/14/81 – 8/28/81	100%Drey 3rd Cent	- 11,056.66	212,011.04
8/28/81 –10/16/81	Money Fund	+ 4,810.04	216,821.08
10/16/81 –12/18/81	100%Drey 3rd Cent	+ 10,607.06	227,428.14
12/18/81 – 3/19/82	Money Fund	+ 7,422.57	234,850.71
3/18/82– 5/21/82	100%Fidelity Fund	+ 11,978.73	246,829.44
5/21/82– 7/2/82	Money Fund	+ 3,889.04	250,718.48
7/2/82 – 8/6/82	100%Fidelity Fund	- 1,602.61	249,115.87
8/6/82 – 8/20/82	Money Fund	+ 1,287.18	250,403.05
8/20/82–10/1/82	100%Fidelity Fund	+ 14,210.73	264,613.78
10/1/82 – 10/15/82	Money Fund	+ 1,047.34	265,661.12
10/15/82–11/15/82	50%Drey Growth	+ 6,354.03	272,015.15
11/15/82– 1/3/83	Money Fund	+ 4,561.93	276,577.08
1/3/83 – 3/11/83	100%Drey Growth	+ 45,700.47	322,277.55
3/11/83– 5/2/83	Money Fund	+ 2,397.40	324,674.95
5/2/83 – 7/13/83	50%Drey 3rd Cent	+ 9,068.40	333,743.35
6/2/83 – 9/12/83	Money Fund	+ 7,691.66	341,435.01
9/12/83–10/19/83	50%Drey Growth	- 7,620.88	333,814.13
9/12/83–11/21/83	Money Fund	+ 4,100.37	337,914.50
9/26/83–10/3/83	100%Drey Growth	- 6,691.27	331,223.23
11/21/83–12/19/83	50%Fidelity Fund	- 4,536.53	326,687.70
11/21/83– 1/9/84	Money Fund	+ 2,931.73	329,619.43
1/9/84 – 1/30/84	50%Fidelity Trend	- 10,235.34	319,384.09
1/9/84 – 5/1/84	Money Fund	+ 8,417.88	327,801.97
5/1/84 – 5/21/84	33%Price New Era	- 4,409.07	323,392.90
5/1/84 – 5/21/84	Money Fund	+ 984.10	324,377.00
5/7/84 – 5/21/84	33%Price New Era	- 2,991.60	321,385.40
5/21/84 – 8/6/84	Money Fund	+ 7,135.98	328,521.38
8/6/84 –10/2/84	25%Nicholas Fund	+ 2,222.47	330,743.85
8/6/84 –10/9/84	25%Nicholas Fund	+ 1,582.67	332,326.52
9/17/84–11/19/84	25%Nicholas Fund	- 98.65	332,227.87
8/6/84 – 1/21/85	Money Fund	+ 8,062.66	340,290.53
11/5/84 – 3/11/85	25%Nicholas Fund	+11,223.39	351,513.92
11/6/84 – 3/11/85 and 5/6/85	25%Nicholas Fund	+12,277.42	363,791.34
1/10/85– 5/6/85 and 7/29/85	25%Nicholas Fund	+16,315.78	380,107.12
1/21/85–7/29/85 and 7/30/85	25%Nicholas Fund	+13,928.42	394,035.54
5/10/85–8/7/85 and 9/13/85	25%Nicholas Fund	+ 3,704.20	397,739.74
5/22/85–9/13/85	15%Nicholas Fund	+ 632.56	398,272.30
3/11/85–10/31/85	Money Fund	+ 10,663.08	408,935.38
11/4/85 – 1/22/86	25%Drey Growth	+ 9,470.44	418,405.82
12/2/86 – 1/22/86	15%Price New Era	+ 2,710.02	421,115.84
2/7/86 – 4/6/86	25%Quasar	+ 10,669.00	431,784.84
11/1/85 – 8/31/86	Money Fund	+ 20,981.04	452,765.88
5/27/86 – 7/9/86	25%Quasar	- 1,659.60	451,106.28
8/31/86 – 12/2/86	Money Fund	+ 4,138.81	455,245.09
12/2/86 – 3/30/87(⅓) 4/1/87(⅓)	20%Neub.Man.	+11,200.07	466,445.16
12/2/86 – 4/1/87(⅓) 4/15/87(⅓)	20%Price New Era	+20,163.78	486,608.94
1/12/87 – 3/30/87(⅓) 4/14/87(⅓)	20%Nicholas Fund	+ 5,230.74	491,839.68
8/31/86 – 11/6/87	Money Fund	+17,222.43	509,062.11
6/8/87 – 6/26/87	10%FinDynamics	- 626.05	508,436.06
6/10/87 – 8/31/87	10%Twen.Cent.Grth	+ 6,591.11	515,027.17
6/12/87 – 9/1/87	10%Neub.Man.	+ 3,147.14	518,174.31
6/15/87 – 9/2/87	10%Fid.Freedom	+ 4,031.80	522,206.11
6/15/87 – 9/4/87	10%Twen.Cent.Grth	+ 4,172.03	526,378.14
6/15/87 – 9/3/87	10%Fid.Contra	+ 3,112.75	529,490.89
9/28/87 – 10/12/87	20%HartwellGrth	- 3,746.00	525,744.89
9/28/87 – 10/9/87	20%USAACornstn	- 1,788.83	523,956.06
10/9/87 – 12/14/87	Money Fund	+ 6,529.46	530,485.52

Hartwell Growth, 515 Madison Ave., New York, NY 10022 (800-645-6405)

Lexington Growth, Park 80 West, Plaza 2, Saddle Brook, NJ 07662 (800-526-0056)

Twentieth Century Growth, 605 West 47 Street, Kansas City, MO 64112 (800-345-2021)

Vanguard Morgan Growth Fund, P.O. Box 2600, Valley Forge, PA 19482 (800-662-7447)

While mutual funds offer great promise, it's important to be aware of a few curves that can be thrown at you. Obviously there's always the potential—as with stocks—for a whipsaw signal. Another point to be aware of is that many funds limit the number of switches you're allowed to make in a given time period. Some of the funds are very reasonable and allow either unlimited or a very large number of switches per year (as long as you don't abuse this privilege by buying and selling in a foolhardy scalping manner). Some funds charge a small penalty fee after a certain number of switches. It's therefore important to get a prospectus for each fund you're charting and familiarize yourself with their rules. Only deal with those funds that allow a reasonable amount of switches.

THE SAME GAME WITH A SLIGHT TWIST

An additional choice was recently added to the switch-fund game. When you buy a mutual fund, you're obviously getting a diversified portfolio of stocks in those sectors currently favored by the fund manager: autos, chemicals, technology, or what have you. But suppose your technical work shows that one particular group is ready to be a real standout? No problem. You can now buy mutual funds that invest strictly in one sector. Although investing in such a narrow fund is obviously more dangerous than going the traditional route of the more diversified fund, the potential rewards are far greater! Several mutual funds have now made these sector funds available. There's usually a low load put on these funds, but when used properly, that's no great deterrent to excellent results.

While certainly not the only mutual fund to offer these sector funds, Fidelity Funds has, in my opinion, the best and most complete overall game plan in this area. First, there's a large choice of funds (35 at last count) that allows you to be quite specific as to sector. In addition, while there's an initial 2 percent fee for entering the plan (and a 1 percent charge if you take the money out of the family of funds), it is a one-time charge. As long as you keep the money within their sector-fund plan and move, for example, from gold to technology (or if you don't like the market at all and move into their Select Money Market Fund), you never have to pay the 2 percent charge again. All you're required to ante up is a $25 transaction fee when you liquidate the sector funds. On a large amount of money this is miniscule. Also, they price their funds on an hourly basis. So if you see an important move starting early in the day, you don't have to wait for the closing price (which can be considerably higher) as you do with most other funds. This is another fine area for your IRAs or pension funds, as well as a portion of your trading funds—especially if you lack the time to check out individual stocks. If you zero in on a winning sector such as energy in 1986–87, your rewards can be fantastic. Fidelity Select Energy gave a strong buy signal at point A on Chart 9–6 back in mid–1986, when it first moved above its 30-week MA. It broke out above resistance at $10.40 as it started a Stage 2 advance. It remained in a bullish Stage 2 uptrend for the next 14 months, finally giving a very timely sell signal in early October 1987, just before the crash.

In addition to supplying you with a choice of 35 different market sectors to buy, Fidelity now also makes available eight (and in the future it's likely to increase) sector funds that you can sell short. Besides being a very profitable trading and investing game, following these 35 sectors also helps you to uncover those one or two areas where you should also do heavy individual stock buying. For both reasons, make sure you pay close attention to these funds.

OPTIONS: A VERY EXCITING BUT RISKY GAME

The next investment vehicle to explore is that of options. If ever the phrase "not for widows and orphans" applied to an investment

CHART 9-6

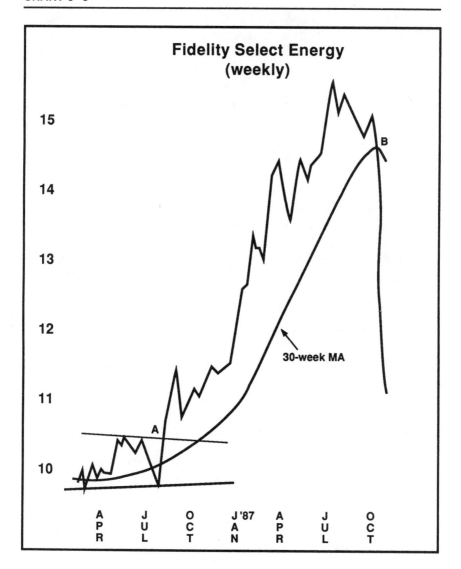

**Fidelity Select Energy
(weekly)**

area, it would certainly apply to options. These instruments are strictly for professionals and high-risk players! Under the best of circumstances, options have a high degree of risk. Of course, the other side of the coin is that when you are right, the payoff can be fabulous! While I cannot teach you how to bring the risk level of options down to that of a utility stock, I have a few tips that will make them a bit less risky. And, more importantly, these concepts will increase your winning percentage.

For those of you who aren't familiar with them, here's a nutshell description of *call and put options*.[4] Owning a call gives you the right to buy a stock at a given price (the striking price) for a specified time period (until the expiration date). The price you pay for an option is called a *premium*. When you buy a call, you are hoping that the underlying stock upon which the call is written will advance in a hurry, which is what makes this vehicle so tricky. Very often you can be right about the stock advancing, but if it doesn't happen before your call expires, you're out of luck. If you buy a call that expires in 90 days, a big jump on the 91st or 92nd day is of no benefit to you whatsoever. While you can buy calls with three, six, and nine-month expirations, the longer the time period that you contract for, the more expensive it is. In addition, the longer-term options lack the liquidity of short-term contracts. There is much more active trading in three-month options because of the short-term orientation of most option players.

When you buy a three-month call on stock XYZ with a striking price of 25, its intrinsic value is one dollar if the underlying common stock is trading at 26 (the price of the common minus the striking price equals intrinsic value; i.e., $26 - 25 = 1$). This isn't some fancy formula, it's market reality. If you want, you can sell the common at 26 and simultaneously exercise your option privilege to buy at 25. In the real world, the option will almost always sell at a price above the intrinsic value.[5] In this case, if the common is at 26 while the striking price is 25, and the call sells at 1⅞ rather than the intrinsic value of 1, the *time value* is ⅞ of a point.[6] The time value

---

[4] Listed options represent a unique realm of the financial markets, with their own exchanges, terminology, and trading rules. I'm assuming you understand the basics. If you don't, ask your broker for "Characteristics and Risks of Standardized Options," a 62-page booklet made available to the public by the Options Clearing Corporation. Until you understand the contents of this brochure, you should steer clear of options.

[5] If the time is almost up on the option, or the common moves so far above the striking price that very few traders want to play that option anymore, then the option will often trade very close to intrinsic value.

[6] Since option quotes are expressed in 100s, ⅞ means $87.50.

is that extra value above the intrinsic worth at which the market values the call. (The same is true for puts.)

If the common advances to 35 in the weeks before the call expires, the price of the call will have to rise to near 10. If there's still plenty of time before expiration, it will probably sell at an even higher price. While the underlying common advanced a very healthy 40 percent, your option chalked up better than a 400 percent gain. It's this chance to grab the gold ring that keeps the option buyers coming back for more, even though most of them lose in the long run.

A put is the opposite of a call. It's similar to selling short. If you expect the stock to get smashed, buying a put gives you the right to sell stock XYZ at a given price for a specified time. If the striking price for your put is 50 and the stock is currently selling at 49, then the intrinsic value is 1, since you can buy the stock for the current price of 49 and immediately exercise your put at 50. In the next few weeks, if XYZ declines to 40, the market value of the put will move to at least 10, which is the intrinsic value.[7] The drop in the common stock represents a 20 percent decline, which certainly would be a fine short-term profit if you sold the stock short. But your put profit is in excess of 400 percent since it advanced from $1\frac{7}{8}$ to 10!

The positives of buying calls and puts are obvious. If you are right, you can hit a grand-slam home run! Another positive is that you can define your risk. A put represents an option on 100 shares of stock. If each put costs you $200, and you decide to buy 10 puts that sell at $2, you can lose no more than $2000 on that particular transaction. (The same mathematics applies to calls.) The final plus is that for a small outlay of money you can get a big bang for your buck.

Unfortunately, this coin has a flip side to it—the downside. If you buy the put for $2 with a 50 striking price, and at the time of expiration you are still holding it while the stock is at 51, it's worthless. You lose your total investment of $2000. In the same manner, if you buy 10 calls with a 25 striking price for a total outlay

---

[7]It has to sell at least at intrinsic value minus the cost of commissions; so in this case it can trade at no more than a fraction below 10.

of $2000, and they expire with the common at 24, you are out the full amount of your investment. Since the striking price was 25, they have no value.

Another risk is that if you pay too high a premium, you can be right about the stock's trend and still wind up losing money. The stock price may not change enough to make your position profitable. For example, you buy a put with a striking price of 50 when the common is at 50½; the premium is $6. The stock has to drop to at least 44½ before you break even on the put. Another danger is the very thin nature of this market. So be absolutely sure to use limit orders rather than market orders when buying puts and calls. If you don't, the market makers will have a field day with your executions and you'll find it even more difficult to make money in this arena.

Obviously, buying calls and puts isn't for everyone. If you are a long-term conservative investor, don't even think about it. There are hedging strategies that conservative investors can use that entail far less risk, but also less chance for profit. These strategies are for people who cannot decide if they're bullish or bearish. To me, they are half-measures that lead to mediocre returns. I really don't agree with the concept of holding a Stage 4 stock but selling a call against it to cut your loss. I'm also negative on selling a call against a Stage 2 stock to get a few more dollars while cutting the chances of a further large up-side gain. To me, if you're bullish, you buy stocks and calls; if you're negative, you sell stocks short and buy puts.

Even if you're a really aggressive market player, I disagree with the idea of making option trading your primary market activity. Balance is the key to success in the market as well as in life. If you feel comfortable with options, then allocate only a small per-centage of your capital to this volatile area. Even a small position will give you more action than you'll see in a Vegas casino. The major difference between a casino and options trading using my rules is that my method puts the odds in your favor instead of with the house.

Here are the proper ways to increase your probability of success.

1. *Buy a call option only on a stock that is in Stage 2 or is moving into Stage 2.* And only buy a put option on a stock that is in Stage 4 or is first entering that negative phase.

CHART 9–7

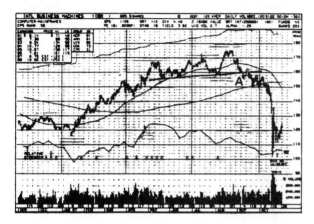

CHART COURTESY: DAILY GRAPHS AND LONG TERM VALUES

Look at this daily chart of IBM (Chart 9–7) in 1987.[8] From the time IBM broke below point A, it was in poor technical shape and had close to a zero chance of becoming a winner on the upside. Yet every day after it broke down at point A, large numbers of calls were purchased. It's therefore not surprising that the overwhelming majority of options expire worthless and most option speculators end up behind the eight ball.

2. *Buy only an option that has big potential.* It's a fact of life that you are going to be wrong with more of your choices in the option sector than when buying stocks. That doesn't mean you won't make good money. In fact, if you strictly follow my methods, you may very well make a greater percentage return on your capital than in stocks themselves. But for this to occur you have to promise yourself that you'll only buy a call or put on an A+ situation with tremendous potential. If you rigorously follow this discipline you can be right much less than 50 percent of the time and still rack

---

[8]This chart is from the Daily Graph Stock Option Guide, P.O. Box 24933, Los Angeles, CA 90024. If you seriously play the options market, this is an excellent service to get. When dealing in this short-term area you need the definition of a daily rather than a weekly chart. In addition, this publication has a chart on almost every underlying common stock. It also lists every option series—month and striking price—for each stock's put and call, along with the option ticker symbol.

up a small fortune. This will happen only if your losses are kept small and your correct calls are home runs. Don't fall into the trap that so many option players do and bet every race because you need the action. *Selectivity is absolutely crucial!* Swing only at the best pitches.

3. *Give yourself a reasonable amount of time before expiration.* It's hard to be right in the options market; it's even tougher to be correct within a limited time span; and it's nearly impossible to be correct within only a few days. So give yourself a break and make sure you buy only options that have a reasonable amount of time left until expiration. Ideally that's three months, but never less than 45 to 50 days. Option players too often choose an option that has a month or less left until expiration because it's cheap (i.e., small time-value premium). Stop looking for bargains. Of course the premium will be small on those options with very little time left. You never get something for nothing. An option is a wasting asset, and the closer it moves to expiration, the less it is worth. Thus the cheaper price is not surprising. If you buy options that have an inadequate amount of time left until expiration, you won't like what your profit and loss sheet will look like down the road!

4. *Buy an option that is close to the striking price and, if possible, in the money.* This is a tricky area. On the one hand, we all want to put up as little cash as possible and, if we're wrong, lose only a small portion of it. That's why so many option players buy options that are way out of the money, which means that the current intrinsic value is negative. If you buy a call with a $50 striking price, but the common is currently $45, your call has no real value. It's out of the money by $5. If it was to expire with the common still down at 45, you'll lose whatever you paid for the call. Yet many speculators buy these far-out-of-the-money calls (and puts) because they can purchase them very cheaply, and every once in a while one of them pays off big. In the above case, if the common takes off and runs up to 55 before expiration, a 50 cent call will increase 1,000 percent to at least 5. So an investment of only $10,000 would be a fast $100,000. These success stories do occur and that's the lure. But it certainly isn't a good probability, anymore than gambling on double zero in a Vegas casino. I don't want you going for the long shot, but rather for the consistent good play.

On the flip side of the coin are those who play it too safe by buying an option too far in the money. If the stock is currently at 50 and you buy a call with a 40 striking price for $10, you have to lay out a lot of money and you lose a good deal of upside leverage. In addition, the reward/risk factor isn't great. If the stock runs from 50 to 60, the call must mathematically increase from $10 to $20. But if the underlying common heads south and you hold it while it drops below 40 by expiration, you'll lose the full $10 per call. In this example, you'd have a one to one reward/risk ratio, which is not acceptable.

So what's the answer? The ideal compromise is to buy a call (or put) that is slightly in the money. For instance, if the common is trading at 50½, then a call with a $50 striking price makes sense as long as the premium isn't ridiculous. (If it is, you must pass on it or wait for the enthusiasm to die down and the price of the call to dip.) If you pay $2 for this call and the stock runs up to 60, you'll make 400 percent on your money because the option will move up to at least $10. If it expires worthless, you'll lose $2. That four to one reward/risk ratio is more exciting than the previous one to one example. Don't make the game even tougher than it has to be. All things being equal, buy an option that's slightly in the money. Or if it's out of the money, make sure it's very close to the striking price. In addition, remember it should have two to three months left before expiration.

5. *Use a very tight protective stop on your option positions.* When buying a call, don't set your sell-stop the way you would an investment stop. Use the rules I showed you for adjusting trading stops and, when possible, be even more aggressive. Don't set your stop on the actual option—they trade too thinly. Instead, use a mental stop (watched by but not physically placed with your broker) on the *underlying common stock.* If the common moves against you, instruct your broker to immediately sell your call (or put).

This daily chart of Digital Equipment (Chart 9–8)—fondly known as DEC on the Street—illustrates how aggressive to be. Because an option's expiration meter is always running, any sign of weakness is a reason to say goodbye to the position, thus locking in your profit or limiting your loss. If you play your hand properly, you should rarely lose all the money you invest in an option. This is another error the average speculator makes. Assume that he buys

CHART 9-8

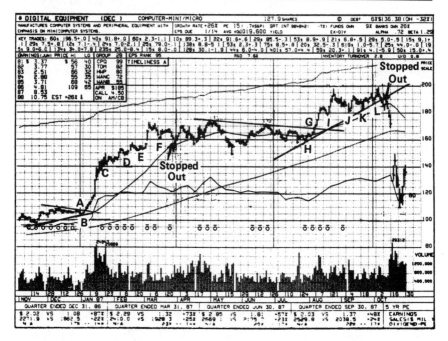

CHART COURTESY: DAILY GRAPHS AND LONG TERM VALUES

a call for $3 and the underlying common fouls up. If there is still plenty of time left on the option, the price might still be $2. But instead of cutting the loss and looking for a new play, our hapless trader figures that 60 to 90 days will be sufficient time for things to work out. When it doesn't, he ends up with nothing. You should exit as soon as the common stock starts to show signs of even short-term weakness. In the case of DEC, the stock should have been bought when it broke out above the downtrend line at point A. A close stop should have been set at B and quickly raised to C, D, E, and so forth. In the following weeks, the stock broke below point F at 160. If you had bought the April 105 call when the common was moving above 108, you would have paid around 9. When your mental stop was hit in March, it was time to exit the position with an excellent profit as the 105 calls were now worth $55. A second good upside trading opportunity was provided in early August when DEC once again broke above an important trendline as it moved above 169 (point G). You could have bought an October 165 call for 9. Then when the uptrend line was violated for the common in early October at 190, you should have exited your call position with another fine gain, as the call was around 26. If you didn't sell, however, the position was soon worthless!

SOME REAL-LIFE EXAMPLES

To see how profitable these speculative vehicles can be, let's follow the progress of a few option recommendations that I made in *PTR*. In early January 1987, I advised subscribers to buy calls on Texas Instruments (Chart 9–9) *if* the common moved above major resistance at 125.[9] When TXN did move above 125½, you could have bought an April 125 call for about $7. In early April, when TXN reached its high of 203 (point B), the call option's intrinsic value was $78. Here's where the exciting power of leverage makes itself felt. While the common chalked up a very respectable 60-percent-plus gain, the call option charged ahead over 1,000 percent!

The same mathematics show up when buying puts. In October 1987, I recommended buying puts on Xerox (Chart 9–10) when the common completed its major top at point A. You could have bought a January 75 put for about 4½. The stock dropped very sharply in the next few sessions to 50. That was a fast 30 percent gain on the short side. But the action of the January 75 put was even more impressive as it skyrocketed from 4½ to 27½ for a fast 500-percent-plus increase.

Obviously, if you're an aggressive trader and love high-risk vehicles this is an area where you should do some selective trading. Under no conditions, however, should even the most aggressive speculator put all of his market capital in options. Options trading is very seductive. A few lucky situations can turn traders into option junkies. Don't let it happen to you. And remember that it's

---

[9]Texas Instruments subsequently split three for one, so all of the numbers on Chart 9–9 are one-third of the prices in the text.

CHART 9–9

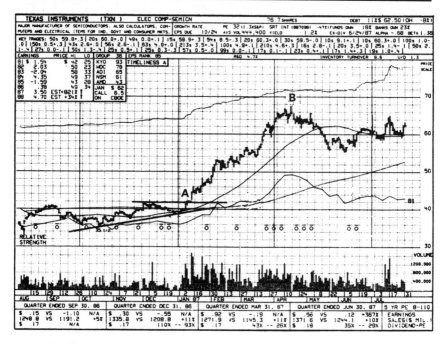

CHART COURTESY: DAILY GRAPHS AND LONG TERM VALUES

imperative for you to follow the rules I've taught you in this chapter if you want to survive and prosper in this speculative jungle.

IT'S NO DIFFERENT WHEN DEALING WITH THE FUTURE(S)

You now possess the ability to spot the start of new trends as they unfold. It's no different than developing any other talent. The more you work at it, the more proficient you'll become. Be aware that the profitability of chart reading isn't limited to stocks. I've already shown you that it's great for mutual funds as well as options. The final area where you can put it to use is with futures contracts.

With a slight alteration in the method (you need a shorter time frame and moving average), you can do amazingly well with any of the futures contracts, be it orange juice or stock index futures.

CHART 9–10

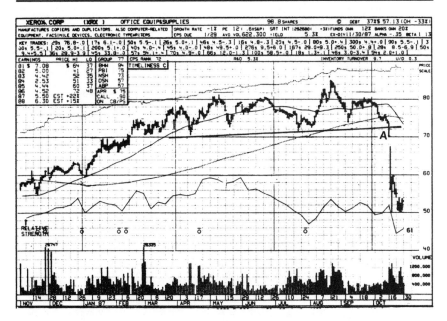

CHART COURTESY: DAILY GRAPHS AND LONG TERM VALUES

If you're going to compete in this area, I suggest that you subscribe to one of the futures chart services.[10]

Look at Chart 9–11 of orange juice futures and note that in the June–August 1987 period, the January 1988 contract formed a small reverse head-and-shoulder bottom. The same formations will occur on futures charts as on stock charts, but with futures the process is far more rapid. It's like playing a record that was recorded at 33⅓ rpm at 78 rpm. You have to be much more sensitive and develop a short-term feel if you're going to stick your toe into the futures pit. This is not an area where you can check your prices only on the weekend. Daily contact is vital! If you purchased orange juice contracts when the futures moved above the neckline (point

[10]One that I like is the Commodity Research Bureau Chart Service, CRB Futures Chart Service, Circulation Department, 30 S. Wacker Drive, Suite 1820, Chicago, IL 60606, 1-800-826-7685.

CHART 9-11

CHART COURTESY: CRB FUTURES CHART SERVICE

A), you would have done very well. If you had wanted to play it on a trading basis, after initially setting the stop right under the reverse right shoulder, you should have pulled it up to points B, C, D, and E. You then would have been stopped out for an excellent profit when this contract broke below the stop at point E.

If you want to play investor, then you could stay with the contract as long as it remained above the 40-day MA (dotted line) on Chart 9–12. The amazing thing is that you can know absolutely nothing about the fundamentals of orange juice, copper, soybeans, or other commodities; yet you can turn out to be far more accurate in your predictions than someone who spends their time reading all the fancy reports put out by the Department of Agriculture.

CHART 9-12

CHART COURTESY: CRB FUTURES CHART SERVICE

Another high-risk but exciting vehicle is the stock index futures contract. There are now several different such contracts trading, each based on a basket of stocks. The best known and most heavily traded futures contract is the Standard & Poor's (S&P) 500, which the institutions love to play. Not quite as active is the Value Line futures contract which, unlike the S&P contract, is weighted toward secondary stocks rather than blue chips.

Many market players and analysts alike were caught in the historic October 1987 crash that they said came out of the blue, but a look at Chart 9-13 shows that this absolutely was not the case. Between June and early October a clear head-and-shoulder top pattern formed. Once the neckline was violated it was truly a case of bombs away! This is even more obvious when you look at Chart 9-14 which is the S&P futures contract charted on a weekly basis. So if you did your technical homework, there was absolutely

CHART 9–13

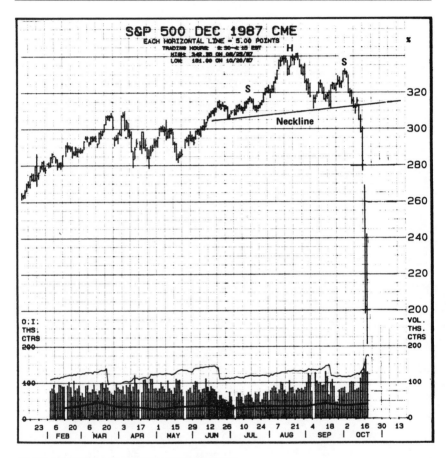

CHART COURTESY: CRB FUTURES CHART SERVICE

no excuse for getting trapped on the long side in that horrible debacle.

I cannot overstress the point that this sector is a high-risk game for professionals and sophisticated traders. The flip side to the high risk is that the payoff can be incredibly big. One contract shorted when the neckline was broken (at that time a margin down payment of $7500 per contract was required) would have yielded a profit of over $66,000 a few days later at the crash low.[11]

---

[11]After the crash, margins were raised to $20,000 per contract.

CHART 9–14

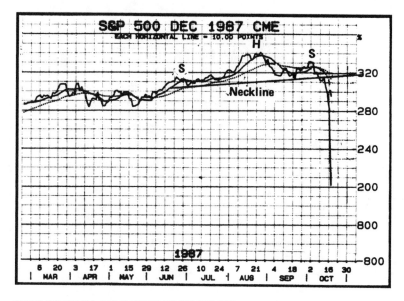

CHART COURTESY: CRB FUTURES CHART SERVICE

The lesson is clear. From now on when trying to predict future prices—whether it be for IBM, a mutual fund, a stock option, gold, or soybeans—forget about reading the financial pages. Instead, grab hold of the chart and study it carefully!

CHAPTER 10

PUTTING IT ALL TOGETHER

In working through the past nine chapters you should have discovered the truth of that Chinese philosopher's famous statement, "A journey of a thousand miles begins with a single step." When you first started reading Chapter 2, my ideal stage chart (10–1) probably looked like a Rorschach test. But if you've done your technical homework, brick by brick has been put into place and the language of technical analysis is now very understandable to you. In addition, some statements that I made earlier in the book probably sounded like heresy (such as "buy high but sell higher") but now should be seen in a much different light.

Promise yourself that you absolutely will never again buy a stock in Stage 4 no matter how exciting the story. Also swear that you'll never hold onto a declining Stage 4 stock no matter what rumors come your way. Also vow that you won't have a change of heart when you see the next exciting earnings report. Your buy and sell decisions are going to be timed from the chart pattern, not from press releases. No longer will you be amazed at seeing Sears rising in 1985 on decreasing earnings and then crashing in 1987 on increasing earnings (Chart 10–2).

You now have a game plan. Don't underestimate its importance. If you follow my tactics in a disciplined manner, you'll never again be behind the eight ball as are so many investors and traders. There will be occasional whipsaws, but you won't ever have to worry that any one position will reverse and wipe out your market capital. By using diversification—both in the number of stocks and market sectors—as well as intelligently placed protective sell-stops, you'll be assured that your negative positions will be more an annoyance than a financial danger. More important, your winners

CHART 10–1

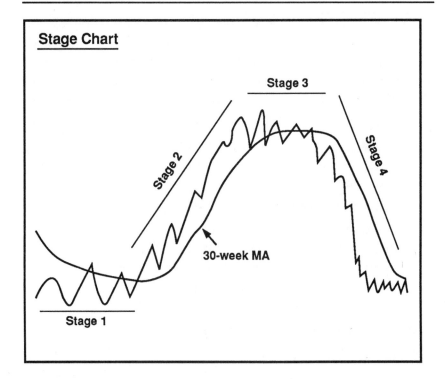

CHART 10–2

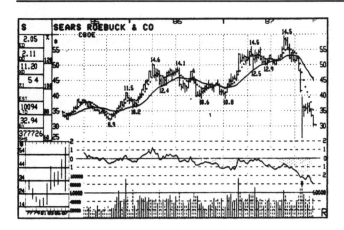

COURTESY OF MANSFIELD STOCK CHARTS

will be home runs rather than singles and give you a very satisfying bottom-line result.

Finally, you'll never suffer the confusion on the upside that most market players do. Even when they turn out to be right, they're filled with anxiety and usually end up selling far too soon, thus missing the lion's share of the gain. And in those cases where they do hang on, they often overstay the move and give most or all of the profit back as the stock plunges into Stage 4. This shouldn't ever be your fate. From now on, whether you're an investor or a trader, vow to be consistent to your system. Do not make any exceptions! Never believe that this time it's different. Always follow these steps:

1. Check the market indicators for overall direction.
2. Scan the groups so you'll know which ones to zero in on.
3. Cull out those few stocks with the most potentially profitable formation within those favorable groups.

Once you've taken these steps, here are some rules to follow:

- If you're an investor, do most of your buying early in Stage 2, when major bases are being completed.
- If you're a trader, concentrate the majority of your buying in continuation-type buy patterns that are already in Stage 2.
- Before entering your buy order, make sure you know where your protective sell-stop will be set. If it's too far away from the purchase price, look for a new buy or wait to purchase the stock when a safer stop level forms. The converse is true when selling short.
- Never sell a stock that's in Stages 1 or 2 (especially Stage 2).
- Never buy a stock that's in Stage 3 or 4 (especially Stage 4).
- Never hold a long or short without a protective stop.
- Don't be afraid to sell short when the overall trend is bearish. Just be sure to protect the position with a buy-stop.
- Be aware that stage analysis can be applied to any and all investments that are governed by supply and demand, which includes stocks, mutual funds, options, futures, and commodities.

- Never guess a bottom. Learn the important lesson that it's better to be late and buy in Stage 2, than to grab a stock that looks cheap but will be 40 to 50 percent cheaper later in Stage 4.
- Don't feel you have to be 100 percent invested at all times. Differentiate between a September 1982 situation, when the indicators and charts strongly suggested a fully invested position, versus a September 1987 position when extreme caution was demanded.
- Buy Stage 2 strength; sell Stage 4 weakness. In other words, always be in harmony with the tape.
- Whenever there's a conflict between the price volume action and the earnings, *always* go with the objective message being supplied by the technical approach.

While I cannot guarantee that you'll make millions in the market, I can assure you that:

- No single commitment will ever wipe you out.
- You'll never have your capital locked into disastrous positions that prohibit you from reversing and getting aboard a profitable new trend.
- You'll always make decisions in a rational manner, which will lead to peace of mind and definitely improve your batting average.
- You'll always be able to objectively judge where and when a given stock should be bought and sold.

All of these important plusses should dramatically improve your market results.

A FEW LAST SUGGESTIONS

Many market books recommend that you first play on paper before risking your capital in the market. I disagree! Many athletes perform incredibly well in warm-ups, only to choke once the actual game begins. It's no different in the market. When there's no pressure on you, it's very easy to cite the proper chapter and verse.

Dealing with the real-life stresses caused by the market's zigs and zags while sticking to your game plan is another case! Therefore, instead of playing on paper, use only a portion of your capital until you sharpen your technical skills and reach a higher level of confidence and proficiency.

A tactic that I used when I first started playing the market was to keep a diary. I strongly suggest you do likewise. In this diary enter only your losing trades. Winners always take care of themselves. While it's nice to have both your pocketbook and ego enhanced, winning teaches you nothing. Losing can be the greatest teacher of all, if properly analyzed. In the final analysis, losing can actually lead to far more winning trades. Write down the date that you bought your losing position and your reason for buying, and be honest with yourself as to why it didn't turn out. If it was merely a whipsaw, say so. But if upon later examination you realize that either the volume was inadequate, or the relative strength was lacking, or the group was negative, or you were influenced by a rumor, write down that error. After several months look for a common denominator in your losses. We all have psychological patterns. When you see what your particular destructive pattern is, it will be easy for you to retrain yourself and deal with it so your investing will become even more profitable.

I also want to stress that you most definitely should not be in awe of the big-money institutions. Too many investors feel they cannot compete in today's marketplace with the so-called financial giants. This is nonsense! You actually have an advantage over the large institutions; most investors just don't realize it. The institutions are like dinosaurs; they have big bodies and move very slowly. You, however, can turn on a dime and act very quickly. In addition, most of the hot-shot money managers really haven't performed that well over a long period of time. So take responsibility for your investments instead of being intellectually lazy and letting someone else manage (or mismanage) your money.

One last fallacy to steer clear of is that you need megabucks to be successful in the market. While it's easier to diversify when you have significant market capital, even a few thousand dollars will allow you to do very well in the market if you combine it with that rare commodity, common sense. If you have a very small starting nest egg, use no-load mutual funds. They will give you diversification and have no commission costs. As your market stake begins to grow, branch out and invest in individual stocks.

In closing, I once again want to use contrary opinion. Don't think of this as an end, but as a new beginning. When I read my first book on technical analysis many years ago (*Technical Analysis of Stock Trends* by Edwards and Magee) it opened my eyes to an entirely new approach. Over the years, as I became more and more proficient in charting, I went back and periodically reread that book. Each new reading gave me greater insights because I was able to view it in terms of my increased market sophistication and experience. So go out and practice what I've taught you, and then return in 18 to 24 months and see if the concepts in this book don't mean even more to you the second time around.

Until the next time we meet in these pages, just remember— that *The Professional Tape Reader* logo is true—"The Tape Tells All."

INDEX

A

Acme United Corporation, 112, 113
Adams-Russell, 111, 112
A-D line. *See* Advance-decline line
Advance-decline line, 275–82
Advancing stage, 31, 34–36
Alfin, 164, 166, 186
Allegis Corporation, 99, 100
Allen, 236
Allied Signal, 104, 105
Alpine Group, 111, 112
Aluminum Company of America, 226, 227
Amdahl, 28, 29
American Barrick Resources, 127, 128
American Capital Management, 207, 208
American Oil & Gas, 86, 87
Anacomp, 172, 174
Anchor Glass Container, 124, 125, 140, 141
Angelica, 220, 221
Anthony Industries, 152
ARA Services, 49, 50, 121
ASA Ltd., 119, 120
Australia, 293
Austria, 292, 293
Avon, 52, 164, 165
Aydin, 202, 204

B

Bally, 81, 82
Banc One Corporation, 238, 239
Bar chart, 22

Barron's, 284, 291, 294, 301
Baruch, Bernard, 257
Basing area, 31, 32–34
Bear, 16
Behavior of Prices on Wall Street, 68
Bethlehem Steel, 33
Beverly Enterprises, 140, 141, 147
Black Monday, 269, 288
Blair, 252, 253
Blocker Energy, 154, 155
Bowmar, 222, 223, 224
Breakdown, 14
Breakout, 14
Brokerage firms, 90
Bull, 17
Burlington Industries, 144, 145
Buying
  ideal time, 58–95
  patterns, 68–73
  quick reference guide, 115–16
  tips, 116–22
  within limits, 66–68
Buy orders, 6
Buy-stop-limit order, 66
Buy-stop order, 65–66
  trailing, 251, 255

C

Caesars World, 81, 83, 148
Call and put options, 322
Campbell Resources, 27, 28
Canada, 293
Cannon Group, 74
Care Enterprises, 114